CONTENTS

BERNARDIN

GUIDE TO

HOME

PRESERVING

When bountiful gardens, fields and orchards explode in brilliantly-coloured, succulent produce, it's time to join Canada's long and delicious tradition of preserving food. Gathering with family and friends to preserve food produces wonderful aromas and one-of-a-kind specialties that store-bought simply can't match. Whether you home can, freeze or dehydrate, you'll enjoy the fruits of your harvest year round.

Even if you didn't learn the art of food preservation as a youngster or young adult, it's never too late! After all, preserving food is just one step beyond cooking!

Use this Guide to learn basic techniques and the reasons why certain steps are essential to success. Then proceed to sample the many delicious options offered by a broad choice of basic and unique recipes. Enjoy!

HOME FOOD PRESERVATION METHODS

All foods exposed to air at room temperature will deteriorate and spoil unless preserved in some way. Microorganisms and enzymes that are part of all foods' natural make-up cause these changes. The air we breathe, the water we drink and the soil in which food is grown, all contain yeasts, molds and bacteria. Although invisible to the human eye, the changes that these microorganisms and enzymes cause as food ages become evident through off-flavours, offensive odours and colour changes.

• One way to control spoilage is to expose the micro-organisms to high temperatures while simultaneously hermetically sealing the food in glass jars. Although no "cans" are involved, the method is commonly known as **home canning**.

• Another time-honoured technique – **dehydration** – removes foods' natural water content by 80 to 95% thus inactivating the growth of bacteria and other spoilage microorganisms.

• Yet another popular home food preservation method is **freezing**. This method is based on the premise that extreme cold temperatures retard growth of microorganisms and slow down enzyme activity and oxidation.

All three preservation methods require specific preparation steps and packaging that control or limit the air to which the prepared food is exposed during storage.

This Guide explores these traditional food preservation methods explaining:

• WHY specific techniques are required for each, and then tells you,

• HOW to succeed in your chosen method.

The Guide provides step-by-step instructions as well as a bevy of delicious recipes to delight your tastebuds.

And to ignite your imagination, we've included intriguing yet practical nonperishable and craft uses for your favourite Bernardin mason jars and SNAP Lids.

SPOILAGE ORGANISMS

Knowing how, when and why microorganisms effect food storage and quality helps in understanding the reasons certain food preservation methods are recommended and necessary.

MOLDS AND YEASTS

Molds are fungi that grow as silken threads and appear as fuzz on food. Some molds can produce mycotoxins that, although invisible to the naked eye, are harmful to eat. i.e molds appear on the surface of foods but actually extend invisibly down through the food. Thus scraping off the top visible mold is not sufficient to prevent potentially harmful affects of certain molds. Molds thrive on the acids that protect against bacteria.

Yeasts, also fungi, cause food to ferment, making it unfit to eat. Fortunately, the acid in foods protects against the growth of bacteria. Molds and yeasts are naturally present in foods and are easily destroyed at temperatures between 140°F and 190°F (60°C and 88°C). Heat processing high acid foods in a boiling water canner heats food in mason jars to 212°F (100°C), more than sufficient to destroy the molds and yeasts without deteriorating the product quality.

BACTERIA

Bacteria are less easily destroyed. Certain bacteria, especially those found in low acid foods, actually thrive at temperatures that destroy molds and yeasts.
- Salmonella is destroyed when held at 140°F (60°C).
- Staphylococcus aureus, or "staph" is destroyed when food is kept above 140°F (60°C). Staph bacteria produce a toxin that must be destroyed by heating the product to 240°F (116°C) for the time specified by a tested home canning recipe.
- Botulism is a food poisoning caused by the bacterium *Clostridium botulinum*. Although this bacteria can be destroyed by long-term boiling, the most practical way to destroy its toxin-producing spores is to heat the food in jars to a temperature of 240°F (116°C). Furthermore, the botulism-causing bacteria thrive on low acid foods held in a moist environment in the absence of air – i.e. the conditions inside a sealed jar of home canned vegetables, meat or seafood.

When home canning, it is ABSOLUTELY ESSENTIAL to heat process low acid foods in a pressure canner at temperatures of 240°F (116°C). This higher heat treatment is the only practical home processing method to effectively disable bacterial spores and the toxins they can produce.

ENZYMES

Enzymes are present in all living things. They act as a catalyst to produce the normal organic changes necessary to the life cycle. Enzymatic action causes food to change flavour, texture and colour. Like molds and yeasts, enzymes are easily inactivated by heat at temperatures beginning at 140°F (60°C) and are therefore effectively treated in a boiling water canner.

Growth And Destruction Of Microorganisms Temperature Degrees °F (°C)

240°F (116°C)
Processing temperature for low-acid foods in a steam-pressure canner when processed at or below 1,000 feet above sea level

212°F (100°C)
Boiling point of water at sea level. Processing temperature for high-acid foods in a boiling-water canner when processed at or below 1,000 feet above sea level

50°-70°F (10°-21°C)
Best storage temperature for home canned and dehydrated foods

240°F (116°C)
220°F (104°C)
200°F (93°C)
180°F (82°C)
160°F (71°C)
140°F (60°C)
120°F (49°C)
100°F (38°C)
80°F (27°C)
60°F (15.5°C)
40°F (4.4°C)
20°F (-6.6°C)

240°F (116°C)
Temperature at which bacterial spores are destroyed in low-acid foods

180°-212°F (82°-100°C)
Temperature at which molds, yeasts and some bacteria are destroyed in high-acid foods

140°-179°F (60°-82°C)
Growth of molds, yeasts and bacteria prevented, but may allow survival of some microorganisms

40°-139°F (4°-59°C)
Active growing range of molds, yeasts and bacteria

32°F (0°C)
Growth of some molds, yeasts and bacteria slowed

HOME CANNING

Home canning is traditional. Yet, as modern as the latest gourmet creation. It's convenient but homemade. Satisfying and rewarding.

Home canners determine not only the origin and quality of the raw ingredients but also recipe proportions, like sugar and salt levels. Many capture the essence of yesteryear by preserving family favourite recipes handed down through generations of fine cooks. Others look to home canned foods to make ethnic specialties not readily available commercially. The results are as diverse as Canada's population.

Not long ago, home canning was a survival necessity. Today, preserving food in mason jars can declare a home canner's individuality. For some, home canning begins with planting a garden. For others it begins with a visit to a pick-your-own location or farmers' market.

HOME CANNING IS "JUST ONE STEP BEYOND COOKING".

It requires the same careful attention to freshness and quality that every successful chef employs. Once food is prepared, spooned into mason jars and closed with a two-piece SNAP Lid it must be heat processed.

"Processing" – heating filled jars –
• destroys microorganisms that lead to food spoilage,
• inactivates enzymatic actions and
• creates a vacuum seal that prevents contamination during storage.

WHY

Air, and all foods, in their normal state, contain naturally occurring microorganisms, such as bacteria, mold and yeasts. Uncontrolled microorganisms cause food spoilage. Proper, safe home canning procedures interrupt normal food spoilage and decay. Heating foods also inactivates naturally occurring enzymes that lead to deterioration in food.

HOW

When food in mason jars closed with two-piece SNAP Lids, is heat processed at the correct temperature and held there for a time determined in scientifically established process control studies, potentially harmful food microorganisms can be destroyed.

Heating filled jars also exhausts or "vents" air from the jar.

Venting exhausts gases from the jar creating a container in which the atmospheric pressure inside the jar is less than that outside. After processing, the jar cools at room temperature where atmospheric pressure is greater than that inside the jar. This pressure pushes the lid down and the softened plastisol conforms to the rim of the jar – creating a hermetic seal.

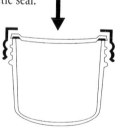

This seal prevents other microorganisms from entering or contaminating the food during storage.

Heat processing all filled jars of home canned foods is not optional! It is essential to create an adequate hermetic or vacuum seal required for food safety as well as delicious taste and quality.

All jars of home canned foods must be heat processed by the appropriate method for the correct time for the food type and jar size. Failure to adequately heat process jars can result in seal failure, food spoilage and substantial health risks.

CLASSIFYING FOODS FOR HOME CANNING

As outlined, some spoilage microorganisms are affected by foods' inherent acidity level. Therefore, acidity or pH is used to divide food for home canning into two groups – high and low acid foods. Each requires a specific heat processing method.

Acidity or pH is determined by the level of acid naturally present in a specific food or the acidification of a recipe mixture. i.e. addition of acid ingredients to borderline or low acid foods such as pickling vegetables.

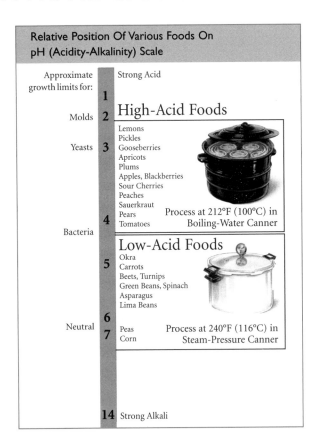

	Relative Position Of Various Foods On pH (Acidity-Alkalinity) Scale
Approximate growth limits for:	Strong Acid
	1
Molds	**2**
	High-Acid Foods
Yeasts	**3** Lemons, Pickles, Gooseberries, Apricots, Plums, Apples, Blackberries, Sour Cherries, Peaches, Sauerkraut
Bacteria	**4** Pears, Tomatoes — Process at 212°F (100°C) in Boiling-Water Canner
	Low-Acid Foods
	5 Okra, Carrots, Beets, Turnips, Green Beans, Spinach, Asparagus, Lima Beans
Neutral	**6**
	7 Peas, Corn — Process at 240°F (116°C) in Steam-Pressure Canner
	14 Strong Alkali

HIGH ACID FOODS

Foods or recipes with a pH of 4.6 or lower are considered **High Acid Foods** and can be safely heat processed in a **boiling water canner**. Fruits, jams, jellies and fruit spreads are high acid foods. Some, like figs and tomatoes, are on the borderline between high and low acid status and therefore require acidification – the addition of acid – to be safely processed in a boiling water canner. Fermented foods, such as sauerkraut and fermented pickles, as well as pickled recipes to which a sufficient quantity of vinegar is added are also considered high acid foods. Other recipes combine high- and low-acid ingredients but include sufficient quantities of added acid ingredients – vinegar, citric acid or lemon juice – to achieve a 4.6 pH or lower. Examples include pickles, relishes, chutney and condiments.

LOW ACID FOODS

Low acid foods have very little natural acid. This group includes vegetables, meats, poultry and seafoods; soups, stews, tomato-vegetable mixtures, tomato-meat and meat sauces. Any food or recipe that has a pH greater than 4.6 is a **Low Acid Food**. **All Low Acid Foods** must be heat processed in a **Pressure Canner** that heats foods to a temperature of 240°F (116°C). This temperature is required to prevent growth of spoilage organisms that can lead to botulism, a deadly form of food poisoning.

HIGH ACID FOODS STEP BY STEP

1
Wash jars & lids. Place jars on a rack in boiling water canner; cover jars with water and heat to a simmer (180°F/82°C).

2
Set screw bands aside; heat SNAP Lids in hot water, NOT boiling (180°F/82°C). Keep jars and SNAP Lids hot until ready to use.

3
Prepare recipe. Ladle hot food into a hot jar leaving recommended headspace.
1/4 inch (0.5 cm) – jams & jellies
1/2 inch (1 cm) – fruit, pickles, tomatoes, chutney, relish

4
Using nonmetallic utensil, remove air bubbles. Readjust headspace if needed. Wipe jar rim removing any stickiness.

5
Centre SNAP Lid on jar; apply screw band **securely & firmly** *until resistance is met – fingertip tight. Do not over tighten.*

6
Place jar in canner. When all jars are filled, adjust hot water in canner so that jars are covered by at least 1 inch (2.5 cm) water.

7
Cover canner; bring water to a full rolling boil. Process – *boil filled jars* – for time in recipe. At altitudes higher than 1,000 ft (305 m) increase processing time (see page 12).

8
When process time has elapsed, turn heat off and remove canner lid. When boil subsides and water is still, approximately 5 minutes, remove jars without tilting. Cool jars upright, undisturbed 24 hours. Do NOT RETIGHTEN screw bands.

9
After cooling 24 hours, check jar seals. *Sealed lids curve downward and do not move when pressed.* Remove screw bands; wipe and dry bands and jars. Store screw bands separately or replace loosely on jars, as desired. Label and store jars in a cool, dark place.

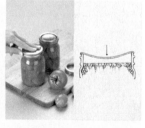

LOW ACID FOODS
STEP BY STEP

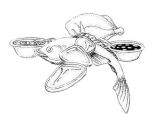

1 Wash jars & lids. Place jars on rack in canner; add 2-3 inches (5-8 cm) water, and heat to a simmer (180°F/82°C).

2 Set screw bands aside; heat SNAP Lids in hot water, NOT boiling (180°F/82°C). Keep jars and SNAP Lids hot until ready to use.

3 Prepare recipe. (**a**) Ladle food into jars leaving **1 inch (2.5 cm) headspace, (b)**. (**c**) Using nonmetallic utensil, remove air bubbles. (**d**) Wipe jar rim removing any stickiness. (**e**) Centre SNAP lid on jar; apply screw band *securely and firmly* until resistance is met – fingertip tight. Do not overtighten.

4 Place jars on rack in pressure canner. Adjust water level as directed by canner manufacturer. Lock canner lid in place. Place over high heat.

5 Vent canner – allow steam to escape – following manufacturer's directions.

6 When pressure reaches required level, begin counting processing time. Regulate heat to maintain required pressure level for your altitude. *Avoid sudden or drastic changes in heat level.*

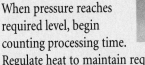

7 When processing time is complete, turn heat off. Let canner stand undisturbed until pressure drops to zero. Wait 2 minutes longer, then remove cover, tilting cover away from face.

8 Remove jars without tilting. Cool jars upright, undisturbed 24 hours. Do NOT RETIGHTEN screw bands.

9 After cooling 24 hours, check jar seals. *Sealed lids curve downward and do not move when pressed.* Remove screw bands; wipe and dry bands and jars. Store screw bands separately or replace loosely on jars, as desired. Label and store jars in a cool, dark place.

EQUIPMENT

Other than mason jars and two-piece SNAP Lids, most equipment needed for home canning high acid foods is readily available in a well-equipped kitchen.

MASON JARS

True "mason jars" are specifically designed to be sealed with a two-piece SNAP lid and to withstand the repeated heating, cooling and handling demanded by the home canning process. While some commercial jars may look like a canning jar or may be embossed with the word "mason",

not all jars are manufactured for reuse and not all are constructed in volume capacities or shapes that are compatible with established heat processing methods and times. It is always more prudent to purchase Bernardin mason jars. These jars are made specifically for home canning in shape configurations and volume capacities that comply with well-established heat processing methods and times… and thus, are safe for home canning.

SNAP LIDS

Two-piece Bernardin SNAP Lids and screws bands and one-piece replacement SNAP Lids are made of specially coated tinplated steel to prevent rusting and resist food acids.

SNAP Lids have a unique red sealing compound – plastisol – built into the flanged edge. Proper lid and screw band application followed by heat processing allows this plastisol to conform to the mason jar rim creating a hermetically sealed jar. Bernardin home canning closures are available in three diameters to fit mason jars used in Canadian homes:
• Standard 70 mm
• Gem 78 mm
• Wide mouth 86 mm

While screw bands can be used repeatedly, SNAP Lids must be used once only. Vacuum seals create a permanent impression in the plastisol rendering it ineffective if reused. To extend the life of screw bands, always remove, clean and dry the bands after sealed jars have cooled 24 hours. Jars that have an adequate hermetic seal do not require the presence of screw bands during storage. If desired, screw bands, after cleaning, can be loosely re-applied to the jars. To prevent accidental damage to seals, it is a wise idea to apply screw bands loosely to jars that will be transported or given to friends.

BOILING WATER CANNER

High Acid Foods with a pH of 4.6 or lower are safely processed in a boiling water canner. Any large, deep pot that has a rack to lift jars off direct heat and a tight-fitting lid can be used as a boiling water canner. Large porcelain-coated steel pots often come equipped with racks. Large stainless steel stockpots are also popular for use in boiling water heat processing. If you do not have a canning rack

that fits a large stockpot, substitute a cake rack or tie screw bands together to cover the bottom of the pot. Regardless of the pot you choose as a boiling water canner, be sure that it allows water to **cover the jars** by 1 to 2 inches (2.5 to 5 cm) and provides enough extra pot height for a rapid, rolling boil to be maintained throughout the processing time.

PRESSURE CANNER

Jars of low acid foods, with a pH greater than 4.6, must be processed in a pressure canner. This specialized pot utilizes a lid that locks onto the pot. When heated, steam pressurizes the sealed vessel and circulates around the jars, transferring heat and bringing the food to an internal temperature of 240°F (116°C) at altitudes up to 1,000 ft (305 m).

Please note that a pressure cooker and a pressure canner are **not** synonymous! Low acid heat processing times have been established using pressure canners (large vessels). Pressure cookers differ in design and function from pressure canners. Pressure cookers are not suitable for home canning.

There are two types of pressure canners – a "dial gauge" which shows the level of pressure on a gauge and a "weighted gauge" that uses different weights for each required pressure level. *Regardless of the type of pressure canner you select, the pressure level must be* **manually maintained throughout the processing time** *by the user gradually* **increasing or decreasing the heat** *to which the canner is exposed.* i.e. There are no "automatic" pressure canners for home use.

Before using any pressure canner, check to see that the gasket fits properly and is soft and pliable to allow an airtight seal when the lid is locked in place. Place a rack at the bottom of the canner to lift jars off direct heat. A second rack must be placed between layers of jars when jars are stacked in a pressure canner.

Test **Dial Gauge Pressure Canners** for accuracy prior to each canning season. Replace gauges that register high by 1 lb (psi) or more than at 5, 10 or 15 lb pressure. All of the bacterial spores that emit toxins may not be destroyed during processing in a pressure canner fitted with an inaccurate gauge.

Weighted Gauge Pressure Canner

The movement of the weighted gauge during processing indicates pressure levels in this type of pressure canner. A three-piece weighted gauge and some styles of one-piece weighted gauge have adjustments for 10 and 15 lb (75 and 102 kPa) pressure. A one-piece weighted gauge that does not adjust for different pressure levels is designed to process only at 15 lb (102 kPa) pressure.

To establish the proper pressure level and processing time, use only recipes that designate both the type of pressure canner as well as the pressure level for the altitude at which you are home canning.

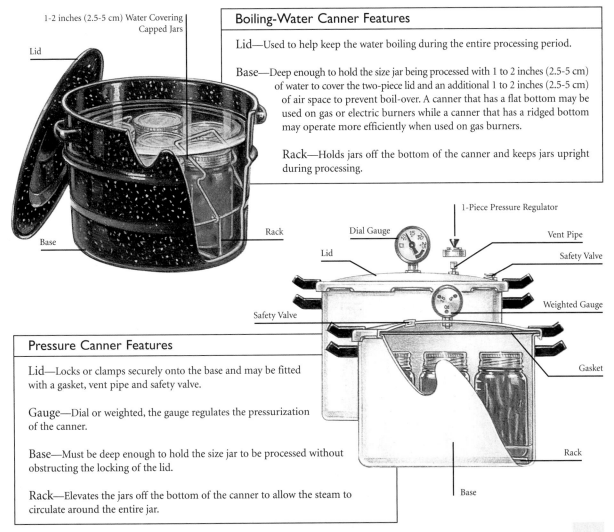

1-2 inches (2.5-5 cm) Water Covering Capped Jars

Lid

Rack

Base

Boiling-Water Canner Features

Lid—Used to help keep the water boiling during the entire processing period.

Base—Deep enough to hold the size jar being processed with 1 to 2 inches (2.5-5 cm) of water to cover the two-piece lid and an additional 1 to 2 inches (2.5-5 cm) of air space to prevent boil-over. A canner that has a flat bottom may be used on gas or electric burners while a canner that has a ridged bottom may operate more efficiently when used on gas burners.

Rack—Holds jars off the bottom of the canner and keeps jars upright during processing.

1-Piece Pressure Regulator

Dial Gauge

Lid

Vent Pipe

Safety Valve

Weighted Gauge

Gasket

Safety Valve

Rack

Base

Pressure Canner Features

Lid—Locks or clamps securely onto the base and may be fitted with a gasket, vent pipe and safety valve.

Gauge—Dial or weighted, the gauge regulates the pressurization of the canner.

Base—Must be deep enough to hold the size jar to be processed without obstructing the locking of the lid.

Rack—Elevates the jars off the bottom of the canner to allow the steam to circulate around the entire jar.

GETTING STARTED

Logic and attention to detail are essential to all successful cooking endeavors. Home canning is no different! Shortcuts easily compromise quality and food safety when preserving food at home. It is always safer and far more prudent to use **only** those methods recommended by established food authorities that use the equipment, jars, lids and ingredients that match those you are using today. Each recipe in this Guide includes detailed start to finish, step-by-step instructions. In some cases, several similar recipes that use different ingredients, specific quantities and preparation procedures but similar "home canning" steps are combined on a two-page spread. Within the two-page spreads complete step-by-step techniques prevent paging back and forth for beginners as well as experienced home canners.

These general procedures apply to home canning both low and high acid foods.

RECIPE

Start with a tested "home canning" recipe from a reliable source that uses the jars, lids and ingredients you are using. In addition to ingredient quantities and food preparation, trustworthy home canning recipes must include specific instructions for: mason jar size and estimated yield, headspace, heat processing method and time appropriate for the type of food – low acid or high acid – and size of jars being home canned. Recipes that do not include these critical factors are not recommended.

Before you begin, read the recipe and assemble ALL required equipment and ingredients.

MASON JAR PREPARATION

Wash and rinse mason jars required for each recipe. Place the required number of clean mason jars, of the volume capacity specified in your recipe, on a rack in your canner. Add water. The quantity of water added depends on the type of canner you are using. To avoid thermal shock, clean jars are heated prior to filling with hot foods.

SNAP LID PREPARATION

Wash and rinse SNAP Lids required for each recipe. Set screw bands aside; heat SNAP Lids in hot water, NOT boiling (180°F/82°C). Keep jars and SNAP Lids hot until ready to use. Note, screw bands do not require heating as they do not come in contact with the food. Their sole purpose is to hold the SNAP Lid in place during heat processing and cooling until the vacuum seal is created. Bands are obviously easier to handle and apply when not heated.

HEADSPACE

Headspace is the space in the jar between the top of the food or liquid and the inside of the lid. If you are packing solid foods & liquid into a jar, add 1/4 inch (0.5 cm) to the recipe's headspace; pack solids to this level. Then, add liquid to the level recommended for the type of food being canned.

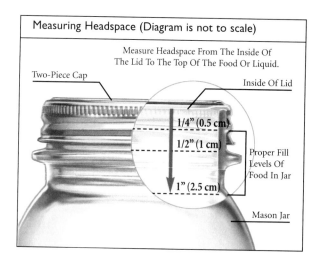

Measuring Headspace (Diagram is not to scale)

Measure Headspace From The Inside Of The Lid To The Top Of The Food Or Liquid.

Two-Piece Cap

Inside Of Lid

1/4" (0.5 cm)

1/2" (1 cm)

1" (2.5 cm)

Proper Fill Levels Of Food In Jar

Mason Jar

Pickles and fruit require 1/2 inch (1 cm) headspace. Because these foods are packed with solids and liquid, pack solids to within 3/4 inch (2 cm) of the top rim, then add liquid to the 1/2 inch (1 cm) level.

Relishes, fruit juices, chutney, condiments require a 1/2 inch (1 cm) headspace.

Jams, jellies, soft spreads and fruit juice should be filled to within 1/4 inch (0.5 cm) of the top rim.

Low acid foods require 1 inch (2.5 cm) headspace.

BUBBLE REMOVAL

Ladle food into jar leaving recommended headspace. Using a nonmetallic utensil, remove air bubbles. Readjust headspace if required.

CLEANING JAR RIMS

Wipe the rim of the jar to remove all stickiness or food particles. The presence of food particles between the jar rim and plastisol on the lid can prevent the formation of a strong vacuum seal.

SCREW BAND APPLICATION

Centre the hot SNAP Lid on the jar; apply screw band *securely & firmly until resistance is met – fingertip tight. Do not overtighten.* Place the jar **upright** in canner; fill and close remaining jars until canner is filled. It is essential that jars remain upright throughout the heat processing time.

HEAT PROCESSING

Place lid on canner and proceed as directed for the type of canner you are using.

BOILING WATER CANNER – HIGH ACID FOODS

Place filled jars **upright** on rack in boiling water canner. Arrange jars so water can circulate around each jar. Jars must remain upright throughout heat processing time. When all jars are in canner, place lid on boiling water canner. Place canner over high heat. When water reaches a full rolling boil begin counting processing time. When allotted recommended processing time has elapsed, turn heat off and remove lid. If possible, move canner off heating element. Let the canner cool 5 minutes before removing jars – especially when canning fruit and tomatoes in larger volume jars.

PRESSURE CANNER – LOW ACID FOODS

Place filled jars on rack in pressure canner. Arrange jars so steam can circulate around each jar. If stacking jars in canner, place a second rack on top of first layer of jars before adding jars to second layer. When canner is filled, adjust water level as directed in pressure canner manufacturer's instructions. Lock canner lid in place leaving vent open. Place canner over high heat.

Vent canner – allow steam to escape steadily for 10 minutes. Close the vent, using the weight or method described for your canner. Regulate heat to achieve the required pressure level.

When this required pressure level is attained, begin counting processing time. Monitor pressure level and regulate heat to maintain the recommended pressure level throughout the processing period. Adjust heat gradually with small changes to heat level. Drastic changes in heat level can result in rapid pressure changes inside the canner. This in turn can cause loss of liquid from the jars that can lead to seal failure.

When processing time has elapsed, turn heat off and remove canner from heat. *Let canner stand undisturbed until pressure drops to zero.* Do not tamper with lid or do anything that will interfere with the natural cooling and pressure drop of the canner.

When dial gauge registers zero or when no steam escapes when weighted gauge canner's weight is nudged – wait 2 minutes longer! Then unlock and remove lid, tilting cover away from yourself as it is lifted.

COOLING JARS AND SEAL FORMATION

When processing is complete and the canner has cooled as specified, remove jars without tilting. Lift jars straight up and place **upright** on a padded surface, in a draft-free place. If desired, cover jars loosely with a towel. Allow jars to cool, undisturbed 24 hours.

Note: Some screw bands may appear to have loosened – this is completely natural! DO NOT RETIGHTEN screw bands. Retightening screw bands after processing can cause seal failure. Lids that have been properly applied and heat processed will form a vacuum as the jars cool.

CHECKING SEAL

After 24 hours, check seals. Sealed lids curve downward and show no movement when pressed with fingertips. *Unsealed jars must be reprocessed immediately or refrigerated.*

Remove screw bands. Rinse and dry bands and wipe jars with a damp cloth. Store screw bands separately or replace bands loosely on jars, as desired. Label jars with content and preparation date.

STORAGE

Store sealed jars of home canned foods in a cool, dark place. The ideal storage room temperature is 50°F to 70°F (10°C to 21°C).

For best quality, use home canned foods within 1 year. Food canned following tested recipes, correct processing methods and times can be stored safely for one year. After 12 months, natural chemical changes – in flavour, colour, texture or nutritional value – may occur that can diminish quality. Rotate home canned foods by date, using the oldest products first.

Even foods that are properly processed can lose some of their quality over extended time. This loss will be accelerated when foods are stored at temperatures above 70°F (21°C). On the other hand, do not allow jars of home canned foods to freeze. Freezing causes food to expand, which in turn can break jars and/or the seal.

Do not store jars in direct sunlight. Shelves in a dark storage area or cupboard are best. Light hastens oxidation, destroys certain vitamins and causes colours in certain foods to fade.

ALTITUDE

Just as it does when you bake, altitude affects canning recipes. In most home canning recipes, recommended processing times are stated for use at elevations of sea level 0 to 1,000 ft (305 m). At higher elevations, water boils at temperatures lower than 212°F (100°C). Lower temperatures are less effective in destroying microorganisms, therefore adjustments must be made to heat processing instructions to extend exposure to adequate heat to destroy microorganisms.

Note – the method of adjustment differs between high and low acid foods.

At elevations higher than 1,000 ft (305 m):
• **Increase** processing **time** for **high acid foods**.

Boiling Water Canner (high acid) — Altitude Adjustments		
Altitude		**INCREASE**
Feet	**Meters**	**Processing Time**
1,001 – 3,000	306 – 915	5 minutes
3,001 – 6,000	916 – 1,830	10 minutes
6,001 – 8,000	1,831 – 2,440	15 minutes
8,001 – 10,000	2,441 – 3,050	20 minutes

At elevations higher than 1,000 ft (305 m):
• Based on the type of pressure canner used, **increase** the **pressure level**, as indicated in chart, for **low acid foods**. *Processing time does **not** change.*

Pressure Canner (low acid) — Altitude Adjustments					
Altitude		**Weighted Gauge**		**Dial Gauge**	
Feet	**Meters**	**lb**	**kPa**	**lb**	**kPa**
0 – 1,000	0 – 305	10	68	11	75
1,001 – 2,000	306 – 609	15	102	11	75
2,001 – 4,000	610 – 1,219	15	102	12	82
4,001 – 6,000	1,220 – 1,828	15	102	13	89
6,001 – 8,000	1,829 – 2,438	15	102	14	95
8,001 – 10,000	2,439 – 3,048	15	102	15	102

USING HOME CANNED FOODS

When up-to-date tested guidelines are followed, there should be little concern about the quality or safety of home canned foods. Before using jars of food, it is always prudent to visually examine each jar to ensure no unexpected changes have occurred. Stored jars that have a secure, hermetic seal and those that you are certain have been processed correctly using up-to-date guidelines generally pose no problem. If you have any question about a particular jar, the age-old adage – *"If in doubt, throw it out"* – is often the most prudent course of action.

Breaking the vacuum seal allows the SNAP Lid to be lifted easily from the jar. To release the vacuum, use a bottle opener to gently lift one edge of the SNAP lid. Take care to avoid damage to the jar rim as jars with chipped rims can not be used for future home canning.

ALTITUDES OF MAJOR CANADIAN CITIES		
	Altitude	
City	**Feet**	**Meters**
Victoria-BC	63	19
Vancouver	14	4
Kamloops	1,133	345
Kelowna	1,409	429
Prince George	2,268	691
Terrace	713	217
Edmonton-AB	2,373	723
Calgary	3,557	1,084
Red Deer	2,968	904
Lethbridge	3,047	928
Medicine Hat	2,352	716
Vermilion	2,025	617
Regina-SK	1,894	577
Saskatoon	1,653	503
Swift Current	2,682	817
Winnipeg-MB	783	239
Brandon	1,343	409
Toronto-ON	569	173
Kenora	1,344	409
Thunder Bay	653	199
Sault Ste. Marie	630	192
Barrie	968	295
North Bay	1,215	370
Ottawa	374	114
Québec City-QC	244	74
Montréal	270	82
Chicoutimi	544	166
Sherbrooke	792	241
Trois-Rivières	199	61
Gaspé	108	33
Fredericton-NB	67	20
Saint John	357	109
Moncton	232	71
Halifax-NS	477	145
Sydney	203	62
Charlottetown-PE	160	49
St. John's-NF	461	141
Gander	496	151
Whitehorse-YT	2,317	706
Yellowknife-NT	675	206
Iqaluit-NU	110	33

Just like commercially processed foods, home canned jars of food – once opened – have a shortened life expectancy. If the entire content of a jar is not used, refrigerate leftovers and use within a few days or freeze until used again. Soft spreads and pickled products may be refrigerated for somewhat longer periods – similar to their commercial counterparts.

A FoodSaver® used with a FoodSaver® Jar Sealer attachment is a good way to extend the quality and shelf life of perishable foods refrigerated or frozen in mason jars. This device can also be used to vacuum pack nonperishables in mason jars. Like home canning, vacuum sealing with the FoodSaver® removes air from the jar, keeping most foods fresh three to five times longer than their normal storage life. Vacuum packaging with the FoodSaver® is **not** a substitute for heat processing or home canning. Vacuum packed perishable food still requires refrigerated or frozen storage.

INCREDIBLE SPREADABLES

A culinary activity that knows no bounds – where the flavour combinations are endless. We call it jam and jelly-making. It's a culinary art in which you add your own spark of creativity to Mother Nature's handiwork. Like traditions, making soft spreads also lets us hold on to the best of the past – fabulous taste plus the fun of picking and jamming with friends and family.

GELLING ESSENTIALS

Gels form when pectin is combined in proper proportions with fruit, sugar and acid under suitable conditions. In simple terms, pectin is the "glue" that binds sugar, fruit and acid into a flexible structure. This structure captures and immobilizes the liquid – water and/or juice, the major component of the gel. Balancing these ingredients is essential for gel formation. Too much or too little of a component weakens the structure and can cause gel failure. *Imagine a perfectly balanced pyramid, each level representing an ingredient. If you take away individuals from one level and/or add more players to another level, the pyramid becomes unbalanced and collapses. This is what happens when ingredients are improperly balanced in a spread recipe – the gel fails.*

Fruits contain different levels of natural pectin that can vary by variety or due to growing conditions. The most basic jam and jelly preparation technique is the *long boil method*. Fruit and sugar are cooked to concentrate the pectin and evaporate moisture until a gel forms. (See gel tests.) This method, however, requires extended cooking times and works best with fruits that are high in pectin and acid. The fruit flavour in long boil spreads tends to have a caramelized flavour as opposed to the fresh-picked taste of products that require little or no cooking.

PECTIN

Pectin is a natural carbohydrate that occurs in all land plants as a cell wall constituent.

Commercial pectins are extracted from the pomace that remains when apples or citrus fruits are pressed for juices. By altering the extraction conditions, manufacturers produce different types of pectin for specific needs. Regardless of the production method used, commercial pectins are natural carbohydrates created by physical processes much like those used to extract sugar from beets or cane. Each pectin product, however, requires its own preparation techniques and ingredient proportions. Specific types of pectin are NOT interchangeable in recipes.

ACID

In addition to adequate pectin, gels require a proper acid level. Acid concentrations that are too high cause gels to form too quickly and result in products that "weep" as moisture is squeezed out of the gel during storage. Citrus fruit, used in marmalade, is naturally high in acid. Thus baking soda is sometimes added in these recipes to reduce the acid level.

PECTIN AND ACID CONTENT OF COMMON FRUITS

High Pectin/High Acid: sour apples, sour cherries, crabapples, cranberries, black currants, red currants, gooseberries, grapefruit, grapes, kiwifruit, lemons, limes, oranges, some varieties of plums.
High Pectin: sweet apples, sweet cherries, some varieties of plums, quince.
Low Pectin/High Acid: apricots, raspberries, rhubarb, strawberries.
Low Pectin: blueberries, elderberries, figs, nectarines, peaches, pears, pineapple.

ADDED PECTIN SOFT SPREADS

Adding commercial pectin, such as those sold by Bernardin Ltd., is a quick, easy and foolproof method of creating gels. Even those fruits with higher pectin concentrations benefit from added pectin as cooking time is reduced or eliminated to yield a spread with the ultimate in fresh-picked, full-bodied fruit flavour. Using a Bernardin pectin allows you to gel products made with any kind of fruit or juice, even vegetable juices, provided the recipe is followed exactly. Products made with added pectin also have higher yields per quantity of fruit used compared to long boil recipes. Each of the four Bernardin pectin products come with recipes and tips for a variety of soft spreads made with common ingredients. So pick a fruit, and start jammin!

JAMMIN' TIPS

Making incredible spreadables is fun and easy. Like all endeavors, success stems from attention to detail. For delicious results every time:
• Use only the best quality produce, free of blemishes.
  – For products made with added pectin, use **only fully ripe** fruit or berries. Use of lower quality, under or overripe fruit produces less flavourful products and can cause gel failure.
  – For long boil recipes, 25% of the fruit may be slightly under ripe.

- Partially thawed, frozen unsweetened fruit may be substituted for fresh. Thaw frozen fruit in refrigerator just until crushable; some ice crystals should still be present.
- Prepare ONE recipe at a time. Do not double batch.
- Measure with precision. Accurate measures ensure success!
  - DO NOT alter ingredient measures, especially sugar. If you want to reduce sugar, use a recipe and pectin specifically formulated for less sugar.
  - Use "liquid measures" (see through glass or plastic) to measure prepared fruit and liquids. Measures for dry ingredients come in sets and are leveled using a straight-edge spatula.
- Thoroughly wash and dry all produce. Unclean fruits can cause spoilage growth in jams. Excess moisture left on fruit may reduce gel strength.
- Prepare and measure fruit or juice as specified in each recipe.
  - Use a potato masher to crush fruit one layer at a time.
  - Unless specified in a recipe, do not purée fruit. Doing so may cause poor texture or gel failure.
- Cook recipes in a large DEEP stainless steel saucepan that allows space for a full rolling boil. When using added pectin, bring the mixture to a full ROLLING BOIL (220°F/104°C) that **cannot** be stirred down, **before** beginning to count the prescribed boiling time.
- To assure good vacuum seals and to destroy microorganisms that can cause food spoilage, HEAT PROCESS all filled jars of cooked soft spreads in a Boiling Water Canner. Freezer jams are stored frozen and do not require heat processing.

JUICE FOR JELLY

Select top-quality fruit. Prepare juice as directed and pour mixture into a dampened jelly bag or cheesecloth-lined sieve. For clear jellies, prepare fruit as directed, place in a jelly bag and allow juices to drip naturally; do not squeeze bag. Commercial juicers do not release sufficient solids into the juice to create good gelling results. Fruits with peels must be cooked to release pectin from the skins into the juice.

Hard Fruit – *Apples, Pears, Nectarines etc.* Wash fruit; remove stem and blossom ends but do not peel or core. Chop fruit; measure. For each slightly rounded 4 cups (1 L) prepared fruit add 1 cup (250 ml) water. Combine fruit and water in stainless steel saucepan; cover and boil gently until fruit is soft.

Soft Fruit – *Grapes, Cherries, Berries, etc.* Wash and stem fruit. Slightly crush fruit or follow specific recipe guidelines for fruit preparation; measure. For each slightly round 4 cups (1 L) prepared fruit add 1/4 to 1/2 cup (50-125 ml) water. Combine fruit and water in stainless steel saucepan; cover and boil gently until fruit is soft.

Use juice fresh, can or freeze for later use. When canning juice, heat juice to a boil before ladling into clean hot jars; follow filling and heat processing directions for Fruit Juice, page 44.

REDUCING FOAM

Cooking certain fruits, especially strawberries, peaches and jellies with lots of sugar can create considerable foam. This foam must be skimmed off prior to ladling the product into jars. To reduce this foaming action, add 1/2 tsp (2 ml) butter, margarine or vegetable oil to the fruit mixture before cooking.

GEL TESTS

Fruit spreads made without added pectin must be tested to establish a gel point. To avoid overcooking, remove the product from heat while conducting your choice of gel tests.

Sheet Test – Dip a cool, metal spoon into the boiling jelly. Lift spoon, moving it away from steam. Gel stage is reached when jelly "sheets" off spoon.

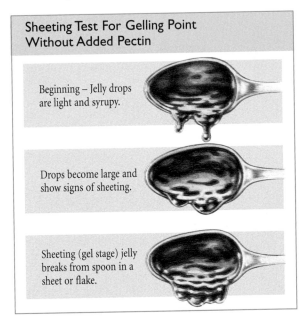

Sheeting Test For Gelling Point Without Added Pectin

Beginning – Jelly drops are light and syrupy.

Drops become large and show signs of sheeting.

Sheeting (gel stage) jelly breaks from spoon in a sheet or flake.

Plate Test – Before cooking jam, refrigerate 2 or 3 saucers. When mixture thickens, place a spoonful of hot mixture on cold plate and place in freezer until cooled to room temperature. A gel has been achieved when the product does not run together when separated.

Thermometer – Use candy/jelly thermometer. To determine gel temperature, first establish the boiling point of water at your location. This temperature plus 8°F (4°C) = the median gel stage at your location. *[The median gel stage temperature is 220°F (104°C), but ranges from 218° to 222°F (103°- 105°C). It depends on the pectin content of the individual fruit.]* When reading the temperature, hold the thermometer vertical in the mixture and read markings at eye level. Once gel temperature has been reached, immediately remove mixture from heat.

Super simple! Scrumptious! Just crush, stir and freeze. Make fruit spreads that taste like freshly-picked berries and fruit with only a few minutes effort with Bernardin Freezer Jam Pectin. These no-cook jams also require substantially less sugar than regular or liquid pectin freezer jams.

BLUSHING PEACH ALMOND CONSERVE

3 1/2 cups (875 ml) finely chopped, peeled & pitted peaches
4 tbsp (60 ml) chopped maraschino cherries
3 tbsp (45 ml) slivered almonds, toasted
1/4 tsp (1 ml) almond extract
1 1/2 cups (375 ml) granulated sugar
1 pouch (45 g) BERNARDIN *Freezer Jam* Pectin

 Prepare and measure peaches into bowl. Add maraschino cherries, almonds and almond extract. ◀◀◀

BANANA STRAWBERRY FREEZER JAM

3 large bananas
3 cups (750 ml) crushed strawberries
1 1/2 cups (375 ml) granulated sugar
1 pouch (45 g) BERNARDIN *Freezer Jam* Pectin

Place unpeeled bananas on baking sheet; bake in 400°F (200°C) oven. Cool. Peel and mash bananas; measure 1 cup (250 ml). *(Heating bananas is optional. It prevents jam from darkening during storage.)* Combine bananas and crushed strawberries. ◀◀◀

PLUM-ORANGE FREEZER JAM

10 medium plums, pitted & chopped
1/2 cup (125 ml) water
1 tsp (5 ml) grated orange peel
1/4 cup (50 ml) finely chopped orange pulp
1 1/2 cups (375 ml) granulated sugar
1 pouch (45 g) BERNARDIN *Freezer Jam* Pectin

Combine plums and water in saucepan. Cover, boil gently 5 minutes. Measure 3 3/4 cups (900 ml) into bowl. Add orange peel and pulp. ◀◀◀

FREEZER JAMS

• Wash and rinse five 250 ml mason jars and BERNARDIN Storage or 2-piece SNAP Lids.

Prepare and measure fruit as directed. Place in a bowl with other specified ingredients, where indicated.

▶▶▶ **Stir in sugar;** let stand 15 minutes.

• Stirring constantly, gradually add BERNARDIN *Freezer Jam* Pectin to fruit mixture. Stir 3 minutes longer.

• Let stand 5 minutes.

• Ladle jam into clean 250 ml mason jars to within 1/2 inch (1 cm) of top rim (headspace). Wipe jar rims removing any stickiness. Apply lids tightly.

• Store in freezer up to 1 year. Refrigerate up to 3 weeks or serve immediately.

Each recipe makes about 5 x 250 ml jars.

BUMBLEBERRY FREEZER JAM

2 cups (500 ml) hulled & crushed strawberries,
  about 1 quart (1 L)
1 cup (250 ml) crushed raspberries, about 1 pint
  (500 ml)
1 cup (250 ml) crushed blueberries, about 1 pint
  (500 ml)
1 1/2 cups (375 ml) granulated sugar
1 pouch (45 g) BERNARDIN *Freezer Jam* Pectin

Wash and prepare berries; measure into a
large bowl. ◀◀◀

BLUEBERRY ORANGE FREEZER JAM

4 cups (1000 ml) crushed blueberries, about
  4 pt (2 L)
2 tsp (10 ml) lightly packed, finely grated
  orange zest
1 1/2 cups (375 ml) granulated sugar
1 pouch (45 g) BERNARDIN *Freezer Jam* Pectin

Wash, thoroughly drain and crush blueberries.
Measure 4 cups (1000 ml); in microwave or on
stovetop, heat and stir blueberries to a boil.
*(Heating berries is optional. It softens skins and yields
a smoother, thicker, intensely coloured jam.)* Add
orange zest. ◀◀◀

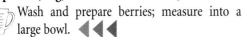

PEACH RASPBERRY FREEZER JAM

2 1/2 cups (625 ml) crushed, peeled & pitted
  peaches or nectarines
1 1/2 cups (375 ml) crushed raspberries
1 1/2 cups (375 ml) granulated sugar
1 pouch (45 g) BERNARDIN *Freezer Jam* Pectin

Prepare and measure peaches and raspberries
into bowl. ◀◀◀

TROPICAL STRAWBERRY FREEZER JAM

2 1/2 cups (625 ml) crushed strawberries,
  about 2 pints
1 1/2 cups (375 ml) prepared fresh pineapple
Grated peel of 1 medium orange
2 tbsp (25 ml) dark rum
1 1/2 cups (375 ml) granulated sugar
1 pouch (45 g) BERNARDIN *Freezer Jam* Pectin

Crush and measure strawberries into bowl. Peel
and core pineapple; pulse in food processor until
a few chunks remain, measure 1 1/2 cups (375 ml).
Add to strawberries with peel and rum. ◀◀◀

MANGO BERRY FREEZER JAM

3 cups (750 ml) crushed strawberries
1 cup (250 ml) mashed mango, 1 to 2 mangos
Grated peel and juice of 1 lime
1 1/2 cups (375 ml) granulated sugar
1 pouch (45 g) BERNARDIN *Freezer Jam* Pectin

Crush and measure strawberries into bowl.
Peel and pit mango; mash or pulse in food
processor until a few chunks remain; measure 1 cup
(250 ml) into strawberries. Add peel and 1 tbsp
(15 ml) lime juice. ◀◀◀

A TOUCH OF CLASS

Use spices, nuts and extracts to personalize, flavour
and add texture to soft spreads. Before adding to a
mixture, lightly toast nuts to boost their natural
flavour. Grated citrus peel or gingerroot also make
excellent additions to soft spreads. To avoid
darkening pastel fruit colour in cooked spreads, use
whole spices, tied in a spice bag. They won't alter
colour like ground spices can. Remove spice bag
before ladling mixture into jars.

As a general rule, ADD:
• grated peel, gingerroot or spices before cooking,
• nuts during the last 5 minutes of cooking,
• flavourings containing alcohol after cooking is
  completed.

This powdered pectin is stirred into prepared fruit and brought to a boil to dissolve the pectin. Sugar is then added and the mixture is returned to a full rolling boil for 1 minute.

JAMS – ORIGINAL PECTIN

• Place required number of clean 250 or 236 ml mason jars on a rack in a boiling water canner; cover jars with water and heat to a simmer (180°F/82°C). Set screw bands aside; heat SNAP Lids in hot water, NOT boiling (180°F/82°C). Keep jars and SNAP Lids hot until ready to use.

Prepare and measure fruit as directed. *Combine fruit, juice and other specified ingredients (except sugar) in a large, deep stainless steel saucepan. If desired, to reduce foaming, add 1/2 tsp (2 ml) butter or vegetable oil to mixture.*
• Measure sugar; set aside.

▶▶▶ **Whisk Fruit Pectin into Fruit Mixture until dissolved.** Stirring frequently, bring mixture to a boil over high heat. Add sugar.
• Stirring constantly, return mixture to a full rolling boil that can't be stirred down. Boil hard 1 minute. Remove from heat; skim foam.
• Ladle jam into a hot jar to within 1/4 inch (0.5 cm) of top rim (headspace). Using nonmetallic utensil, remove air bubbles. Wipe jar rim removing any stickiness. Centre SNAP Lid on jar; apply screw band *securely & firmly until resistance is met – fingertip tight. Do not overtighten.* Place jar in canner; repeat for remaining jam.
• Cover canner; bring water to a boil. At altitudes up to 1,000 ft (305 m), process – *boil filled jars* – **10 minutes**. Remove jars without tilting. Cool upright, undisturbed 24 hours; DO NOT RETIGHTEN screw bands. After cooling check jar seals. *Sealed lids curve downward.* Remove screw bands; wipe and dry bands and jars. Store screw bands separately or replace loosely on jars, as desired. Label and store jars in a cool, dark place.

APRICOT JAM

2 1/2 cups (625 ml) dried apricots, about 14 oz (400 g)
1 1/2 cups (375 ml) water
1 cup (250 ml) orange juice
1 tbsp (15 ml) bottled lemon juice
3 1/2 cups (875 ml) granulated sugar
1 pkg (57 g) BERNARDIN *Original Fruit Pectin*

In a large, deep stainless steel saucepan, combine apricots, water and orange juice; bring to a boil. Cover and boil gently until softened, about 20 minutes.
• Purée apricots with cooking liquid in food processor. Measure 3 cups (750 ml); add lemon juice. ◀◀◀
Yield – 4 x 250 or 236 ml jars

CHERRY JAM

4 cups (1000 ml) prepared sweet OR sour cherries, about 3 lb (1.4 kg)
5 cups (1250 ml) granulated sugar
1/4 cup (50 ml) bottled lemon juice – for sweet cherries, only
1 pkg (57 g) BERNARDIN *Original Fruit Pectin*

Wash, stem, pit and finely chop cherries. Measure 4 cups (1000 ml) cherries. If using sweet cherries, add lemon juice. ◀◀◀
Yield – 6 x 250 or 236 ml jars

BLACK CURRANT JAM

YOU MUST BE ON YOUR TOES TO MAKE THIS SWEET-TART JAM. THESE BERRIES ARE ONLY AVAILABLE FOR A COUPLE OF WEEKS THROUGH-OUT THE YEAR.
8 cups (2000 ml) black currants
3/4 cup (175 ml) water
6 1/2 cups (1625 ml) granulated sugar
1 pkg (57 g) BERNARDIN *Original Fruit Pectin*

Wash and stem currants. Combine currants and water in a saucepan; simmer, covered, 15 minutes. Thoroughly crush and measure 5 cups (1250 ml). ◀◀◀
Yield – 7 x 250 or 236 ml jars

BLUEBERRY LIME JAM

4 cups (1000 ml) crushed blueberries
1-2 limes
4 cups (1000 ml) granulated sugar
1 pkg (57 g) BERNARDIN *Original Fruit Pectin*

• Wash and crush blueberries, one layer at a time. Measure 4 cups (1000 ml).

Wash and finely grate zest from lime(s); measure 2 tbsp (30 ml). Squeeze lime(s); measure 2 tbsp (30 ml) juice. ◀◀◀

Yield – 6 x 250 or 236 ml jars

FABULOUS FIG JAM

3 1/2 cups (875 ml) dried figs, about 18 oz (500 g)
3 1/4 cups (800 ml) water
3 1/2 cups (875 ml) granulated sugar
1/3 cup (75 ml) orange juice
1 tbsp (15 ml) bottled lemon juice
1 pkg (57 g) BERNARDIN *Original Fruit Pectin*
1/3 cup (75 ml) orange liqueur, *optional*

Combine figs and water in a large, deep stainless steel saucepan. Stirring frequently, bring to a boil; cover and reduce heat. Boil gently until soft, about 20 minutes. Purée figs with cooking liquid. Measure 3 cups (750 ml). Add orange and lemon juices.

• If using, stir orange liqueur into **cooked** jam just before ladling into jars. ◀◀◀

Yield – 6 x 250 or 236 ml jars

KIWI DAIQUIRI JAM

1 3/4 cups (425 ml) mashed kiwifruit, about 8-9 medium
2/3 cup (150 ml) unsweetened pineapple juice
1/3 cup (75 ml) lime juice
3 cups (750 ml) granulated sugar
1 pkg (57 g) BERNARDIN *Original Fruit Pectin*
1/4 cup (50 ml) rum
5-6 drops green food colouring, *optional*

Peel and mash kiwifruit, one layer at a time. Measure 1 3/4 cups (425 ml). Add pineapple and lime juices.

• If using, stir rum and food colouring into **cooked** jam just before ladling into jars. ◀◀◀

Yield – 4 x 250 or 236 ml jars

MULBERRY JAM

3 cups (750 ml) crushed mulberries
1/2 cup (125 ml) bottled lemon juice
6 cups (1500 ml) granulated sugar
1 pkg (57 g) BERNARDIN *Original Fruit Pectin*

Wash, stem and crush berries, one layer at a time; measure 3 cups (750 ml). ◀◀◀

Yield – 6 x 250 or 236 ml jars

PEACH AND BLACKBERRY JAM

3 cups (750 ml) crushed, peeled & pitted peaches
2 cups (500 ml) blackberries, about 3/4 lb (350 g)
2 tbsp (30 ml) bottled lemon juice
1/2 tsp (2 ml) ground cinnamon
1/4 tsp (1 ml) ground ginger
6 cups (1500 ml) granulated sugar
1 pkg (57 g) BERNARDIN *Original Fruit Pectin*

Blanch, peel, pit and finely chop or crush peaches, one layer at a time. Measure 3 cups (750 ml).

• Combine peaches, blackberries, lemon juice and spices in a large, deep stainless steel saucepan. ◀◀◀

Yield – 6 x 250 or 236 ml jars

STRAWBERRY RHUBARB JAM

2 cups (500 ml) crushed strawberries, about 1 quart (1 L)
2 cups (500 ml) finely chopped rhubarb, 1 lb (454 g)
1/4 cup (50 ml) bottled lemon juice
5 1/2 cups (1375 ml) granulated sugar
1 pkg (57 g) BERNARDIN *Original Fruit Pectin*

Wash, hull and crush strawberries, one layer at a time. Measure 2 cups (500 ml). Wash and finely chop rhubarb. Measure 2 cups (500 ml). ◀◀◀

Yield – 6 x 250 or 236 ml jars

This rapid-set pectin is fully dissolved and ready to stir into both cooked and uncooked (freezer) fruit-sugar mixtures. Because cooking time is shorter than any other method, liquid pectin delivers the freshest possible flavour.

APRICOT RED CURRANT JAM

2 3/4 cups (675 ml) finely chopped apricots, about 1.7 lb (750 g) fresh
1 cup (250 ml) red currants
Peel and juice of 1 large lemon
6 cups (1500 ml) granulated sugar
1 pouch (85 ml) BERNARDIN *Liquid* Pectin

Wash, pit and finely chop apricots; measure 2 3/4 cups (675 ml). Wash and stem red currants; measure 1 cup (250 ml); add to apricots. Remove 2 tsp (10 ml) finely grated peel and 1/4 cup (50 ml) juice; add both to apricot mixture.

• Stir sugar into apricot mixture and let stand 5 minutes for juices to flow. ◀◀◀
Yield – 6 x 250 or 236 ml jars

LIQUID PECTIN JAMS

• Place required number of clean 250 or 236 ml mason jars on a rack in a boiling water canner; cover jars with water and heat to a simmer (180°F/82°C). Set screw bands aside; heat SNAP Lids in hot water, NOT boiling (180°F/82°C). Keep jars and SNAP Lids hot until ready to use.

Prepare and measure fruit as directed in individual recipes.

Combine fruit, juice and seasonings, if required, in a large, deep stainless steel saucepan.

▶▶▶ **Stir sugar into fruit mixture.** *If desired, to reduce foaming, add 1/2 tsp (2 ml) butter or vegetable oil to mixture.*

• Over high heat, bring mixture to a full rolling boil. Stirring constantly, boil hard 1 minute. Remove from heat.

• Immediately stir in *Liquid* Pectin, mixing well. Stir and skim foam.

• Ladle jam into a hot jar to within 1/4 inch (0.5 cm) of top rim (headspace). Using nonmetallic utensil, remove air bubbles. Wipe jar rim removing any stickiness. Centre SNAP Lid on jar; apply screw band *securely & firmly* until resistance is met – *fingertip tight. Do not overtighten.* Place jar in canner; repeat for remaining jam.

• Cover canner; bring water to a boil. At altitudes up to 1,000 ft (305 m), process – *boil filled jars* – **10 minutes.** Remove jars without tilting. Cool upright, undisturbed 24 hours; DO NOT RETIGHTEN screw bands. After cooling check jar seals. *Sealed lids curve downward.* Remove screw bands; wipe and dry bands and jars. Store screw bands separately or replace loosely on jars, as desired. Label and store jars in a cool, dark place.

BLACKBERRY JAM

3 3/4 cups (925 ml) crushed blackberries, about 4 pints (2 L)
1/3 cup (75 ml) bottled lemon juice
7 1/3 cups (1800 ml) granulated sugar
1 pouch (85 ml) BERNARDIN *Liquid* Pectin

Wash and crush berries, one layer at a time. Sieve part of the pulp to remove seeds, if desired. Measure 3 3/4 cups (925 ml). ◀◀◀
Yield – 8 x 250 or 236 ml jars

BLUEBERRY JAM

4 1/2 cups (1125 ml) crushed blueberries, about 4 pints (2 L)
1/4 cup (50 ml) bottled lemon juice
7 cups (1750 ml) granulated sugar
2 pouches (170 ml) BERNARDIN *Liquid* Pectin

Wash and crush blueberries, one layer at a time. Measure 4 1/2 cups (1125 ml). ◀◀◀
Yield – 8 x 250 or 236 ml jars

AUTUMN CRANBERRY PEAR JAM

2.2 lb (1 kg) fully ripe pears, about 4 large
2/3 cup (150 ml) chopped dried cranberries
1/4 cup (50 ml) unsweetened apple juice
1/4 cup (50 ml) bottled lemon juice
5 1/2 cups (1375 ml) granulated sugar
1 tsp (5 ml) ground cinnamon
1 pouch (85 ml) BERNARDIN *Liquid* Pectin

Peel, core and crush pears; measure 3 cups (750 ml). ◄◄◄

Yield – 6 x 250 or 236 ml jars

CORONATION GRAPE JAM

3.3 lb (1.5 kg) Sovereign (seedless) Coronation
  Grapes or seeded Concord Grapes
1/2 cup (125 ml) water
7 1/2 cups (1875 ml) granulated sugar
1 pouch (85 ml) BERNARDIN *Liquid* Pectin

Wash and stem grapes. Combine with water in large deep stainless steel saucepan. Bring mixture to a boil; reduce heat. Crush and boil gently 5 minutes; measure 4 1/2 cups (1125 ml). Wash saucepan and return measured grapes to pan. ◄◄◄

Yield – 8 x 250 or 236 ml jars

CINNAMON PEAR JAM

4 cups (1000 ml) prepared pears
1/3 cup (75 ml) bottled lemon juice
1 tsp (5 ml) ground cinnamon
7 1/2 cups (1875 ml) granulated sugar
1 pouch (85 ml) BERNARDIN *Liquid* Pectin

Peel, core and finely chop pears or crush fully ripe pears; measure 4 cups (1000 ml). ◄◄◄

Yield – 6 x 250 or 236 ml jars

GOLDEN SPICED PLUM JAM

3.3 lb (1.5 kg) golden plums
1/2 cup (125 ml) apple juice
4 inch (10 cm) cinnamon stick
4 to 6 cardamom pods
6 2/3 cups (1650 ml) granulated sugar
1 pouch (85 ml) BERNARDIN *Liquid* Pectin
4 tbsp (60 ml) dark rum, *optional*

Wash, pit and coarsely chop plums. Combine plums and apple juice in a large, deep stainless steel saucepan. Tie cinnamon and cardamom in a square of cheesecloth creating a spice bag; add to plums. Bring to a boil; reduce heat and boil gently, covered, 5 minutes. Discard spice bag.
• Measure 4 1/2 cups (1125 ml) cooked plums. Add rum after cooking. ◄◄◄

Yield – 7 x 250 or 236 ml jars

STRAWBERRY JAM

3 3/4 cups (925 ml) crushed strawberries, about
  2 quarts (2 L)
1/4 cup (50 ml) bottled lemon juice
7 cups (1750 ml) granulated sugar
1 pouch (85 ml) BERNARDIN *Liquid* Pectin

Wash, hull and crush strawberries, one layer at a time. Measure 3 3/4 cups (925 ml). ◄◄◄

Yield – 7 x 250 or 236 ml jars

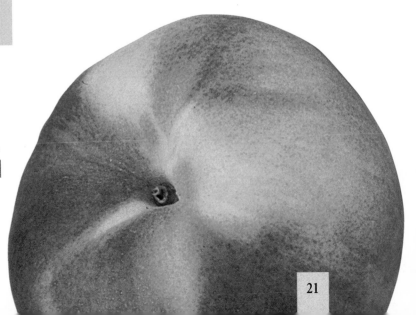

Cooking fruit-sugar mixtures concentrates the naturally occurring pectin. To enhance natural pectin content in long-boil jams, prepare recipe using a mixture of 3/4 fully ripe and 1/4 slightly underripe fruit. These "long boil" soft spreads require longer cooking periods and a gel test (page 15).

JAMS – LONG BOIL (NO ADDED PECTIN)

• Place required number of clean 250 or 236 ml mason jars on a rack in a boiling water canner; cover jars with water and heat to a simmer (180°F/82°C). Set screw bands aside; heat SNAP Lids in hot water, NOT boiling (180°F/82°C). Keep jars and SNAP Lids hot until ready to use.

Prepare fruit mixture as directed. *To reduce foaming, add 1/2 tsp (2 ml) butter or vegetable oil to mixture, if desired.*

▶▶▶ **Bring mixture to boiling point slowly, stirring until sugar dissolves.** Increase heat, boil vigorously – **approximate Cook Time indicated in each recipe** – until mixture reaches gel point. As mixture thickens, stir frequently to prevent sticking. When conducting gel test, remove mixture from heat to prevent over-cooking or scorching.

• Remove from heat; skim foam and ladle jam into a hot jar to within 1/4 inch (0.5 cm) of top rim (headspace). Using nonmetallic utensil, remove air bubbles. Wipe jar rim removing any stickiness. Centre SNAP Lid on jar; apply screw band *securely & firmly* until resistance is met – fingertip tight. Do not overtighten. Place jar in canner; repeat for remaining jam.

• Cover canner; bring water to a boil. At altitudes up to 1,000 ft (305 m), process – *boil filled jars* – **10 minutes**. Remove jars without tilting. Cool upright, undisturbed 24 hours; DO NOT RETIGHTEN screw bands. After cooling check jar seals. *Sealed lids curve downward.* Remove screw bands; wipe and dry bands and jars. Store screw bands separately or replace loosely on jars, as desired. Label and store jars in a cool, dark place.

APRICOT JAM

8 cups (2000 ml) finely chopped, peeled pitted apricots
4 tbsp (60 ml) lemon juice
6 cups (1500 ml) granulated sugar

Combine apricots, lemon juice and sugar in a large, deep stainless steel saucepan. ◀◀◀
• Cook: 25 minutes   **Yield – 9 x 250 or 236 ml jars**

BERRY JAM

9 cups (2250 ml) crushed berries
6 cups (1500 ml) granulated sugar

Use one or a combination of berries. Wash, dry and crush berries. To remove a portion of or all of seeds, press berries through sieve before measuring. Measure berries and sugar into a large, deep stainless steel saucepan. ◀◀◀
• Cook: 20 minutes   **Yield – 7 x 250 or 236 ml jars**

GINGERED CITRUS-RHUBARB JAM

8 cups (2000 ml) prepared rhubarb, about 2 lb (1 kg)
Grated peel and juice of 2 oranges
Grated peel and juice of 1 lime
6 cups (1500 ml) granulated sugar
2 tsp (10 ml) grated fresh gingerroot

Wash and trim rhubarb; cut into 1/2 inch (1 cm) pieces. Measure 8 cups (2000 ml) into a large, deep stainless steel saucepan.
• Wash oranges & lime; grate peel. Squeeze juice from oranges and lime; measure 3/4 cup (175 ml), adding water if necessary. Add peel and juice to rhubarb with grated gingerroot. ◀◀◀
• Cook: 30-35 minutes **Yield – 5 x 250 or 236 ml jars**

GRAPE JAM

8 cups (2000 ml) Concord grapes
1/2 cup (125 ml) water
6 cups (1500 ml) granulated sugar

Pinch grapes to separate pulp from skins of grapes. Chop skins, if desired. Combine skins and water; cook gently 15 to 20 minutes. In separate saucepan, cook pulp until soft; press pulp through sieve to remove seeds.

• Combine pulp, skins and sugar in a large, deep stainless steel saucepan. ◀◀◀
• Cook: 10 minutes **Yield – 6 x 250 or 236 ml jars**

PEACH OR PEAR JAM

8 cups (2000 ml) crushed, peeled, pitted peaches
  or pears
2 tbsp (25 ml) lemon juice
1/2 cup (125 ml) water
6 cups (1500 ml) granulated sugar

Combine fruit, lemon juice and water in a large, deep stainless steel saucepan; cook gently 10 minutes. Add sugar. ◀◀◀
• Cook: 15 minutes **Yield – 8 x 250 or 236 ml jars**

SPICED PEACH OR PEAR JAM

Tie 1 tsp (5 ml) whole cloves, 1 stick cinnamon and 1/2 tsp (2 ml) whole allspice or cracked nutmeg in spice bag. Cook spices with fruit mixture; remove spice bag before ladling jam into jars.

ELDERBERRY JAM

8 cups (2000 ml) crushed elderberries
4 tbsp (60 ml) vinegar
6 cups (1500 ml) granulated sugar

Wash elderberries. Crush and measure into a large, deep stainless steel saucepan. Add vinegar and sugar. ◀◀◀
• Cook: 20 minutes **Yield – 6 x 250 or 236 ml jars**

RASPBERRY RED CURRANT JAM

6 cups (1500 ml) red currants
2 cups (500 ml) crushed raspberries
3 cups (750 ml) granulated sugar

Wash currants. Cook with 1/4 cup (50 ml) water until softened; press through sieve to remove seeds.

• Measure 2 cups (500 ml) currant pulp into large, deep stainless steel saucepan. Add raspberries and sugar. ◀◀◀
• Cook: 30 minutes **Yield – 4 x 250 or 236 ml jars**

PLUM JAM

4 lb (1.8 kg) tart plums, stems removed
1 1/2 cups (375 ml) water
4 tbsp (60 ml) lemon juice
6 cups (1500 ml) granulated sugar

Wash and pit plums; chop coarsely and place in a large, deep stainless steel saucepan. Add water, lemon juice and sugar. ◀◀◀
• Cook: 20 minutes **Yield – 8 x 250 or 236 ml jars**

STRAWBERRY JAM

8 cups (2000 ml) crushed strawberries
1/3 cup (75 ml) lemon juice
6 cups (1500 ml) granulated sugar

Wash and hull strawberries. Crush and measure into a large, deep stainless steel saucepan. Add lemon juice and sugar. ◀◀◀
• Cook: 40 minutes **Yield – 8 x 250 or 236 ml jars**

JELLY BAG

A high quality mesh bag used to strain juice for making jellies. Each bag has an elasticised top to stretch over a jelly stand or bowl. To clean rinse the reusable bag in warm soapy water. A cheesecloth-lined strainer may be substituted.

Have it your way! Fruit spreads without additional sweetener or lightly sweetened with sugar substitutes (artificial sweeteners) or small quantities of sugar, corn syrup or honey. Unique to Bernardin, this special pectin gels fruit mixtures with no added sugar. Before you begin, please read the recipe preparation steps carefully. The **order of ingredient addition** is dependent upon the type of sweetener you choose. i.e. sugar replacements are added after completion of the boiling step; sugar is added to the hot fruit-pectin mixture which is then boiled. For best results, when making Light (sugar added) Spreads, add no more than of 3 cups (750 ml) granulated sugar. Each package of Bernardin *NO SUGAR NEEDED* Pectin contains recipes for the most popular fruits used in Ultra Light, Very Light and Light spreads and jellies.

LIGHT and NO SUGAR ADDED FRUIT SPREADS

• Place required number of clean 250 or 236 ml mason jars on a rack in a boiling water canner; cover jars with water and heat to a simmer (180°F/82°C). Set screw bands aside; heat SNAP Lids in hot water, NOT boiling (180°F/82°C). Keep jars and SNAP Lids hot until ready to use.

Prepare and measure fruit as directed. *Combine fruit, juice and other specified ingredients (**except sugar and/or sweetener**) in a large, deep stainless steel saucepan. If desired, to reduce foaming, add 1/2 tsp (2 ml) butter or vegetable oil to mixture.*

• If required in chosen recipe, measure sugar OR granular sugar replacement (artificial sweetener); set aside.

▶▶▶ **Whisk NO SUGAR NEEDED Fruit Pectin into fruit mixture,** stirring until pectin is completely dissolved. Stirring occasionally, bring mixture to a boil over high heat.

• **ULTRA LIGHT** *(no sweetener or sugar added)* – stirring constantly, boil fruit **spreads** – 5 minutes; **jellies** – 1 minute. Remove from heat.

• **VERY LIGHT** *(with artificial sweetener)* – stirring constantly, boil fruit **spreads** – 5 minutes; **jellies** – 1 minute. Remove from heat. Add artificial sweetener, stirring until well mixed.

• **LIGHT** *(sugar added)* – add sugar to hot mixture. Stirring constantly, return mixture to a boil; boil fruit **spreads** and **jellies** – 5 minutes. Remove from heat; skim foam.

• Ladle fruit spread into a hot jar to within 1/4 inch (0.5 cm) of top rim (headspace). Using nonmetallic utensil, remove air bubbles. Wipe jar rim removing any stickiness. Centre SNAP Lid on jar; apply screw band *securely & firmly until resistance is met – fingertip tight. Do not overtighten.* Place jar in canner; repeat for remaining fruit spread.

• Cover canner; bring water to a boil. At altitudes up to 1,000 ft (305 m), process – *boil filled jars* – **10 minutes**. Remove jars without tilting. Cool upright, undisturbed 24 hours; DO NOT RETIGHTEN screw bands. After cooling check jar seals. *Sealed lids curve downward.* Remove screw bands; wipe and dry bands and jars. Store screw bands separately or replace loosely on jars, as desired. Label and store jars in a cool, dark place.

ULTRA LIGHT

BUMBLEBERRY SPREAD

1 1/2 cups (375 ml) crushed fully ripe strawberries
1 cup (250 ml) crushed raspberries
1 cup (250 ml) crushed blackberries
1/2 cup (125 ml) unsweetened cherry juice
1 pkg (49 g) Bernardin NO SUGAR NEEDED Pectin

If desired, press raspberries and blackberries through a coarse sieve to remove most of seeds before measuring.

• Crush and measure berries individually. Combine strawberries, raspberries, blackberries and cherry juice in a stainless steel saucepan. Whisk in pectin; proceed as directed in main recipe. ◀◀◀

Yield – 3 to 4 x 250 or 236 ml jars

HERB JELLY

1 large bunch fresh herbs – basil, mint, thyme, sage
3 3/4 cups (925 ml) unsweetened apple or white grape juice
1 pkg (49 g) Bernardin NO SUGAR NEEDED Pectin

Wash herbs, shake off excess moisture and place in a stainless steel saucepan. Press herbs with spoon or masher to bruise leaves and release flavour. Add juice, heat to a boil; cover and let steep 30 minutes or longer. Pour juice through cheesecloth lined strainer. Measure 3 1/2 cups into clean saucepan. Whisk in pectin. Bring to a full rolling boil; boil 1 minute. Proceed as directed in main recipe. ◀◀◀

Yield – 3 x 250 or 236 ml jars

PEACH BERRY SPREAD

3 cups (750 ml) crushed, peeled fully ripe peaches
1 cup (250 ml) whole raspberries
1/2 cup (125 ml) unsweetened apple or white grape juice
1/4 cup (50 ml) lemon juice
1 pkg (49 g) Bernardin NO SUGAR NEEDED Pectin

Crush peaches; measure peaches and raspberries separately. Combine fruit and juices in a stainless steel saucepan. Whisk in pectin; proceed as directed in main recipe. ◀◀◀

Yield – 3 to 4 x 250 or 236 ml jars

VERY LIGHT

MOM'S APPLE PIE IN A JAR

6 cups (1500 ml) chopped, peeled Granny Smith apples
Juice and grated peel of 1 large lemon
2 cups (500 ml) unsweetened apple juice
3/4 cup (175 ml) raisins or dried cranberries
1 tsp (5 ml) ground cinnamon
1 pkg (49 g) Bernardin NO SUGAR NEEDED Pectin
1 1/2 cups (375 ml) granular sugar replacement
   (artificial sweetener)

Combine apples, lemon peel and juices in stainless steel saucepan. Bring to a boil, boil gently several minutes until apples begin to soften. Remove from heat, whisk in pectin; add dried fruit and cinnamon. Return mixture to a boil; boil 5 minutes. Remove from heat; stir in sweetener. Proceed as directed in main recipe. ◀◀◀
Yield – 4 to 5 x 250 or 236 ml jars

RASPBERRY JELLY

12 cups (3000 ml) raspberries
3 cups (750 ml) water
1 pkg (49 g) Bernardin NO SUGAR NEEDED Pectin
1 1/2 cups (375 ml) granular sugar replacement
   (artificial sweetener)

Combine raspberries and water in a stainless steel saucepan; cook 5 minutes and crush berries. Pour into damped jelly bag suspended over bowl. Let drip to collect juice. Measure 3 3/4 cups (950 ml) juice into saucepan. Whisk in pectin until dissolved. Bring to a full rolling boil; boil 1 minute. Remove from heat; stir in sweetener. Proceed as directed in main recipe. ◀◀◀
Yield – 3 to 4 x 250 or 236 ml jars

CHERRY APRICOT SPREAD

2 1/2 cups (625 ml) pitted, chopped sour cherries
1 cup (250 ml) finely chopped, pitted apricots
1/2 cup (125 ml) unsweetened apple juice
2 tbsp (25 ml) lemon juice
1 pkg (49 g) Bernardin NO SUGAR NEEDED Pectin
1 1/2 cups (375 ml) granular sugar replacement
   (artificial sweetener)

Combine cherries, apricots and juices in a stainless steel saucepan. Whisk in pectin. Bring to a full rolling boil; boil 5 minutes. Remove from heat; stir in sweetener. Proceed as directed in main recipe. ◀◀◀
Yield – about 4 x 250 or 236 ml jars

LIGHT

CANDIED APPLE SPREAD

1 small lemon
3 MacIntosh apples, peeled, cored & chopped
2 tart Granny Smith apples, peeled, cored & chopped
2 cups (500 ml) unsweetened apple or white grape
   juice, divided
4 inch (10 cm) cinnamon stick
1 pkg (49 g) Bernardin NO SUGAR NEEDED Pectin
150 g cinnamon hearts candy (about 3/4 cup/175 ml)

Chop lemon, including peel. Combine lemon, apples, 1/2 cup (125 ml) juice and cinnamon stick in a large stainless steel saucepan. Bring to a boil; cover and cook, stirring occasionally, until apples are tender. Discard cinnamon stick.
• Press fruit mixture through a coarse sieve; measure 4 1/2 cups (1125 ml) applesauce and return to saucepan with remaining 1 1/2 cups (375 ml) juice. Whisk in pectin until dissolved. Bring to a boil; add candy and proceed as directed in main recipe. ◀◀◀
Yield – about 5 x 250 or 236 ml jars

CHERRY JELLY

3 1/2 lb (1.6 kg) sour cherries, stemmed
1/2 cup (125 ml) water
1 pkg (49 g) Bernardin NO SUGAR NEEDED Pectin
2 cups (500 ml) granulated sugar

Combine cherries and water in stainless steel saucepan; boil gently, covered, 5 minutes. Crush, cook 5 minutes longer. Pour into jelly bag suspended over bowl; let drip to collect juice.
• Measure 3 1/2 cups (875 ml) juice into clean stainless steel saucepan. Whisk in pectin until dissolved. Bring to a boil, add sugar and proceed as directed in main recipe. ◀◀◀
Yield – about 5 x 250 or 236 ml jars

AUTUMN GLORY
FRUIT SPREAD

2 cups (500 ml) crushed, fully ripe peeled pears
1 1/4 cups (300 ml) finely chopped plums
1 cup (250 ml) unsweetened white grape juice
1/4 cup (50 ml) lemon juice
1 pkg (49 g) Bernardin NO SUGAR NEEDED Pectin
2 1/2 cups (625 ml) granulated sugar

Combine pears, plums, grape and lemon juices in stainless steel saucepan. Whisk in pectin until dissolved. Bring to a boil; add sugar and proceed as directed in main recipe. ◀◀◀
Yield – about 5 x 250 or 236 ml jars

Light and luscious, these spreads showcase fruit's natural sweetness and flavour – no sugar is added! Apples boost the pectin-content and add body to these spreads.

SPREADABLE FRUIT

• Place required number of clean 250 or 236 ml mason jars on a rack in a boiling water canner; cover jars with water and heat to a simmer (180°F/82°C). Set screw bands aside; heat SNAP Lids in hot water, NOT boiling (180°F/82°C). Keep jars and SNAP Lids hot until ready to use.

 Wash, prepare and measure Specific Fruit and apples as directed.

 **Combine fruit, apples, juice concentrate and any other ingredients for Specific Fruit recipes in a large deep stainless steel saucepan.** Bring mixture to a boil, stirring occasionally. Boil gently, stirring frequently – **approximate Cook Time indicated in each recipe** – *until mixture thickens to spreadable consistency.*

• Ladle spread into a hot jar to within 1/4 inch (0.5 cm) of top rim (headspace). Using nonmetallic utensil, remove air bubbles. Wipe jar rim removing any stickiness. Centre SNAP Lid on jar; apply screw band *securely & firmly until resistance is met – fingertip tight. Do not overtighten.* Place jar in canner; repeat for remaining jam.

• Cover canner; bring water to a boil. At altitudes up to 1,000 ft (305 m), process – *boil filled jars* – **10 minutes.** Remove jars without tilting. Cool upright, undisturbed 24 hours; DO NOT RETIGHTEN screw bands. After cooling check jar seals. *Sealed lids curve downward.* Remove screw bands; wipe and dry bands and jars. Store screw bands separately or replace loosely on jars, as desired. Label and store jars in a cool, dark place.

26

SPREADABLE BERRIES

6 cups (1500 ml) hulled strawberries
5 tart apples, peeled, cored & chopped
3 cups (750 ml) pitted cherries
3 cups (750 ml) raspberries
2 cans (each 355 ml) undiluted frozen apple juice concentrate, thawed

 Cook: 45 minutes ◀◀◀
    Yield – 7 x 250 or 236 ml jars

SPREADABLE BLUEBERRIES

10 cups (2500 ml) blueberries
4 tart apples, peeled, cored & chopped
2 cans (each 355 ml) undiluted frozen grape juice concentrate, thawed

 Cook: 60 minutes ◀◀◀
    Yield – 6 x 250 or 236 ml jars

SPICY SPREADABLE PEACHES

5 cups (1250 ml) peeled, pitted, chopped peaches
4 tart apples, peeled, cored & chopped
1 can undiluted frozen apple juice concentrate, thawed
2 tbsp (30 ml) lemon juice
1/2 tsp (2 ml) grated lemon peel
1/2 tsp (2 ml) *Each:* ground nutmeg & ginger

 Cook: 30 minutes ◀◀◀
    Yield – 5 x 250 or 236 ml jars

SPREADABLE RHUBERRIES

5 cups (1250 ml) hulled, halved strawberries
2 cups (500 ml) finely chopped rhubarb
4 tart apples, peeled, cored & chopped
2 cans (each 355 ml) undiluted frozen apple juice concentrate, thawed
Red food colouring, *optional*

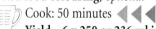 Cook: 50 minutes ◀◀◀
    Yield – 6 x 250 or 236 ml jars

SPREADABLE STRAWBERRIES

12 cups (3000 ml) hulled strawberries
5 tart apples, peeled, cored & chopped
2 cans (each 355 ml) undiluted frozen apple juice concentrate, thawed

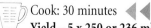 Cook: 30 minutes ◀◀◀
    Yield – 5 x 250 or 236 ml jars

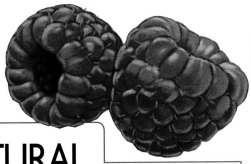

NATURAL SUMMER FRUIT JAM

5 tart apples, unpeeled
2 cups (500 ml) water
1 medium lemon, zest, pulp and juice
Specific FRUIT & granulated sugar

• Place required number of clean 250 or 236 ml mason jars on a rack in a boiling water canner; cover jars with water and heat to a simmer (180°F/82°C). Set screw bands aside; heat SNAP Lids in hot water, NOT boiling (180°F/82°C). Keep jars and SNAP Lids hot until ready to use.

• Remove apple blossom and stem ends; chop apples (including cores); place in a large, deep stainless steel saucepan with 2 cups (500 ml) water.

• Remove lemon peel in one long piece; squeeze juice; set both aside. Chop remaining lemon pith/pulp and add to apples. Bring mixture to a boil; cover and simmer 20 minutes.

• Pour cooked apple mixture, including liquid, into a fine sieve. With back of spoon, press mixture through sieve to yield 2 cups (500 ml) applesauce; return to saucepan.

Wash, prepare and measure Specific FRUIT and sugar. Add Specific FRUIT to applesauce with reserved lemon peel; bring to a boil.

▶▶▶ Maintaining a constant boil, gradually add required quantity of sugar to mixture, stirring until sugar is completely dissolved. Stirring frequently to prevent scorching, boil vigorously – **approximate Cook Time indicated in each recipe** – *until mixture reaches gel stage. (page 15)*

• Add reserved lemon juice; boil 1 minute longer. Remove from heat and skim foam. Discard lemon peel.

• Ladle jam into a hot jar to within 1/4 inch (0.5 cm) of top rim (headspace). Using nonmetallic utensil, remove air bubbles. Wipe jar rim removing any stickiness. Centre SNAP Lid on jar; apply screw band *securely & firmly until resistance is met – fingertip tight. Do not overtighten.* Place jar in canner; repeat for remaining jam.

• Cover canner; bring water to a boil. At altitudes up to 1,000 ft (305 m), process – *boil filled jars* – **10 minutes**. Remove jars without tilting. Cool upright, undisturbed 24 hours; DO NOT RETIGHTEN screw bands. After cooling check jar seals. *Sealed lids curve downward.* Remove screw bands; wipe and dry bands and jars. Store screw bands separately or replace loosely on jars, as desired. Label and store jars in a cool, dark place.

BLUEBERRY

4 cups (1000 ml) blueberries (whole)
Juice and grated peel of 1 lime
3 cups (750 ml) granulated sugar
Cook: 15-20 minutes ◀◀◀
Yield – 5 x 250 or 236 ml jars

RED CURRANT

6 cups (1500 ml) red currants (whole)
5 1/2 cups (1375 ml) granulated sugar
Cook: 15-20 minutes ◀◀◀
Yield – 7 x 250 or 236 ml jars

PEACH/NECTARINE

6 cups (1500 ml) chopped, peeled & pitted
  peaches or nectarines
2 tbsp (25 ml) lemon juice
5 1/2 cups (1375 ml) granulated sugar
Cook: 15-20 minutes ◀◀◀
Yield – 7 x 250 or 236 ml jars

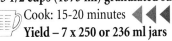

PLUM

6 cups (1500 ml) chopped & pitted plums
5 1/2 cups (1375 ml) granulated sugar
Cook: 30 minutes ◀◀◀
Yield – 8 x 250 or 236 ml jars

RASPBERRY

4 cups (1000 ml) raspberries (whole)
5 cups (1250 ml) granulated sugar
Cook: 15-20 minutes ◀◀◀
Yield – 6 x 250 or 236 ml jars

STRAWBERRY

8 cups (2000 ml) halved strawberries, about
  2 1/2 quarts
5 1/2 cups (1375 ml) granulated sugar
Cook: 20 minutes ◀◀◀
Yield – 8 x 250 or 236 ml jars

These delicious spreads add delicious variety to your home canning repertoire.

SPECIALTIES de la maison

• Place required number of mason jars on a rack in a boiling water canner; cover jars with water and heat to a simmer (180°F/82°C). Set screw bands aside; heat SNAP Lids in hot water, NOT boiling (180°F/82°C). Keep jars and SNAP Lids hot until ready to use.

 Prepare, measure and cook selected recipe ingredients as directed.

▶▶▶ **Ladle hot cooked mixture into a hot jar to within 1/4 inch (0.5 cm) of top rim (headspace).** Using nonmetallic utensil, remove air bubbles. Wipe jar rim removing any stickiness. Centre SNAP Lid on jar; apply screw band *securely & firmly* until resistance is met – *fingertip tight. Do not overtighten.* Place jar in canner; repeat for remaining cooked mixture.

• Cover canner; bring water to a boil. At altitudes up to 1,000 ft (305 m), process – *boil filled jars* – **10 minutes.** Remove jars without tilting. Cool upright, undisturbed 24 hours; DO NOT RETIGHTEN screw bands. After cooling check jar seals. *Sealed lids curve downward.* Remove screw bands; wipe and dry bands and jars. Store screw bands separately or replace loosely on jars, as desired. Label and store jars in a cool, dark place.

SOUR CHERRY WALNUT CONSERVE

CHERRIES AND WALNUTS PRODUCE A LUSCIOUS CONSERVE WORTHY OF ANY ROYAL TABLE. IF YOU PREFER CONSERVES WITH A TART FLAVOUR, OMIT THE AMARETTO AS IT ADDS A TOUCH OF SWEETNESS.

2 cups (500 ml) prepared tart apples, 4 medium
5 cups (1250 ml) pitted sour cherries, about 3 1/4 lb (1.5 kg)
3/4 cup (175 ml) water
3 medium oranges and 3 lemons
3 1/2 cups (875 ml) granulated sugar
3/4 cup (175 ml) chopped toasted walnuts
1/4 cup (50 ml) amaretto liqueur, *optional*

Peel, core and chop apples; measure 2 cups (500 ml). Combine cherries with their juice, apples and water in a large stainless steel saucepan. Using a zester or grater, remove zest from oranges and one lemon; add to cherries. Remove remaining white membrane and peel from citrus fruit, discard seeds and chop fruit; add to cherries.

• Bring fruit mixture to a full boil, stirring constantly. Stirring frequently, gently boil 10 to 15 minutes or until cherries are soft. Stir in sugar until dissolved. Boil gently, stirring occasionally until mixture thickens and reaches a gel stage, about 30-40 minutes. (See gel test page 15.)

• Stir in walnuts. If using liqueur, remove conserve from heat and stir in amaretto. Return conserve to a boil; stirring constantly, boil until mixture reaches desired consistency, about 3 to 5 minutes. Remove from heat. ◀◀◀

Yield – about 7 x 250 or 236 ml jars

PAPAYA GRAPEFRUIT PRESERVES

HOME CANNING NEED NOT BE LIMITED TO SUMMER & FALL. THESE WINTER SPRING SEASONAL FRUITS MAKE DELICIOUS SOFT SPREADS.

2 large grapefruit
2 cups (500 ml) chopped papaya or mango
3 1/2 cups (875 ml) granulated sugar
1/4 cup (50 ml) water
2 tbsp (25 ml) orange liqueur, *optional*
1 pkg (57 g) BERNARDIN *Original Fruit Pectin*

Grate 2 tbsp (25 ml) grapefruit peel. With a sharp knife, remove remaining peel and pith from grapefruit. Working over a bowl to catch juice, remove grapefruit segments; discard membrane. Measure 2 cups (500 ml) grapefruit, including juice. Measure sugar; set aside.

• Combine, grapefruit segments and grated peel with papaya and water in a large, deep stainless steel saucepan. Whisk in Fruit Pectin until dissolved.

• Stirring frequently, bring mixture to a boil over high heat. Add sugar. Stirring constantly, return mixture to a full rolling boil; boil hard 1 minute. Remove from heat; skim foam. Stir in orange liqueur, if using. ◀◀◀

Yield – about 7 x 250 or 236 ml jars

CRANBERRY GRAPE PRESERVES

CRANBERRIES ADD A ZIPPY FLAVOUR AND CHUNKY TWIST TO TRADITIONAL GRAPE JELLY!

4 cups (1000 ml) grape juice
4 cups (1000 ml) chopped cranberries
1 tsp (5 ml) finely grated orange zest
5 cups (1250 ml) granulated sugar

Combine grape juice, cranberries and orange zest in a large stainless steel saucepan. Bring mixture to a boil. Add sugar. Stirring frequently, return mixture to a boil. Boil hard, stirring constantly, until mixture reaches gel stage, about 12 minutes. (See gel test page 15.) Remove from heat. ◀◀◀

Yield – about 5 x 250 or 236 ml jars

ELDERBERRY PEACH PRESERVES

GO WILD! PEACHES COMBINED WITH ELDERBERRY JELLY GIVE THIS PRESERVE A CHUNKY TEXTURE. IT'S LUSCIOUS ON BREAD BUT MAKES A PLEASING DESSERT OR BREAKFAST SAUCE AS WELL.

6 1/2 cups (1625 ml) elderberries, about
  1.8 lb (800 g)
2 cups (500 ml) chopped, peeled peaches, about
  1.5 lb (700 g)
1/2 cup (125 ml) bottled lemon juice
7 cups (1750 ml) granulated sugar
2 pouches (170 ml) BERNARDIN *Liquid* Pectin

Place elderberries in a large stainless steel saucepan; crush thoroughly. Bring to a boil; cover and reduce heat; boil gently 5 minutes. Remove from heat; pour into dampened Jelly Bag or cheese cloth-lined sieve suspended over a deep container. Let drip to collect 1 1/2 cups (325 ml) juice.
• Combine elderberry juice, peaches, lemon juice and sugar in a large, deep stainless steel saucepan. Over high heat, bring mixture to a full rolling boil. Stirring constantly, boil hard 1 minute. Remove from heat.
• Immediately add Liquid Pectin; stir 3 minutes and skim foam. ◀◀◀

Yield – about 8 x 250 or 236 ml jars

CARROT CAKE CONSERVE

THIS SUNNY CONSERVE, SWEETENED WITH CRUSHED PINEAPPLE AND SPICES, TASTES JUST LIKE CARROT CAKE. COME CHRISTMAS, IT WILL MAKES A WONDERFUL GIFT.

1 1/2 cups (375 ml) finely grated carrots, 3 large
1 1/2 cups (375 ml) peeled, chopped pears, 2 large
1 can (14 oz/398 ml) crushed pineapple, undrained
3 tbsp (45 ml) bottled lemon juice
1 tsp (5 ml) ground cinnamon
1/2 tsp (2 ml) *Each:* ground nutmeg and ground
  cloves
1 pkg (57 g) BERNARDIN *Original Fruit Pectin*
6 1/2 cups (1625 ml) granulated sugar
2/3 cup (150 ml) chopped toasted pecans

Combine carrots, pears, pineapple (including juice), lemon juice and spices in a large, deep stainless steel saucepan. Stirring frequently, bring mixture to a boil; cover and reduce heat. Boil gently 20 minutes, stirring occasionally. Measure sugar; set aside.
• Whisk Fruit Pectin into carrot mixture until dissolved. Stirring frequently, bring to a boil over high heat. Add sugar. Stirring constantly, return mixture to a full rolling boil; boil hard 1 minute. Stir in pecans. Remove from heat; skim foam. ◀◀◀

Yield – about 6 x 250 or 236 ml jars

RASPBERRY CRANBERRY PRESERVES

SWEET PRESERVES ARE THE PERFECT WAY TO ENJOY TART BERRIES LIKE THESE. WHOLE CRANBERRIES ADD CHUNKINESS AND A UNIQUE TOUCH TO RASPBERRY JAM.

2 1/2 cups (625 ml) whole raspberries
2 cups (500 ml) whole cranberries
1 cup (250 ml) finely chopped, peeled apple
3 1/2 cups (875 ml) granulated sugar
1 cup (250 ml) liquid honey
1 tsp (5 ml) butter
1 pouch (85 ml) BERNARDIN *Liquid* Pectin

Measure raspberries, cranberries, prepared apple, sugar, honey and butter into a large, deep stainless steel saucepan. Let stand 15 minutes. Slowly bring mixture to a full rolling boil. Stirring constantly, boil hard 1 minute. Remove from heat.
• Immediately add Liquid Pectin; stir 3 minutes and skim foam. ◀◀◀

Yield – about 6 x 250 or 236 ml jars

A golden suspension of peel and pulp, marmalade is truly an international preserve!

SEVILLE MARMALADE

1 kg (2.2 lb) Seville oranges, 5 or 6
2 clementines and 2 lemons
12 1/2 cups (3000 ml) hot water
11 1/2 cups (2750 ml) granulated sugar
1/3 cup (75 ml) brandy, *optional*

Place a 12-inch (30 cm) square of dampened cheesecloth in a bowl. Cut oranges, clementines and lemons in half lengthwise. Squeeze juice from each half into cheesecloth lined bowl; using spoon or grapefruit knife, scoop seeds and pulp into bowl. With a sharp knife, thinly slice peel, placing it in a deep stainless steel saucepan. Tie cheesecloth around pulp and seeds; add juice, pulp-seed bag and water to sliced peel. If desired, cover and let stand 24 hours.

• Bring fruit-water mixture to a boil. Reduce heat; boil gently uncovered about 2 hours until peel is tender and mixture is reduced to about 10 cups (2.5 L). Check frequently to be sure bubbles continue to gently break surface during this cooking time.

• Meanwhile, place 11 clean 250 or 236 ml mason jars in a boiling water canner; cover with water, heat to a simmer. Set screw bands aside; heat SNAP Lids in hot water, NOT boiling (180°F/82°C). Keep jars and SNAP Lids hot until ready to use.

• When peel is tender, remove pulp-seed bag to a bowl to cool. With fruit mixture over medium low heat, add sugar; cook and stir until sugar dissolves. Squeeze pulp-seed bag extracting as much liquid as possible; add liquid to fruit-sugar mixture and discard bag. Add 1/2 tsp (2 ml) butter or vegetable oil to reduce foaming.

• **When sugar is completely dissolved, increase heat to maximum.** *When mixture reaches a full rolling boil that cannot be stirred down,* cook about 15 minutes or until it reaches gel stage (page 15). Add brandy, if using, stir and cook 2 minutes. Skim off foam.

▶▶▶ **Ladle marmalade into a hot jar to within 1/4 inch (6 mm) of top rim (headspace).** Using nonmetallic utensil, remove air bubbles. Wipe jar rim removing any stickiness. Centre SNAP Lid on jar; apply screw band *securely & firmly until resistance is met – fingertip tight. Do not overtighten.* Place jar in canner; repeat for remaining marmalade
• Cover canner; bring water to a boil. At altitudes up to 1,000 ft (305 m), process – *boil filled jars –* **10 minutes.** Remove jars without tilting. Cool upright, undisturbed 24 hours; DO NOT RETIGHTEN screw bands. After cooling check jar seals. *Sealed lids curve downward.* Remove screw bands; wipe and dry bands and jars. Store screw bands separately or replace loosely on jars, as desired. Label and store in a cool, dark place.
Yield – 10-11 x 250 or 236 ml jars

EASIEST EVER MARMALADE

3 oranges, small
1 lemon
1 grapefruit, small
1 can (19 oz, 540 ml) crushed pineapple, undrained
6 cups (1500 ml) granulated sugar
1/2 cup (125 ml) chopped maraschino cherries

Prepare 6 mason jars and lids as indicated in Seville Marmalade. Wash, remove seeds and coarsely chop unpeeled oranges, lemon and grapefruit – by hand or in food processor.

• Combine prepared fruit, pineapple and sugar in a large stainless steel saucepan. Bring to a boil, stirring until sugar dissolves. Stirring frequently to prevent scorching, boil gently, uncovered, 25 minutes or until marmalade reaches gel stage (page 15). Stir in cherries during the last 5 minutes. ◀◀◀

• Ladle marmalade into jars and heat process as indicated in Seville Marmalade.
Yield – 6 x 250 or 236 ml jars

GINGERED ZUCCHINI MARMALADE

2 oranges
2 lemons
2-3 inch (5-7.5 cm) piece of gingerroot, peeled & chopped
5 cups (1250 ml) shredded zucchini
1 tart apple, cored & shredded
4 cups (1000 ml) granulated sugar

Prepare 4 mason jars and lids as indicated in Seville Marmalade. Thoroughly wash citrus fruit. With a vegetable peeler, remove coloured peel from oranges; thinly slice orange peel and place in a large, deep stainless steel saucepan. With a sharp knife, cut white pith and any remaining peel from oranges and lemons. Tie pith, peel and gingerroot in a large square of cheesecloth, creating a spice bag; add to peel in saucepan. Finely chop orange and lemon pulp; add to saucepan with zucchini, apple and sugar.

• Over medium-high heat, bring mixture to a boil, stirring until sugar dissolves. Stirring frequently, boil uncovered until mixture reaches gel stage (page 15), about 45 minutes.

• Ladle marmalade into jars and heat process as indicated in Seville Marmalade. ◀◀◀
Yield – 4 x 250 or 236 ml jars

SALUTE TO CANADIAN ENTREPRENEURS

For more than few Canadians, a love of home canning led to successful business ventures. Here is a very small sampling of their stories and a few recipes to whet your appetite and inspire your own endeavours.

THE FEASTING TABLE

When is a jelly NOT made for bread. When Bob Rouleau makes it! Retired from one of several careers in Ottawa, Bob turned to his kitchen for something to do. The result was Habanero Gold and 'The Feasting Table', a line of fiery jellies designed for use as marinades and cooking aids. Bob generously shares a cornucopia of these unique, homemade boldly-flavoured suspensions. NOTE – Bob employs a manual manipulation of the hot jars to make these jellies – it must be done with extreme care to avoid disturbing the formation of the vacuum seal.

FEASTING TABLE JELLIES

• Place 3 clean 250 or 236 ml mason jars on a rack in a boiling water canner; cover jars with water and heat to a simmer (180°F/82°C). Set screw bands aside; heat SNAP Lids in hot water, NOT boiling (180°F/82°C). Keep jars and SNAP Lids hot until ready to use.

Measure ingredients for selected recipe – *except Liquid Pectin* – and combine in a large, deep stainless steel saucepan.

▶▶▶ **Over high heat, bring mixture to a full rolling boil.** *Stirring constantly,* boil hard 1 minute. Remove from heat. Immediately stir in one pouch *Liquid* Pectin, mixing well.

• Pour jelly into a hot jar, dividing solids equally among jars and filling each jar to within 1/4 inch (0.5 cm) of top rim (headspace). Wipe jar rims removing any stickiness. Centre SNAP Lid on jar; apply screw band *securely & firmly until resistance is met – fingertip tight. Do not overtighten.* Place jar in canner.

• Cover canner; bring water to a boil. At altitudes up to 1,000 ft (305 m), process – *boil filled jars* – **10 minutes.** Remove jars without tilting.

• Cool upright, until lids pop down, about 30 minutes. DO NOT RETIGHTEN screw bands.

• When lids are concave but the jelly is still hot, carefully grasp the jar without disturbing the screw band or lid and invert, twist or rotate each jar to distribute solids throughout the jelly. The jar can be inverted **temporarily** but do not allow it to stand upside-down for prolonged periods. Repeat as needed during the cooling/setting time, until solids are nicely suspended in the jelly.

• After 24 hours check jar seals. *Sealed lids curve downward.* Remove screw bands; wipe and dry bands and jars. Store screw bands separately or replace loosely on jars, as desired. Label and store jars in a cool, dark place.

BASIL BANANA PEPPER JELLY

ALMOST ANY PEPPERS WILL DO, AS LONG AS IT'S A COLOURFUL MIXTURE. BOB USES HOT AND MILD, FRESH PEPPERS AND COMMER-CIALLY PICKLED MIXED PEPPERS. AMONG THE PEPPERS HE USES – BANANA, CUBANELLE, HUNGARIAN, RED AND GREEN CHILIES, JAMAICAN. DON'T BE AFRAID TO USE PEPPERS WITH LOTS OF FLAVOUR AND HEAT. THE SUGAR AND VINEGAR TAME SOME OF THE HEAT ESPECIALLY WHEN THE JELLY IS USED AS A MARINADE OR GLAZE.

1/2 cup (125 ml) thinly sliced, seeded mild banana peppers (fresh or pickled)

1/4 cup (50 ml) thinly sliced, fresh hot peppers (most of seeds removed)

1/4 cup (50 ml) finely diced red onion

3 to 4 large fresh basil leaves, cut into thin ribbons

1/4 tsp (1 ml) dried basil

3/4 cup (175 ml) white vinegar

3 cups (750 ml) granulated sugar

1 pouch (85 ml) BERNARDIN *Liquid* Pectin

Combine mild and hot peppers, red onion, fresh and dried basil in a large, deep stainless steel saucepan. Stir in vinegar and sugar. ◀◀◀

ZESTY RED ONION JELLY

A HOUSE SPECIALTY DESIGNED ESPECIALLY FOR AN OTTAWA NEWSPAPER. FOR JELLY WITH A LOVELY PINK HUE, MAKE THE JELLY IN AUGUST WHEN THE RED ONIONS ARE FRESH. BOB SAYS THAT WHEN HE MAKES THIS JELLY IN JANUARY, IT LACKS THE BEAUTIFUL ROSE HUE OF THE SAME RECIPE MADE WITH FRESHLY PICKED PRODUCE.

1 cup (250 ml) diced red onion
2 tsp (10 ml) lemon zest
3/4 cup (175 ml) white vinegar
3 cups (750 ml) granulated sugar
1 pouch (85 ml) BERNARDIN *Liquid* Pectin

Cut red onion into 1/8 inch (3 mm) slices; cut slices into 1/4 inch (0.5 cm) dice. Measure 1 cup (250 ml) into a large, deep stainless steel saucepan. With a sharp knife, cut a wide strip of paper-thin yellow peel from lemon; cut into thin strips and measure 2 tsp (10 ml) into saucepan. Stir in vinegar and sugar. ◀◀◀

HABANERO GOLD JELLY

COLOURFUL PEPPERS SUSPENDED THROUGH-OUT THE PALE GOLDEN JELLY – THIS IS THE FOUNDATION ON WHICH THE FEASTING TABLE ESTABLISHED ITS INNOVATIVE REPUTATION.

1/3 cup (75 ml) finely sliced dried apricots
3/4 cup (175 ml) white vinegar
1/4 cup (50 ml) finely diced red onion
1/4 cup (50 ml) finely diced sweet red pepper
1/4 cup (50 ml) finely diced habanero peppers
   including seeds
OR 1/4 cup (50 ml) diced, combined jalapeño
   and Scotch bonnet peppers
3 cups (750 ml) granulated sugar
1 pouch (85 ml) BERNARDIN *Liquid* Pectin

With scissors or knife, cut apricots into 1/8 inch (0.3 cm) slices. Measure into a large deep stainless steel saucepan with vinegar; let stand 4 hours. Individually, cut onion and seeded peppers into 1/8 inch (0.3 cm) slices; cut slices into 1/4 inch (0.5 cm) dice. Measure each ingredient; add to apricots. Stir in sugar. ◀◀◀

RED PEPPER & GARLIC JELLY

THIS JELLY IS FLECKED WITH BITS OF SWEET RED PEPPER. ADJUST THE GARLIC INTENSITY BY CHOOSING LARGER OR SMALLER CLOVES OF GARLIC.

1 cup (250 ml) finely diced red pepper
3 large cloves garlic
3/4 cup (175 ml) apple cider vinegar
3 cups (750 ml) granulated sugar
1 pouch (85 ml) BERNARDIN *Liquid* Pectin

Cut red pepper into 1/8 inch slices; cut slices into 1/4 inch (0.5 cm) dice. If desired, pepper can be chopped in a mechanical chopper, but take care to avoid puréeing peppers. Measure 1 cup (250 ml) diced red pepper into a large, deep stainless steel saucepan. Finely slice garlic cloves, then cut slices into slivers. Garlic can also be ground or crushed, if desired. Add to red pepper with sugar and cider vinegar. ◀◀◀

CURRY RAISIN JELLY

USE ANY TYPE OF RAISINS, BUT BOB PREFERS GOLDEN. FOR A MORE TRANSLUCENT JELLY, INFUSE VINEGAR WITH WHOLE SPICES – BLACK PEPPER, CORIANDER, CUMIN SEEDS, CLOVES, CINNAMON – IN PLACE OF CURRY POWDER.

3 cups (750 ml) granulated sugar
1 to 2 tsp (5 to 10 ml) curry powder
1/2 cup (125 ml) golden raisins
1/2 cup (125 ml) very finely chopped Spanish onion
3/4 cup (175 ml) white vinegar
1 pouch (85 ml) BERNARDIN *Liquid* Pectin

Combine sugar and curry powder in a large, deep stainless steel saucepan. Stir in raisins, onion and vinegar. ◀◀◀

LAST MOUNTAIN BERRY FARMS

Saskatchewan based, Barry and Barbara Isaac produce thousands of jars fruit spreads proudly labeled with Last Mountain Berry Farms brand. Their successful venture is a joint effort that is an outgrowth of Barbara's knack for home canning and their entrepreneurial talents. Although not part of their current successful line of products, Barbara shared one of her favourite homemade recipes, adapted here for your home canning pleasure.

LAST MOUNTAIN'S SPICED APPLE BUTTER

6 lb (2.7 kg) cooking apples (Spy, Courtland, Russet or Spartan)
2 cups (500 ml) apple cider
2-3 cups (500-750 ml) granulated sugar
2-3 cups (500-750 ml) packed brown sugar
1/4 cup (50 ml) lemon juice
1 1/2 tsp (7 ml) ground cinnamon
1/2 tsp (2 ml) *Each:* ground nutmeg, ground cloves
1/4 tsp (1 ml) ground allspice
1 tbsp (15 ml) finely grated lemon rind

• Cut apples into eighths, removing stems and blossom ends. Combine apples and apple cider in a large stainless steel saucepan; cook, covered over medium heat until the apples are soft, about 20 minutes. Remove from heat and press mixture through a sieve or food mill.

• Place 8 clean 250 ml mason jars on a rack in a boiling water canner; cover jars with water and heat to a simmer (180°F/82°C). Set screw bands aside; heat SNAP Lids in hot water, NOT boiling (180°F/82°C). Keep jars and SNAP Lids hot until ready to use.

• Measure the purée back into the saucepan. Depending on the tartness of the apples, add 1/2 to 3/4 cup (125 to 175 ml) of each of the sugars for each cup (250 ml) of purée. Add the lemon juice and bring to a boil, stirring constantly. Reduce the heat and boil gently uncovered for 40-50 minutes or until the mixture is thickened. Stir in the spices and lemon rind during the last 5-10 minutes of the cooking time. Remove from heat.

• Ladle jam into a hot jar to within 1/4 inch (0.5 cm) of top rim (headspace). Using nonmetallic utensil, remove air bubbles. Wipe jar rim removing any stickiness. Centre SNAP Lid on jar; apply screw band **securely & firmly** until resistance is met – *fingertip tight. Do not overtighten.* Place jar in canner; repeat for remaining jam.

• Cover canner; bring water to a boil. At altitudes up to 1,000 ft (305 m), process – *boil filled jars* – **10 minutes**. Remove jars without tilting. Cool upright, undisturbed 24 hours; DO NOT RETIGHTEN screw bands. After cooling check jar seals. *Sealed lids curve downward.* Remove screw bands; wipe and dry bands and jars. Store screw bands separately or replace loosely on jars, as desired. Label and store jars in a cool, dark place.
Yield – 8 x 250 ml jars

SHIRLEY'S HOMEMADE PRESERVES

Shirley Morrison's business success illustrates the profit potential of simple, homemade preserves. Shirley's extensive line of fruit spreads are centered around basic recipes made in small batches with locally grown, top quality produce. Shirley's business was initiated with a contractor who came to do renovations and noticed her well-stocked pantry. He suggested she sell her preserves to a local store. She did, word spread and the business grew. Here's a sample of one of Shirley's preserves.

SHIRLEY'S HOMEMADE APRICOT JAM

6 cups (1500 ml) pitted and crushed, unpeeled apricots
4 cups (1000 ml) granulated sugar
2 pkg (each 57 g) BERNARDIN *Original Fruit Pectin*

• Place 7 clean 250 or 236 ml mason jars on a rack in a boiling water canner; cover jars with water and heat to a simmer (180°F/82°C). Set screw bands aside; heat SNAP Lids in hot water, NOT boiling (180°F/82°C). Keep jars and SNAP Lids hot until ready to use.

• Measure apricots into a deep stainless steel saucepan. Add the pectin and mix thoroughly. Stirring constantly, bring the mixture to a boil taking care to avoid scorching the mixture.

• Stirring constantly, add sugar and return mixture to a rolling boil; boil 2 minutes. Remove from heat and stir 1 minute longer.

• Ladle jam into a hot jar to within 1/4 inch (0.5 cm) of top rim (headspace). Using nonmetallic utensil, remove air bubbles. Wipe jar rim removing any stickiness. Centre SNAP Lid on jar; apply screw band *securely & firmly* until resistance is met – *fingertip tight. Do not overtighten.* Place jar in canner; repeat for remaining jam.

• Cover canner; bring water to a boil. At altitudes up to 1,000 ft (305 m), process – *boil filled jars* – **10 minutes.** Remove jars without tilting. Cool

upright, undisturbed 24 hours; DO NOT RETIGHTEN screw bands. After cooling check jar seals. *Sealed lids curve downward.* Remove screw bands; wipe and dry bands and jars. Store screw bands separately or replace loosely on jars, as desired. Label and store jars in a cool, dark place.
Yield – about 7 x 250 ml jars

KINCADES FINE FOODS

A musician and song writer, Larry Kincade is also an entrepreneurial lover of fine food and a fine chef. His line of gourmet spreads, toppings and condiments have captured prestigious awards in professional food competitions such as those sponsored by the Canadian Association of Specialty Foods.

KINCADES LIME MINT JELLY

4 to 5 limes
3.5 oz (100 g) mint leaves & stems
4 1/4 cups (1050 ml) water
7 cups (1750 ml) granulated sugar
3 pouches (each 85 ml) BERNARDIN *Liquid* Pectin
4 tbsp (60 ml) crème de menthe liqueur

• With vegetable peeler, sharp knife or zester, remove zest from limes; measure 3 1/2 tbsp (50 ml). Cut limes in half, squeeze juice; measure 1/2 cup (125 ml). Wash mint removing any brown leaves and discard stem bottoms. Chop mint, by hand or in blender, until it resembles tea leaves. Combine lime zest, mint and water in a stainless steel saucepan. Bring to a boil, reduce heat and simmer 15 minutes. Turn off heat, cover and let steep 20 minutes. Pour mint infusion through a jelly bag or cheesecloth lined sieve to collect juice. For clear jelly, strain 2 to 3 times through dampened triple-layer cheesecloth to remove mint particles.

• Place 10 clean 250 or 236 ml mason jars on a rack in a boiling water canner; cover jars with water and heat to a simmer (180°F/82°C). Set screw bands aside; heat SNAP Lids in hot water, NOT boiling (180°F/82°C). Keep jars and SNAP Lids hot until ready to use.

• Combine mint juice, sugar, mint liqueur and lime juice in a deep stainless steel saucepan; bring to a rolling boil; boil very hard 1 minute. Remove from heat, add liquid pectin and stir 1 minute.

• Pour jelly into hot jars to within 1/4 inch (0.5 cm) of top rim (headspace). Using nonmetallic utensil, remove air bubbles. Wipe jar rim removing any stickiness. Centre SNAP Lid on jar; apply screw band ***securely & firmly*** until resistance is met – *fingertip tight. Do not overtighten.* Place jars in canner.

• Cover canner; bring water to a boil. At altitudes up to 1,000 ft (305 m), process – *boil filled jars* – **10 minutes**. Remove jars without tilting. Cool upright, undisturbed 24 hours; DO NOT RETIGHTEN screw bands. After cooling check jar seals. *Sealed lids curve downward.* Remove screw bands; wipe and dry bands and jars. Store screw bands separately or replace loosely on jars, as desired. Label and store jars in a cool, dark place.
Yield – 10 x 250 ml jars

FABULOUS FRUIT

Sun-soaked, succulent fruits – are one of Mother Nature's best summer gifts. Alas, the season is always too short! Home canning fresh fruit lets you add enjoyment, colour, variety and juicy flavour to meals and snacks year round.

Fruit falls into the high acid food category but the acidity of individual fruits varies. Specific recipes and boiling water canner processing times must be followed for each fruit. Like jams and jellies, home canned fruits are also susceptible to spoilage by yeasts and molds. Unless inactivated, enzymes will diminish the fruit's quality over time. Yeasts, molds and enzymes are destroyed or inactivated at a temperature of 212°F (100°C) – a temperature which is easily attained when filled jars are heat processed in a boiling water canner.

PREVENT DARKENING

Colour is one of the most appealing aspects of home canned fruits. Apples, apricots, peaches, pears and other light-colour fruits tend to darken when peeled or cut and exposed to air. To prevent darkening, place fruit in a colour protection solution as soon as it is peeled or cut. When all the fruit is prepared, drain the fruit and proceed as directed in the recipe.

Either of these two simple treatments will reduce unwanted colour changes.

• Dissolve 4 tbsp (60 ml) Fruit-Fresh® Colour Protector in 8 cups (2000 ml) water. *Fruit-Fresh® Colour Protector also preserves the fresh colour of fruit for salads and snacks. Simply sprinkle it onto the cut fruit as it is prepared.*

• Mix 1/4 cup (50 ml) bottled lemon juice with 4 cups (1000 ml) water.

HOT PACK VERSES RAW PACK

Fruit has very porous tissues. While these pores contain the juice we love, they also hold air that, if not exhausted, from the fruit can cause discolouration as well as floatation. Hot packing fruit helps exhaust this air. Hot packing requires prepared fruit to be heated to a boil in the hot canning liquid. Raw packing skips this heating step and often results in an inferior product. One of the goals of home canning is the removal of excess air from the jars during heat processing. The less air in the jar to begin with, the better the results will be. Removing air from fruit tissues shrinks the fruit so that you will be able to put more fruit in each jar. It also prevents fruit from floating to the top of the jar, increases the vacuum in sealed jars and improves shelf-life.

FILLING JARS

For maximum flavour and colour retention, be sure that fruit at the top of the jar is covered with canning liquid and that the total headspace allowed in each jar is 1/2 inch (1 cm). Fruit that is not covered with liquid tends to darken during storage. When packing fruit, layer fruit in jar to within 3/4 inch (2 cm) of the jar rim. Then add hot canning liquid to cover the fruit to within 1/2 inch (1 cm) of the jar rim. Remove air bubbles with a rubber spatula and readjust the headspace to 1/2 inch (1 cm).

SYRUPS AND SWEETENERS

Fruits may be canned in syrups with or without added sweeteners. Sugar syrups help fruit retain its flavour, colour and texture but do not prevent spoilage.

A syrup, sweetened with sugar or a combination of sugar and honey or corn syrup, is used most often. Corn syrup or honey may be substituted for a portion of the sugar.

Fruit may also be canned in fruit juice, plain water or liquids sweetened with certain sugar substitutes.

Fruit juice may be substituted for sugar-syrups. Fruit juice adds flavour and is generally lower in total sugar content than sugar syrup. Commercial unsweetened apple, pineapple or white grape juice make good packing liquids for many fruits. These juices may be used uncut or may be diluted with water. Juice can also be extracted from some of the fruit that is being canned or from fresh apples, pineapple or grapes. Always use the **HOT PACK** method when canning fruit without added sugar.

SPECIAL DIETS

Persons following sugar-restricted diets can use plain water in place of syrup or juice. The fruit, however, will not be as plump, flavourful or colourful as fruit canned with a sweetened syrup. Sugar substitutes may be used to sweeten home canned fruit. Follow manufacturer's directions for measuring each type of sweetener. Because some artificial sweeteners can develop off-flavours or lose their sweetening power when heated or during storage, it can be more satisfactory to preserve the fruit without added sugar and use sugar substitutes to sweeten to taste at serving time.

Whatever your choice of canning liquid, it must be hot when added to the jars. To make syrup, measure sugar and liquid into a saucepan. Cook until syrup is hot throughout. Keep syrup hot until needed, but do not let it boil down. Allow 1 to 1 1/2 cups (250 to 375 ml) syrup for each 1 L jar of fruit.

Type of Syrup	Approx % Sugar	Granulated Sugar	Syrup	Water	Syrup Yield
Ultra Light – approximates natural sugar level in most fruits; adds fewest calories	10	1/2 cup (125 ml)		5 cups (1250 ml)	5 1/4 cups (1300 ml)
Extra Light – Use with very sweet fruit. Try small quantity first to be sure family likes it.	20	1 1/4 cups (300 ml)		5 1/2 cups (1375 ml)	6 cups (1500 ml)
Light – Sweet apples, sweet cherries, berries, grapes.	30	2 1/4 cups (550 ml)		5 1/4 cups (1300 ml)	7 cups (1750 ml)
Medium – Tart apples, apricots, sour cherries, gooseberries, nectarines, peaches, pears, plums.	40	3 1/4 cups (800 ml)		5 cups (1250 ml)	7 cups (1750 ml)
Heavy – Very sour fruit. Try small quantity first to be sure family likes it.	50	4 1/4 cups (1050 ml)		4 1/4 cups (1125 ml)	7 cups (1750 ml)
Corn Syrup		1 1/2 cups (375 ml)	corn syrup – 1 cup (250 ml)	3 cups (750 ml)	6 cups (1500 ml)
Honey		1 cup (250 ml)	liquid honey – 1 cup (250 ml)	4 cups (1000 ml)	5 cups (1250 ml)

Many fruits that were historically packed in heavy syrup are excellent and tasteful products canned in lighter syrups.

FRUIT

- Prepare **syrup or canning liquid** in canner batch quantities – approximately 5 cups (1250 ml) for 7 – 500 ml jars; 10 1/2 cups (2650 ml) for 7 – 1 L jars; 9 cups (2250 ml) for 4 – 1.5 L jars.
- Place required number of clean mason jars on a rack in a boiling water canner; cover jars with water and heat to a simmer (180°F/82°C). Set screw bands aside; heat SNAP Lids in hot water, NOT boiling (180°F/82°C). Keep jars and SNAP Lids hot until ready to use.

 Prepare selected fruit as directed.

▶▶▶ **Pack fruit into a hot jar to within 3/4 inch (2 cm) of top rim. Add hot canning syrup to cover fruit** *to within 1/2 inch (1 cm) of top rim (headspace).* Using nonmetallic utensil, remove air bubbles. Readjust headspace if required. Wipe jar rim removing any stickiness. Centre SNAP Lid on jar; apply screw band ***securely & firmly*** *until resistance is met – fingertip tight. Do not overtighten.* Place jar in canner. Repeat for remaining fruit and syrup.
- Cover canner; bring water to a boil. At altitudes up to 1,000 ft (305 m), process – *boil filled jars* – **for the times indicated for pack method, fruit and jar size.**
- At end of processing time, turn heat off and remove canner lid. Wait until water is still and no more bubbles rise to surface, about 5 minutes. Remove jars without tilting. Cool upright, undisturbed 24 hours; DO NOT RETIGHTEN screw bands. After cooling check jar seals. *Sealed lids curve downward.* Remove screw bands; wipe and dry bands and jars. Store screw bands separately or replace loosely on jars, as desired. Label and store jars in a cool, dark place.

APPLES

For each 1 L jar, select 2 1/2 to 3 lb (1.1 to 1.4 kg) crisp, juicy apples. Use combination of sweet and tart apples. Wash, peel and core apples. Cut into 1/4 inch (5 mm) slices, quarters or halves. As you work, place prepared apples in a colour protection solution (page 38). Prepare a light or medium syrup and bring to a boil in a large stainless steel saucepan. *(When canning apples for baking, use an extra light syrup or water.)* Drain apples, place in syrup and return to a boil. Boil 5 minutes. Pack hot apples into hot jars. ◀◀◀
Heat Process: 500 ml or 1 L jars – **20 min.**

APRICOTS

For each 1 L jar, select 2 to 2 1/2 lb (900 g to 1.1 kg) ripe, mature apricots. Fruit may be packed in water, apple or white grape juice, very light, light or medium syrup.
RAW PACK – Wash apricots; halve and pit but do not peel, placing fruit in colour protection solution (page 38). Prepare a light or medium syrup and bring to boil. Drain apricots and pack cavity side down, overlapping layers into hot jars. ◀◀◀
Heat process: 500 ml jars – **25 min.**; 1 L jars – **30 min.**

HOT PACK – Wash and blanch apricots; remove peel. Cut in half and pit, placing fruit in colour protection solution (page 38). Prepare and heat a light or medium syrup in large stainless steel saucepan. Drain fruit and place one layer at a time in syrup; return to boil or until fruit is heated through. Pack hot fruit into hot jars. ◀◀◀
Heat process: 500 ml jars – **20 min.**; 1 L jars – **25 min.**

BERRIES

For each 1 L jar, select 1 1/2 to 3 lb (680 g to 1.4 kg) ripe, sweet berries of uniform colour. Use Raw Pack for red raspberries and other berries that do not hold their shape when heated. Berries such as blackberries, Saskatoon berries that hold their shape can be Hot Packed. For each 1 L jar of elderberries, add 1 to 2 tbsp (15 to 25 ml) lemon juice to improve flavour. Wash berries under running water. Drain, cap or stem berries. For Gooseberries, snip off heads and tails with scissors.
RAW PACK – Prepare a light or medium syrup, keep hot. Ladle 1/2 cup (125 ml) hot syrup into a hot jar. Fill with berries, gently shaking jar to pack berries without crushing. ◀◀◀
HOT PACK – Measure and place prepared berries in a large saucepan. For each 1 L berries, add 1/4 to 1/2 cup (50 to 125 ml) sugar; stir. Let stand 2 hours in cool place. Heat mixture slowly until sugar dissolves and berries are heated through. Ladle hot mixture into hot jars.
For berries to be used in baking recipes, eliminate sugar and heat berries with just enough water to prevent sticking. ◀◀◀
Heat Process (*Raw Pack or Hot Pack*): 250 ml or 500 ml jars – **15 min.**; 1 L jars – **20 min.**

CHERRIES

For each 1 L jar, select 2 to 2 1/2 lb (900 g to 1.1 kg) mature, bright, uniformly coloured cherries. Stem, wash and drain cherries. Remove pits, if desired. If pitted, place in colour protection solution (page 38) to prevent stem end discolouration. If unpitted, prick skins on opposite sides with a sterilized needle to reduce splitting.
RAW PACK – For sweet cherries prepare a light or medium syrup; for sour cherries, a medium or heavy syrup. Bring syrup to a boil. Ladle 1/2 cup (125 ml) into a hot jar. Fill with cherries, gently shaking jar to pack cherries without crushing. ◀◀◀
Heat process: 500 ml or 1 L jars – **25 min.**
HOT PACK – Measure and place prepared cherries in a large saucepan. For each 1 L cherries, add 1/2 to 3/4 cup (125 to 175 ml) sugar. Stir and cook slowly until sugar dissolves and mixture is heated through. For unpitted cherries, add just enough water to prevent sticking. When packing into jars, if insufficient juice has accumulated, add boiling water to cover cherries. ◀◀◀
Heat process: 500 ml jars – **15 min.**; 1 L jars – **20 min.**

CRANBERRIES

For each 1 L jar, select about 1.4 lb (625 g) fresh, firm, unblemished cranberries. Wash and remove stems. Prepare heavy syrup and bring to a boil in a large stainless steel saucepan. Add cranberries; return to a boil; boil 3 minutes. Pack hot cranberries into hot jars; add hot syrup to cover fruit. ◀◀◀
Heat process: 500 ml or 1 L jars – **15 min.**

FRUIT PURÉE (BABY FOOD)

Select appropriate fruit. Do not can puréed figs or tomatoes. Stem, wash, drain, peel and remove pits if necessary. Coarsely slice or chop fruit. Measure fruit into a large saucepan, crushing gently if desired. For every 4 cups (1000 ml) fruit, add 1 cup (250 ml) hot water. Stirring frequently, cook slowly until fruit is soft. Press through sieve or food mill. Add sugar to taste, if desired. Return fruit purée to saucepan; bring back to a boil. If sugar is added, boil until sugar dissolves. ◀◀◀
Heat Process: 250 ml or 500 ml jars – **15 min.**

PEARS

For each 1 L jar, select 2 to 3 lb (900 g to 1.4 kg) ripe, mature fruit. Harvest pears when full grown. Store in a cool place (60-75°F/15-18°C) until ripe but not soft. Wash, peel, halve and core pears. Place in colour protection solution (page 38). Pears may be packed in water, apple or white grape juice, very light or light syrup.
HOT PACK – Prepare syrup and bring to a boil in large stainless steel saucepan. Drain fruit and place one layer at a time in syrup; return to boil or until fruit is heated through. Pack hot fruit into hot jars and add hot syrup. Repeat for remaining fruit. ◀◀◀
Heat process: 500 ml jars – **20 min.**; 1 L jars – **25 min.**; 1.5 L jars – **35 min.**

PEACHES, NECTARINES

For each 1 L jar, select 2 to 3 lb (900 g to 1.4 kg) ripe, mature peaches; 2 to 2 1/2 lb (900 g to 1.2 kg) nectarines.
Peaches – blanch in boiling water for 30 to 60 seconds. Dip quickly in cold water and slip off skins. **Nectarines** – wash and drain, do not peel.
Halve and pit fruit; slice if desired. Place fruit into colour protection solution (page 38). Fruit may be packed in water, apple or white grape juice, very light, light or medium syrup.
RAW PACK – Prepare syrup and bring to boil. Pack peaches cavity side down, overlapping layers into hot jars. Ladle hot syrup over fruit. ◀◀◀

Heat process: 500 ml jars – **25 min.**; 1 L jars – **30 min.**
HOT PACK – Prepare and heat syrup in large stainless steel saucepan. Drain fruit and place one layer at a time in syrup; return to boil or until fruit is heated through. Pack hot fruit into hot jars and add hot syrup. Repeat for remaining fruit. ◀◀◀
Heat process: 500 ml jars – **20 min.**; 1 L jars – **25 min.**; 1.5 L jars – **35 min.**

PLUMS (FRESH PRUNES)

For each 1 L jar, select 1 1/2 to 2 1/2 lb (680 g to 1.1 kg) ripe, deeply coloured, mature fruit. Stem and wash plums. For whole plums, prick skin in several places to prevent bursting (peel may still crack when canned). Halve and pit freestone plums, if desired.
Heat process: 500 ml jars – **20 min.**; 1 L jars – **25 min.**
HOT PACK – Prepare and heat medium or heavy syrup in large stainless steel saucepan. Add plums and return to a boil; reduce heat and simmer 5 minutes. Remove from heat and let stand 30 minutes. Remove plums from syrup; return syrup to a boil. Pack hot plums into hot jars and add hot syrup. ◀◀◀
Heat process: 500 ml jars – **20 min.**; 1 L jars – **25 min.**

RHUBARB

For each 1 L jar, select 1 1/2 to 2 lb (680 to 900 g) ripe, deeply coloured, mature fruit. Use young, tender, well-coloured stalks. Trim off leaves. Wash stalks and cut into 1-inch (2.5 cm) pieces. Measure rhubarb in a large saucepan. For each 4 cups (1 L) rhubarb, add 1/2 to 1 cup (125 to 250 ml) sugar. Stir and let stand in a cool place until juice appears – 3 to 4 hours. Slowly bring to a boil; boil 30 seconds. Pack hot rhubarb and syrup into hot jars. ◀◀◀
Heat process: 500 ml or 1 L jars – **15 min.**

STRAWBERRIES

For each 1 L jar, select 2 1/2 to 3 lb (1.1 to 1.4 kg) firm, red-ripe berries which have neither white flesh or hollow centres. Strawberries tend to fade and lose flavour when canned. Wash berries under running water. Drain; remove caps & hulls. Measure and place prepared berries in a large saucepan. For each 1 L berries, add 1/2 to 3/4 cup (125 to 175 ml) sugar. Stir to coat fruit. Let stand 5 to 6 hours in a cool place. Heat mixture slowly until sugar dissolves and berries are heated through. Ladle hot mixture into hot jars. For berries to be used in baking recipes, eliminate sugar and heat berries with just enough water to prevent sticking. ◀◀◀
Heat Process: 500 ml jars – **10 min.**; 1 L jars – **15 min.**

Enjoy the taste of summer all year round. Fruit fillings have many delicious uses beyond pies. Add to pudding, layer into parfaits with whipped sweetened cream cheese or use as cake toppings or fillings.

FRUIT PIE FILLINGS

• Place required number of mason jars on a rack in a boiling water canner; cover jars with water and heat to a simmer (180°F/82°C). Set screw bands aside; heat SNAP Lids in hot water, NOT boiling (180°F/82°C). Keep jars and SNAP Lids hot until ready to use.

Prepare fruit mixture as specified in individual recipe.

▶ ▶ ▶ **Ladle hot fruit mixture into a hot jar to within 1 inch (2.5 cm) of top rim (headspace).** Using nonmetallic utensil, remove air bubbles. Wipe jar rim removing any stickiness. Centre SNAP Lid on jar; apply screw band *securely & firmly until resistance is met – fingertip tight. Do not overtighten.* Place jar in canner; repeat for remaining pie filling.
• Cover canner; bring water to a boil. At altitudes up to 1,000 ft (305 m), process – *boil filled jars* – **as specified in individual recipe.** Remove jars without tilting. Cool upright, undisturbed 24 hours; DO NOT RETIGHTEN screw bands. After cooling check jar seals. *Sealed lids curve downward.* Remove screw bands; wipe and dry bands and jars. Store screw bands separately or replace loosely on jars, as desired. Label and store jars in a cool, dark place.

LOTS OF CHERRIES PIE

10 lb (4.5 kg) frozen red tart cherries (10% sugar added), thawed
3 1/2 cups (875 ml) granulated sugar
1 cup (250 ml) Clear Jel® starch
1/2 tsp (2 ml) ground cinnamon
1/4 cup (50 ml) lemon juice

Thaw cherries in colander. Collect 8 cups (2000 ml) juice. Use extra juice for other recipes.
• In a large, deep stainless steel saucepan, whisk together 4 cups (1000 ml) cherry liquid, sugar, Clear Jel® and cinnamon. Whisking frequently, bring to a boil over medium high heat until mixture thickens. Add lemon juice and boil 1 minute, stirring constantly.
• Stir in entire quantity of drained cherries, approximately 15 cups (3750 ml). Cook and stir until completely heated through and mixture boils. ◀ ◀ ◀
Yield – 4 x 1 L or 8 x 500 ml jars. Heat process – 35 minutes.

Sweet Cherry Pie Filling – Prepare as directed for red tart cherries substituting same quantity of black sweet cherries, Clear Jel, and cinnamon. Reduce sugar to 2 1/2 cups (625 ml) and increase lemon juice to 1/3 cup (75 ml).

PEACH PIE

12 cups (3000 ml) peeled, sliced & pitted peaches
3 inches (7.5 cm) cinnamon stick
2 tsp (10 ml) whole cloves
2 2/3 cups (650 ml) granulated sugar
2 cups (500 ml) peeled & finely chopped apples
1 cup (250 ml) golden raisins
1/2 cup (125 ml) lemon juice
1/4 cup (50 ml) white vinegar
2 tbsp (25 ml) lemon zest
1/2 tsp (2 ml) ground nutmeg

Prepare and measure peaches. Tie cinnamon stick and cloves in a square of cheesecloth creating a spice bag.

• Combine peaches, spice bag, sugar, apples, raisins, lemon juice, vinegar, lemon zest and nutmeg in a large stainless steel saucepan. Bring to a boil; cover and boil gently, stirring occasionally until thickened. Discard spice bag. ◀◀◀

Yield – 4 x 500 ml jars. Heat process – 15 minutes.

RASPBERRY PIE

7 cups (1750 ml) raspberries
1 3/4 cup (425 ml) granulated sugar
2/3 cup (150 ml) Clear Jel® starch
2 cups (500 ml) cold water
Food colouring, *optional*
2 tbsp (25 ml) bottled lemon juice

Wash and drain raspberries. Combine sugar and Clear Jel in a large stainless steel saucepan. Add water and food colouring, if using. Stirring frequently, bring to a boil over medium high heat. Add lemon juice and boil 1 minute, stirring constantly. Quickly fold in raspberries; cook and stir until completely heated through and mixture boils. ◀◀◀

Yield – 5 x 500 ml jars. Heat process – 30 minutes.

RHUBARB STRAWBERRY PIE

7 cups (1750 ml) prepared rhubarb, about 1 3/4 lb (750 g)
3 large cooking apples, peeled & finely chopped
2 cups (500 ml) granulated sugar
1/4 cup (50 ml) orange juice
1 tbsp (15 ml) grated orange peel
4 cups (1000 ml) prepared strawberries, about 1 1/2 qt (1.5 L)

Cut rhubarb into 1-inch (2.5 cm) pieces. Measure 7 cups (1750 ml).

• Combine rhubarb, apples, sugar, orange juice and peel in a large stainless steel saucepan. Bring to a boil; boil gently 10 to 15 minutes or until rhubarb is soft. Set aside.

• Wash, hull and halve strawberries; measure 4 cups (1000 ml). Add strawberries to rhubarb and bring to a boil. Remove from heat. ◀◀◀

Yield – 5 x 500 ml jars. Heat process – 15 minutes.

BLUEBERRY PIE

7 cups (1750) cups blueberries
1 2/3 cups (400 ml) granulated sugar
2/3 cup (150 ml) Clear Jel® starch
2 cups (500 ml) water
2 tbsp (30 ml) lemon juice
1 tsp (5 ml) grated lemon peel, *optional*

Wash & drain blueberries. Bring a large saucepan of water to a rolling boil; add blueberries, blanch 1 minute. Drain and keep warm.

• In a large, deep stainless steel saucepan, combine sugar and ClearJel; whisk in water and bring mixture to a boil. (If desired, tint with a few drops of red & blue food colourings.) Cook, stirring frequently, just until mixture thickens and begins to bubble. Stir in lemon juice and peel, cook 1 minute longer. Fold in heated blueberries and fill jars immediately. ◀◀◀

Yield – 4 x 500 ml or 2 x 1 L jars. Heat process – 30 minutes.

THICKENERS FOR HOME CANNING

Not all cooking starches are suitable for home canning. Reheating causes some to lose viscosity. Making mixtures too thick can interfere with required heat penetration during heat processing. Unlike other starches, ClearJel® retains a smooth consistency during heat processing and is excellent for home canned pie fillings. It also works well in preparing ready-to-eat bakery products, sauces, gravies or any food in which a smooth, short stable texture is desired. This product is available at some specialty food stores and may also be obtained via mail order from Bernardin.

FRUIT JUICE

Prepare fruit as directed in individual recipe.
▶▶▶ Strain cooked mixture through a Jelly Bag or several layers of cheesecloth. *(For greater clarity, pour strained juice through a paper coffee filter.)* Refrigerate juice 12 to 48 hours to allow sediment to settle.

• Place required number of clean mason jars on a rack in a boiling water canner; cover jars with water and heat to a simmer (180°F/82°C). Set screw bands aside; heat SNAP Lids in hot water, NOT boiling (180°F/82°C). Keep jars and SNAP Lids hot until ready to use.

• Without mixing or disturbing sediment, carefully pour juice into saucepan; discard sediment. If desired, measure and sweeten juice as directed. Heat juice 5 minutes to 190°F (88°C); do not boil.

• Ladle hot juice into a hot jar to within 1/4 inch (0.5 cm) of top rim (headspace). Using nonmetallic utensil, remove air bubbles. Wipe jar rim removing any stickiness. Centre SNAP Lid on jar; apply screw band *securely & firmly* until resistance is met – fingertip tight. *Do not overtighten.* Place jar in canner; repeat for remaining juice.

• Cover canner; bring water to a boil. At altitudes up to 1,000 ft (305 m), process – *boil filled jars* – **for time indicated in individual recipes**. Remove jars without tilting. Cool upright, undisturbed 24 hours; DO NOT RETIGHTEN screw bands. After cooling check jar seals. *Sealed lids curve downward.* Remove screw bands; wipe and dry bands and jars. Store screw bands separately or replace loosely on jars, as desired. Label and store jars in a cool, dark place.

APPLE JUICE

Wash 24 lb (10.8 kg) sweet, well-coloured, firm, mature apples; drain. Remove stem and blossom ends. Chop apples; place in large stainless steel saucepan. Add 8 cups (2000 ml) water; cook, stirring occasionally, until apples are tender. ◀◀◀
Yield – 6 x 1 L jars. Heat process 1 L jars – 10 minutes; 1.5 L jars 15 minutes.

BERRY JUICE

Wash and crush boysenberries, loganberries or raspberries. Adding just enough water to prevent sticking, simmer fruit until soft. Measure juice. If desired, sweeten strained juice before reheating. For each 1 cup (250 ml) juice, add 1 to 2 tbsp (15 to 25 ml) sugar. ◀◀◀
Heat process 500 ml or 1 L jars – 15 minutes.

CRANBERRY JUICE

Wash cranberries; drain. Combine equal measures of cranberries and water in a large stainless steel saucepan. Bring to a boil. Reduce heat; cook until cranberries burst. ◀◀◀
If desired, sweeten strained juice to taste with sugar before reheating.
Heat process 500 ml or 1 L jars – 15 minutes.

GRAPE JUICE

Wash grapes; drain. Stem, crush and measure grapes into a stainless steel saucepan. For each 4 cups (1 L) crushed grapes, add 1/4 cup (50 ml) water. Heat mixture 10 minutes at 190°F (88°C). Do not boil. ◀◀◀ *If desired, sweeten strained juice before reheating.* For each 1 L juice, add 1/4 to 1/2 cup (50 to 125 ml) sugar. Heat process 500 ml or 1 L jars – 15 minutes; 1.5 L jars – 20 minutes.

PEACH NECTAR

Wash, peel and pit fully ripe peaches; chop coarsely and measure. For each 4 cups (1000 ml) fruit add 1 cup (250 ml) water. Cook mixture until soft. Purée fruit and liquid; do not strain. Return nectar to saucepan and sweeten to taste with sugar. Stirring occasionally, bring to a boil. ◀◀◀
Heat process 500 ml or 1 L jars – 15 minutes.

AUTUMN GLORY COMPOTE

THIS DELECTABLE COMPOTE EXTENDS THE BRIEF SEASON IN WHICH TO ENJOY MOTHER NATURE'S AUTUMN GIFT OF PUMPKINS.

5 cups (1250 ml) cubed pumpkin, about 3 lb (1.4 kg)
1 large fresh pineapple
2 lemons, peel and juice
1 cup (250 ml) coarsely chopped dried apricots
1 cup (250 ml) golden raisins
2 1/2 cups (625 ml) granulated sugar
1/2 cup (125 ml) water
8 inches (20 cm) cinnamon stick

• Place 4 clean 500 ml mason jars on a rack in a boiling water canner; cover jars with water and heat to a simmer (180°F/82°C). Set screw bands aside; heat SNAP Lids in hot water, NOT boiling (180°F/82°C). Keep jars and SNAP Lids hot until ready to use.

• Halve pumpkin, seed and remove rind or use a melon baller to cut pumpkin from rind. Cut pulp into 3/4 inch (2 cm) cubes. Measure 5 cups (1250 ml) into a large stainless steel saucepan.

• Peel, quarter and core pineapple. Cut pulp into 3/4 inch (2 cm) pieces. Measure 5 cups (1250 ml); add to pumpkin.

• Finely grate enough lemon peel to measure 1 tbsp (15 ml) firmly packed and squeeze enough lemon juice to measure 1/2 cup (125 ml). Add juice and peel to pumpkin mixture. Stir in apricots, raisins, sugar, water and cinnamon. Bring to a boil. Stirring constantly, boil gently, uncovered, 2 minutes. Discard cinnamon stick.

• Pack pumpkin mixture into a hot jar to within 3/4 inch (2 cm) of top rim. Add hot liquid to cover mixture to within 1/2 inch (1 cm) of top rim (headspace). Using nonmetallic utensil, remove air bubbles. Wipe jar rim removing any stickiness. Centre SNAP Lid on jar; apply screw band *securely & firmly* until resistance is met – *fingertip tight. Do not overtighten.* Place jar in canner; repeat for remaining pumpkin mixture and hot liquid.

• Cover canner; bring water to a boil. At altitudes up to 1,000 ft (305 m), process – *boil filled jars* – **25 minutes**. Remove jars without tilting. Cool upright, undisturbed 24 hours; DO NOT RETIGHTEN screw bands. After cooling check jar seals. *Sealed lids curve downward.* Remove screw bands; wipe and dry bands and jars. Store screw bands separately or replace loosely on jars, as desired. Label and store jars in a cool, dark place.

Yield – about 4 x 500 ml jars

Note: *This recipe was specially formulated to allow home canners to preserve pumpkin – a low acid food – in a boiling water canner. Do NOT deviate from the recipe ingredients, quantities, jar size and processing method and time. Changes can affect the safety of the end product.*

JELLIED CRANBERRY SAUCE

4 1/4 cups (1000 ml) cranberries
1 3/4 cups (425 ml) water
2 cups (500 ml) granulated sugar
Cinnamon stick and 1 tsp (5 ml) whole cloves, *optional*

• Place two clean 500 ml or four 250 ml straight-sided mason jars on a rack in a boiling water canner; cover jars with water and heat to a simmer (180°F/82°C). Set screw bands aside; heat SNAP Lids in hot water, NOT boiling (180°F/82°C). Keep jars and SNAP Lids hot until ready to use.

• Wash cranberries; drain. Combine cranberries and water in a large stainless steel saucepan. Bring to a boil; cook until skins burst. Purée mixture and return to a clean saucepan.

• Add sugar. For spicy sauce, tie cinnamon and cloves in cheesecloth square; making a spice bag and add to cranberries. Gradually bring mixture to a boil, stirring until sugar dissolves. Increase heat, boil vigorously until mixture reaches gel point (page 15). Discard spice bag, if using.

• Ladle sauce into a hot jar to within 1/4 inch (0.5 cm) of top rim (headspace). Using nonmetallic utensil, remove air bubbles. Wipe jar rim removing any stickiness. Centre SNAP Lid on jar; apply screw band *securely & firmly until resistance is met – fingertip tight. Do not overtighten.* Place jar in canner; repeat for remaining sauce.

• Cover canner; bring water to a boil. At altitudes up to 1,000 ft (305 m), process – *boil filled 250 ml jars –* **10 minutes**; *500 ml jars –* **15 minutes**. Remove jars without tilting. Cool upright, undisturbed 24 hours; DO NOT RETIGHTEN screw bands. After cooling check jar seals. *Sealed lids curve downward.* Remove screw bands; wipe and dry bands and jars. Store screw bands separately or replace loosely on jars, as desired. Label and store jars in a cool, dark place.

Yield – 4 x 250 ml or 2 x 500 ml jars

WHOLE CRANBERRY SAUCE

8 cups (2000 ml) cranberries
4 cups (1000 ml) water
4 cups (1000 ml) granulated sugar

• Prepare 6 clean 500 ml mason jars and two-piece SNAP Lids as directed for Jellied Cranberry Sauce.

• Combine sugar and water in a large deep stainless steel saucepan. Boil 5 minutes. Add cranberries. Return mixture to the boil; continue cooking without stirring until skins burst.

• Ladle hot sauce into hot jars and heat process as for Jellied Cranberry Sauce.

Yield – 6 x 500 ml jars

Lovely to behold, delicious to eat! Serve these one-of-a-kind delicacies as desserts or accents to the main course for formal and casual eating occasions.

ORCHARD SPECIALTIES

• Place required number of mason jars on a rack in a boiling water canner; cover jars with water and heat to a simmer (180°F/82°C). Set screw bands aside; heat SNAP Lids in hot water, NOT boiling (180°F/82°C). Keep jars and SNAP Lids hot until ready to use.

 Prepare fruit and syrup as directed in individual recipes.

▶▶▶ **Pack or ladle fruit into a hot jar to within 3/4 inch (2 cm) of top rim.** Add hot liquid to cover fruit to within 1/2 inch (1 cm) of top rim (headspace). Using nonmetallic utensil, remove air bubbles. Wipe jar rim removing any stickiness. Centre SNAP Lid on jar; apply screw band *securely & firmly until resistance is met – fingertip tight. Do not overtighten.* Place jar in canner; repeat for remaining fruit and hot liquid.

• Cover canner; bring water to a boil. At altitudes up to 1,000 ft (305 m), process – *boil filled jars* – **for time specified in individual recipes.** Remove jars without tilting. Cool upright, undisturbed 24 hours; DO NOT RETIGHTEN screw bands. After cooling check jar seals. *Sealed lids curve downward.* Remove screw bands; wipe and dry bands and jars. Store screw bands separately or replace loosely on jars, as desired. Label and store jars in a cool, dark place.

SPICED CRABAPPLES

4 1/2 cups (1125 ml) granulated sugar
3 cups (750 ml) water
2 1/2 cups (625 ml) white vinegar
4 inch (10 cm) cinnamon stick
1 tbsp (15 ml) *Each:* whole allspice and whole cloves
8 cups (2 L) crabapples, about 3 3/4 lb (1.7 kg)

Combine sugar, water and vinegar in a large stainless steel saucepan. Tie cinnamon, allspice and cloves in a large square of cheesecloth, creating a spice bag; place in saucepan. Bring mixture to a boil; boil 10 minutes.

• Wash and stem crabapples; drain but do not peel. To reduce bursting fruit, prick each crabapple with a fork. Add crabapples and return to a boil; reduce heat and boil gently 10 to 20 minutes or until crabapples are tender. Do not overcook. Crabapples turn to mush very quickly. Discard spice bag. ◀◀◀

Yield – 6 x 500 ml jars. Heat Process filled 500 ml jars – 20 minutes.

ORANGES IN COINTREAU

9 medium Navel oranges, about 3 1/4 lb (1.5 kg)
10 whole cloves
5 cinnamon sticks, broken in half
3 1/2 cups (875 ml) granulated sugar
2/3 cup (150 ml) water
3/4 cup (175 ml) Cointreau (orange liqueur)
1/2 cup (125 ml) white wine

Wash and cut 1/2 inch (1 cm) off both ends of oranges. Thinly slice oranges with a food processor or sharp knife, creating pinwheels approximately 1/8 inch (3 mm) thick. Carefully remove any seeds. Set orange slices aside.

• Tie cinnamon sticks and cloves in a square of cheesecloth, creating a spice bag. Combine spice bag, sugar and water in a large, stainless steel saucepan. Mix well. Slowly bring to a boil; reduce heat to low and boil gently 10 minutes, stirring occasionally. Remove spice bag. Add orange slices, Cointreau and wine to sugar mixture. Stirring gently, heat until mixture begins to boil. Remove from heat. ◀◀◀

Yield – 8 x 250 ml jars. Heat Process filled 250 ml jars – 15 minutes.

CRIMSON-HONEY GRAPEFRUIT SEGMENTS

16 cups (4000 ml) grapefruit segments
1 can (275 ml) undiluted frozen cranberry
  cocktail concentrate, thawed
2/3 cup (150 ml) liquid honey

With a sharp knife, remove grapefruit peel and pith. Holding fruit over bowl to catch juice, slice down to core on either side of segment. Let segments fall into bowl. Continue with remaining grapefruit. Measure 16 cups (4000 ml).

• Combine cranberry concentrate, honey and juice drained from segments in a large stainless steel saucepan. Bring to a boil; boil until honey dissolves. ◀◀◀

Yield – 7 x 250 ml jars. Heat Process filled 250 ml jars – 10 minutes.

PEAR PORT COMPOTE

10 cups (2500 ml) prepared pears, 4 1/2 lb (2 kg)
1 cup (250 ml) *Each:* dark raisins and golden raisins
1/2 cup (125 ml) coarsely chopped dried apricots
Grated peel & juice of 1 orange & 1 lemon
1/2 cup (125 ml) lightly packed golden brown sugar
2 tsp (10 ml) *Each:* ground cinnamon and nutmeg
1/2 tsp (2 ml) ground ginger
1/4 tsp (1 ml) pickling salt
1 cup (250 ml) slivered blanched almonds, *optional*
1/4 cup (50 ml) port wine

Peel, core and coarsely chop pears. Measure 10 cups (2500 ml); place in colour protection solution (page 38).

• Combine dark and golden raisins, apricots, juice and peel of orange and lemon, brown sugar, cinnamon, nutmeg, ginger and salt in a large stainless steel saucepan.

• Drain and add pears to fruit mixture. Bring to a boil, stirring occasionally. Boil gently, covered, stirring occasionally, 20 minutes. Uncover fruit mixture. Boil until thick, stirring frequently to prevent scorching, about 15 minutes. Stir in almonds, if using, and add port; boil gently 5 minutes longer, stirring constantly. ◀◀◀

Yield – 5 x 500 ml jars. Heat Process filled 500 ml jars – 20 minutes.

SUMMER FRUIT COCKTAIL

6 cups (1500 ml) prepared peaches, about
  10 medium or 2.8 lb (1.2 kg)
3 cups (750 ml) prepared pears, about 6 or
  1.7 lb (750 g)
2 cups (500 ml) seedless grapes, about 1 lb (500 g)
2 tbsp (30 ml) BERNARDIN Fruit-Fresh®
2 cups (500 ml) water
1 1/4 cups (300 ml) granulated sugar
1/4 cup (60 ml) liquid honey
1 cup (250 ml) maraschino cherries, well drained
  & halved
5 fresh mint sprigs

Blanch, peel, pit and chop peaches; measure 6 cups (1500 ml). As you work, place fruit in a colour protection solution (page 38). Peel, core and chop pears; measure 3 cups (750 ml), add to peaches. Remove grapes from stems; measure 2 cups (500 ml).

• Combine water, sugar and honey in a large stainless steel saucepan. Bring to a boil. Drain prepared fruit; add to syrup. Return to boil; boil gently 5 minutes; stir in cherries. Remove from heat. Place 1 mint sprig in each hot jar. ◀◀◀

Yield – 5 x 500 ml jars. Heat Process filled 500 ml jars – 20 minutes.

Fruits infused with liquor, wine or liqueur make delightful gifts to share with friends.

SPIRITED FRUIT

Syrup – for one (fruit) recipe:
  1 cup (250 ml) granulated sugar
  2 cups (500 ml) water
Selected Fruit & Spirits

• Place 7 clean 250 ml mason jars on a rack in a boiling water canner; cover jars with water and heat to a simmer (180°F/82°C). Set screw bands aside; heat SNAP Lids in hot water, NOT boiling (180°F/82°C). Keep jars and SNAP Lids hot until ready to use.

 Prepare selected fruit as directed. *Set aside.*

▶▶▶ **Combine sugar and water in a large stainless steel saucepan.** Bring to a boil. Add fruit and return mixture to a boil; boil gently 5 minutes.

• Drain fruit and pack into a hot jar to within 3/4 inch (2 cm) of top rim. Pour specified quantity of chosen Spirits over fruit in jar.

• Add hot syrup to cover fruit to within 1/2 inch (1 cm) of top rim (headspace). Using nonmetallic utensil, remove air bubbles. Wipe jar rim removing any stickiness. Centre SNAP Lid on jar; apply screw band *securely & firmly until resistance is met – fingertip tight. Do not overtighten.* Place jar in canner; repeat for remaining fruit and hot syrup.

• Cover canner; bring water to a boil. At altitudes up to 1,000 ft (305 m), process – *boil filled jars –* **for the Process Time indicated in each Fruit Specific recipe.** Remove jars without tilting. Cool upright, undisturbed 24 hours; DO NOT RETIGHTEN screw bands. After cooling check jar seals. *Sealed lids curve downward.* Remove screw bands; wipe and dry bands and jars. Store screw bands separately or replace loosely on jars, as desired. Label and store jars in a cool, dark place.

Each recipe makes about 7 x 250 ml jars.

BLACKBERRIES

12 cups (3000 ml) blackberries
PER JAR: 1 tbsp (15 ml) rum, brandy or vodka OR
1 1/2 tsp (7 ml) crème de cassis or marsala

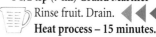 Wash berries in cold or ice water to firm fruit. Drain. ◀◀◀
Heat process – 15 minutes.

BLUEBERRIES

12 cups (3000 ml) blueberries
PER JAR: 1 tbsp (15 ml) rum, brandy or vodka OR
1 1/2 tsp (7 ml) Grand Marnier

Rinse fruit. Drain. ◀◀◀
Heat process – 15 minutes.

CHERRIES

5 cups (1250 ml) cherries
PER JAR: 1 tbsp (15 ml) rum, brandy or vodka OR
1 1/2 tsp (7 ml) kirsch, brandy or amaretto

Wash fruit. If desired, remove pits.
(If pits are removed, increase quantity of cherries by 50%). ◀◀◀
Heat process – 10 minutes.

PEACHES

7 cups (1750 ml) prepared peaches, about 10 medium
PER JAR: 1 tbsp (15 ml) rum or brandy OR
1 1/2 tsp (7 ml) Dubonnet or schnapps

Blanch, peel, pit and slice peaches.
As you work, place peaches in a colour protection solution. (page 38) ◀◀◀
Heat process – 20 minutes.

APRICOTS

4 cups (1000 ml) prepared apricots, about 40
PER JAR: 1 tbsp (15 ml) rum, brandy or white wine OR
1 1/2 tsp (7 ml) apricot brandy, amaretto or port wine

Blanch, peel, pit and slice apricots. As you work, place apricots in colour protection solution. (page 38) ◀◀◀
Heat process – 20 minutes.

PEARS

8 1/2 cups (2125 ml) prepared pears, about 10 medium
PER JAR: 1 tbsp (15 ml) rum, brandy or red wine OR
1 1/2 tsp (7 ml) Kahlua, cognac or crème de menthe

Peel, halve and core pears. Cut into quarters, if desired. As you work, place pears in colour protection solution. (page 38) ◀◀◀
Heat process – 20 minutes.

TERRIFIC TOMATOES

On their own – whole or sauced – as well as in a wealth of savoury and sweet recipes, tomatoes find their way into more Canadian home canned specialties than any other single fruit or vegetable.

A vegetable of many monikers, scientists know them as Lycopersicon lycopersicum. The French called them "pommes d'amour" (love apples) while Germans referred to tomatoes as "apples of paradise." Upon introduction into Italy, tomatoes were yellow and gained fame as "pomo d'oro" (golden apples).

As diverse as their endless culinary uses, these adaptable, juicy "fruits of a vine" come in red, pink, orange, white, green, and yellow varieties. Their shapes vary from round globes to plum-shaped (paste) tomatoes. While both are suitable for home canning, plum tomatoes produce thicker, meatier sauces with less cooking than globe varieties. Plum tomatoes also contain elevated levels of sugar, acid and pectin; varieties include Mamma Mia, La Roma, Roma, San Marzano, Saucy and Viva Italia. Round slicing tomatoes are noted for their juicy eating quality. They can also be used in home canning recipes, but may require extra cooking to reach preferred consistencies.

SELECTION

Choose uniformly coloured, firm but not hard, tomatoes that are heavy for their size, have a good fragrance and are free of bruises, cracks and discolourations. Tomatoes that are heavy for their size will be the juiciest. Do not home can tomatoes from frost-killed vines. While hot house and imported tomatoes are available year round, home canners prefer locally grown garden-ripened tomatoes for ultimate flavour and economy.

Round/globe:
1 lb (454 g) = 2 large or 3 medium or 4 small
1 bushel = 53 lb (24 kg)
Paste/plum:
1 lb (454 g) = 4 large or 5 medium or 6 to 7 small
1 bushel = 53 lb (24 kg)
Prepared tomatoes:
1 lb = 2 cups (500 ml) chopped or 2 1/2 cups (625 ml) sliced or 1 1/2 cups (375 ml) crushed or puréed (peeled)
Store fresh tomatoes at room temperature (55°- 70°F/ 13°- 21°C), away from direct sunlight. Do not refrigerate! Refrigeration causes mealy texture and bland taste. Ripen green tomatoes in a paper bag. Store home canned tomatoes in a cool, dark place.

PREPARATION & HANDLING

Wash tomatoes thoroughly under cool running water. Peeling tomatoes enhances their eating quality and reduces the bacteria load. A vegetable peeler can be used to remove skins. However, blanching is the most efficient way to remove skins from large numbers of tomatoes.

To blanch tomatoes, half-fill a deep stainless steel saucepan with water and bring to a boil. Score tomatoes with an 'X' at the base. Working with small batches, dip tomatoes into boiling water for 30 to 60 seconds, just until skins loosen or begin to curl. Remove and immediately plunge in cold water. Ice water works best. Slip off skins.

Large batches of tomatoes may also be pressed through a food mill or Victorio-type strainer. These devices crush the pulp and separate it from seeds and skins all in one hand-cranked operation.

Seeding tomatoes eliminates excess moisture and reduces cooking time required to thicken or cook off excess liquids. Food mills are the most efficient way to seed tomatoes for a large quantity of sauced tomato ingredient. When seeded "chopped" tomatoes are the objective, cut tomato in half and squeeze out seeds or use a spoon or your fingers to scoop out seeds.

TOMATO CANNING ESSENTIALS

While each family has its tomato favourites, all home canned tomatoes require certain procedures to preserve their goodness.

• Because tomatoes have pH values that fall close to 4.6 (the dividing line between high and low acid foods) precautions must be taken to can them safely. Acidity levels also vary due to variety and growing conditions. *For these reasons, **tomatoes preserved in a boiling water canner must have acid** – citric acid, lemon juice or 5% vinegar – **added to each jar.***

• **Citric acid** is a natural acid found in citrus fruits. When added to tomatoes, this powdered product elevates acidity with little if any change to colour or taste of the final product. It is available in the spice section of some stores and can be ordered by mail from BERNARDIN Ltd.

• **Lemon juice** – bottled juice is preferred because the commercial product has a standardized pH (acidity) level. Adding lemon juice may have a tendency to cause slight clouding of canned whole or half tomatoes.

• **Vinegar** can cause an off-flavour in the final product and is not recommended.

Jar size	Lemon juice	Citric acid
500 ml	1 tbsp (15 ml)	1/4 tsp (1 ml)
1 L	2 tbsp (30 ml)	1/2 tsp (2 ml)
1.5 L	3 tbsp (45 ml)	3/4 tsp (4 ml)

Acids also act as natural flavour enhancers, similar to salt. If you fear that lemon juice will adversely affect tomatoes' flavour, add a small spoonful of sugar to each jar.

• In most cases, *adding vegetables to tomatoes lowers acidity creating a "low acid food" that must be heat processed in a pressure canner.* Some home canning recipes combine tomatoes with vegetables and are processed in a boiling water canner. The ingredient proportions and procedures in such recipes must be designed and tested to maintain a "high acid" food classification. When selecting combination tomato-vegetable "high acid" recipes, always be sure the recipe comes from a reliable source that can verify its acidity and safety. *Do not alter ingredient proportions.* Doing so can change the pH and create a product that can not be safely processed in a boiling water canner.

• Natural acids in tomatoes react with aluminum copper, brass and iron cooking utensils. This reaction causes undesirable colour changes and bitter flavour development. Always use glass or stainless steel utensils and saucepans. Avoid use of wooden utensils that absorb flavour or colour and carry them to other foods.

• During storage, pulp and juice in home canned tomatoes may separate, especially in sauce or juice made with crushed or puréed tomatoes. Separation is caused by an enzyme, Pectase (Pectinesterase), found in high concentrations in tomatoes. The enzyme is activated when tomatoes are cut. To reduce separation, heat tomatoes quickly over high heat to 180°F (82°C) to destroy the enzyme.

Try this technique:

Place a layer of tomatoes in a deep stainless steel saucepan, over high heat. When the mixture begins to boil, cut and add additional tomatoes, crushing them into the cooking mixture. To minimize separation, be sure to add tomatoes as soon as they are cut. Continue until all tomatoes are in the pot and heated.

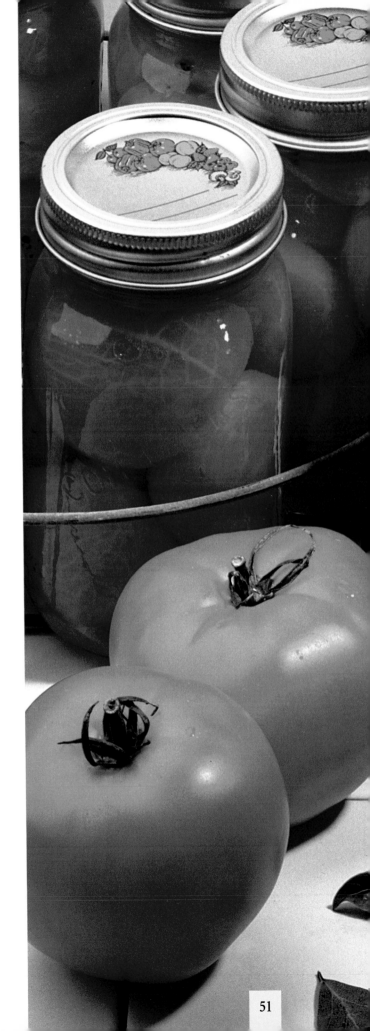

Home canned, garden fresh tomatoes have long been a staple of winter meals. Put up a few or many jars but follow safe home canning procedures and processing times to guarantee quality and safety.

CRUSHED TOMATOES

Tomatoes, prepared
Bottled lemon juice or citric acid
Salt

• Place required number of clean 500 ml or 1 L mason jars on a rack in a boiling water canner; cover jars with water and heat to a simmer (180°F/82°C). Set screw bands aside; heat SNAP Lids in hot water, NOT boiling (180°F/82°C). Keep jars and SNAP Lids hot until ready to use.

• Blanch, peel, core and quarter tomatoes removing bruised or discoloured portions.

• Place 2 cups (500 ml) tomato quarters in a large stainless steel saucepan. Bring to a boil while crushing and stirring to extract juice. Boil gently, stirring constantly; add remaining tomato quarters, 2 cups (500 ml) at a time. DO NOT pre-crush or purée crushed tomatoes, as they will soften with heating and stirring. When all tomatoes are added, boil gently 5 minutes.

• Place 1 tbsp (15 ml) lemon juice or 1/4 tsp citric acid and 1/2 tsp (2 ml) salt, if using, in hot 500 ml jar or 2 tbsp (30 ml) lemon juice or 1/2 tsp (2 ml) citric acid and 1 tsp (5 ml) salt, if using, in hot 1 L jar.

• Ladle tomatoes into a hot jar to within 1/2 inch (1 cm) of top rim (headspace). Using nonmetallic utensil, remove air bubbles. Wipe jar rim removing any stickiness. Centre SNAP Lid on jar; apply screw band *securely & firmly* until resistance is met – fingertip tight. Do not overtighten. Place jar in canner; repeat for remaining tomatoes.

• Cover boiling water canner; bring water to a boil. At altitudes up to 1,000 ft (305 m), process – *boil filled jars* – **35 minutes** for 500 ml; **45 minutes** for 1 L. Remove jars without tilting. Cool upright, undisturbed 24 hours; DO NOT RETIGHTEN screw bands. After cooling check jar seals. *Sealed lids curve downward.* Remove screw bands; wipe and dry bands and jars. Store screw bands separately or replace loosely on jars, as desired. Label and store jars in a cool, dark place.

Whole or halved tomatoes can be packed in a variety of ways but heat processing times must be adjusted to the packing method. To assure a safe, shelf-stable product, be sure to follow all the steps for your packing method, i.e. don't mix and match.

WHOLE OR HALVED TOMATOES

Tomatoes
Tomato juice, *optional*
Bottled lemon juice or citric acid
Salt, *optional*

• Place required number of clean 500 ml, 1 L or 1.5 L mason jars on a rack in a boiling water canner; cover jars with water and heat to a simmer (180°F/82°C). Set screw bands aside; heat SNAP Lids in hot water, NOT boiling (180°F/82°C). Keep jars and SNAP Lids hot until ready to use.
• Wash and blanch tomatoes. Slip off skins; remove cores and any bruised or discoloured portions. Leave whole or halve.
• Add quantity of lemon juice **or** citric acid specified below to each hot mason jar before packing tomatoes. If using, add salt to jar prior to filling.

Jar size	Lemon juice or		Citric acid	Salt, *optional*
500 ml	1 tbsp (15 ml)	**or**	1/4 tsp (1 ml)	1/2 tsp (2 ml)
1 L	2 tbsp (30 ml)	**or**	1/2 tsp (2 ml)	1 tsp (5 ml)
1.5 L	3 tbsp (45 ml)	**or**	3/4 tsp (4 ml)	1 1/4 tsp (7 ml)

Raw Pack with no added liquid:
• Pack raw, peeled tomatoes into a hot jar to within 1/2 inch (1 cm) of top rim. Press tomatoes in the jar until spaces between them fill with juice. Leave 1/2 inch (1 cm) of top rim (headspace).

Hot Pack with Water:
• Place tomatoes in a large stainless steel saucepan. Add enough water to cover; bring to a boil; boil gently for 5 minutes.
• Pack tomatoes into a hot jar to within 3/4 inch (2 cm) of top rim. Add hot cooking liquid to cover tomatoes to within 1/2 inch (1 cm) of top rim (headspace).

Hot Pack with Tomato Juice:
• Place tomatoes in a large stainless steel saucepan. Add enough tomato juice to cover; bring to a boil; boil gently for 5 minutes.
• Pack tomatoes into a hot jar to within 3/4 inch (2 cm) of top rim. Add hot tomato juice to cover tomatoes to within 1/2 inch (1 cm) of top rim (headspace).
• Using nonmetallic utensil, remove air bubbles. Wipe jar rim removing any stickiness. Centre SNAP Lid on jar; apply screw band *securely & firmly until resistance is met – fingertip tight. Do not overtighten.* Place jar in canner; repeat for remaining tomatoes and hot cooking liquid if indicated.
• Cover boiling water canner; bring water to a boil. At altitudes up to 1,000 ft (305 m), process – *boil filled jars* – **for the time indicated for the jar size and packing method used.**

Jar Size	Raw Pack	Hot Pack with Water	Hot Pack with Tomato Juice
500 ml	85 minutes	40 minutes	85 minutes
1 L	85 minutes	45 minutes	85 minutes
1.5 L	110 minutes	45 minutes	No processing time available

• Remove jars without tilting. Cool upright, undisturbed 24 hours; DO NOT RETIGHTEN screw bands. After cooling check jar seals. *Sealed lids curve downward.* Remove screw bands; wipe and dry bands and jars. Store screw bands separately or replace loosely on jars, as desired. Label and store jars in a cool, dark place.

Basic tomato sauce is handy to have on hand to add to pasta sauces, chili, soups or stews. When ready to use this sauce, add any combination of seasonings you desire. For thin sauce, an average of 35 lb (15.8 kg) is needed for seven 1 L jars. For thick sauce, an average of 46 lb (20.8 kg) for seven 1 L jar is required.

TOMATO SAUCE

Tomatoes
Bottled lemon juice or citric acid
Salt, *optional*
Dried herbs, to taste, *optional*

• Place required number of clean 500 ml, 1 L or 1.5 L mason jars on a rack in a boiling water canner; cover jars with water and heat to a simmer (180°F/82°C). Set screw bands aside; heat SNAP Lids in hot water, NOT boiling (180°F/82°C). Keep jars and SNAP Lids hot until ready to use.

• Wash tomatoes, remove cores and trim off bruised or discoloured portions.

• **Option 1** – Quarter tomatoes and pass through a food mill or victorio strainer that separates out seeds and skins from tomato pulp and juice. Heat sauce to a boil.

• **Option 2** – Quarter 1 lb (500 g) tomatoes (about 2 cups/ 500 ml) and place in a large stainless steel saucepan over high heat. Stir and crush tomatoes until mixture boils rapidly. Then continue to slowly add and crush freshly cut tomato quarters to the boiling mixture. Be sure to maintain a constant, vigorous boil while adding remaining tomatoes. Remove from heat and cool slightly. Press mixture through a fine sieve or food mill to remove seeds and skins.

• Return 4 cups (1 L) of sieved mixture to large diameter, deep stainless steel saucepan. Bring to a vigorous boil. Add additional tomato mixture 1 cup (250 ml) at a time, maintaining a steady boil. When all of mixture has been returned to pan, continue stirring occasionally and boiling gently until sauce reaches desired consistency. Boil until volume is reduced by about one-third for thin sauce or by one-half for thick sauce.

• Add quantity of lemon juice or citric acid specified below to each hot mason jar before filling with sauce. If using, add salt and dried herbs to jar prior to filling:

Jar size	Lemon juice	or	Citric acid	Salt, *optional*	Dried herbs, *optional*
500 ml	1 tbsp (15 ml)	**or**	1/4 tsp (1 ml)	1/2 tsp (2 ml)	1-2 tsp (5-10 ml)
1 L	2 tbsp (30 ml)	**or**	1/2 tsp (2 ml)	1 tsp (5 ml)	2-3 tsp (10-15 ml)
1.5 L	3 tbsp (45 ml)	**or**	3/4 tsp (4 ml)	1 1/4 tsp (7 ml)	1 1/2 tbsp (25 ml)

• Ladle sauce into a hot jar to within 1/2 inch (1 cm) of top rim (headspace). Using nonmetallic utensil, remove air bubbles. Wipe jar rim removing any stickiness. Centre SNAP Lid on jar; apply screw band *securely & firmly* until resistance is met – *fingertip tight. Do not overtighten.* Place jar in canner; repeat for remaining sauce.

• Cover canner; bring water to a boil. At altitudes up to 1,000 ft (305 m), process – *boil filled jars* –

Jar size	Processing time
500 ml	35 minutes
1 L	40 minutes
1.5 L	50 minutes

• Remove jars without tilting. Cool upright, undisturbed 24 hours; DO NOT RETIGHTEN screw bands. After cooling check jar seals. *Sealed lids curve downward.* Remove screw bands; wipe and dry bands and jars. Store screw bands separately or replace loosely on jars, as desired. Label and store jars in a cool, dark place.

Any quantity of tomatoes can be used. An average of 3 to 3 1/4 lb (1.4 to 1.5 kg) of tomatoes is needed to make 1 L of juice.

TOMATO JUICE

Tomatoes

Bottled lemon juice or citric acid

Salt, *optional*

• Place required number of clean 500 ml, 1 L or 1.5 L mason jars on a rack in a boiling water canner; cover jars with water and heat to a simmer (180°F/82°C). Set screw bands aside; heat SNAP Lids in hot water, NOT boiling (180°F/82°C). Keep jars and SNAP Lids hot until ready to use.

• Wash tomatoes, remove stems and trim off bruised or discoloured portions.

• To prevent juice from separating, quarter 1 lb (500 g) tomatoes (about 2 cup [500 ml]) and place in a large stainless steel saucepan over high heat. Stir and crush mixture until it boils rapidly. Then continue to slowly add and crush freshly-cut tomato quarters to the boiling mixture. Be sure to maintain a constant, vigorous boil while adding remaining tomatoes. When all pieces have been added and crushed, boil gently for 5 minutes before juicing.

• If juice separation is not a concern, simply slice or quarter tomatoes into a large stainless steel saucepan. Crush, heat and boil gently for 5 minutes before juicing.

• To remove skins and seeds, press through a fine sieve or food mill. Discard seeds and skins. Return juice to saucepan; heat to boiling.

• Add quantity of lemon juice or citric acid specified below to each hot mason jar before filling with juice. If using, add salt to jar prior to filling:

Jar size	Lemon juice	or	Citric acid	Salt, *optional*
500 ml	1 tbsp (15 ml)	or	1/4 tsp (1 ml)	1/2 tsp (2 ml)
1 L	2 tbsp (30 ml)	or	1/2 tsp (2 ml)	1 tsp (5 ml)
1.5 L	3 tbsp (45 ml)	or	3/4 tsp (4 ml)	1 1/4 tsp (7 ml)

• Ladle juice into a hot jar to within 1/2 inch (1 cm) of top rim (headspace). Using nonmetallic utensil, remove air bubbles. Wipe jar rim removing any stickiness. Centre SNAP Lid on jar; apply screw band **securely & firmly** *until resistance is met – fingertip tight. Do not overtighten.* Place jar in canner; repeat for remaining juice.

• Cover canner; bring water to a boil. At altitudes up to 1,000 ft (305 m), process – *boil filled jars* –

Jar size	Processing time
500 ml	35 minutes
1 L	40 minutes
1.5 L	50 minutes

• Remove jars without tilting. Cool upright, undisturbed 24 hours; DO NOT RETIGHTEN screw bands. After cooling check jar seals. *Sealed lids curve downward.* Remove screw bands; wipe and dry bands and jars. Store screw bands separately or replace loosely on jars, as desired. Label and store jars in a cool, dark place.

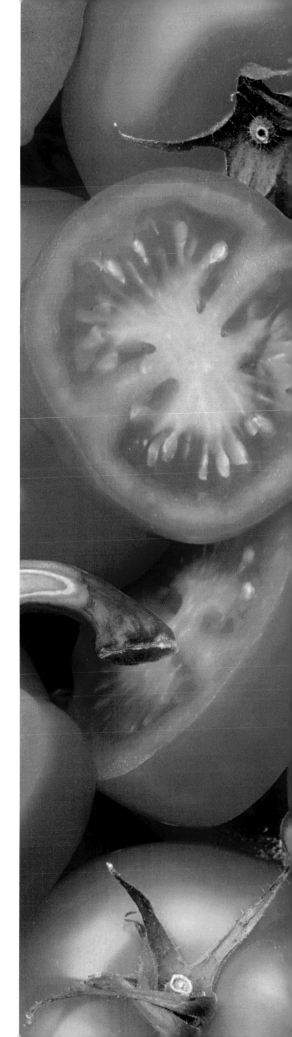

Use this homemade basic to jazz up soups, stews and tomato sauces. Cooking concentrates this recipe's acid content, so unlike other home canned tomato recipes added acid is not required.

TOMATO PASTE

32 cups (8000 ml) chopped tomatoes, about 16 lb (11 kg),
  48 medium-large
1 1/2 cups (375 ml) chopped red pepper, about 3 medium
2 bay leaves
1 tsp (5 ml) salt
1 clove garlic, *optional*

• Place 9 clean 250 ml mason jars on a rack in a boiling water canner; cover jars with water and heat to a simmer (180°F/82°C). Set screw bands aside; heat SNAP Lids in hot water, NOT boiling (180°F/82°C). Keep jars and SNAP Lids hot until ready to use.

• In a large stainless steel saucepan combine tomatoes and pepper. Cook slowly 1 hour, stirring occasionally. Press mixture through a fine sieve or food mill.

• Return mixture to saucepan; add bay leaves, salt and garlic, if using. Cook slowly, stirring frequently, until mixture is thick enough to mound on a spoon, about 2 1/2 hours. Remove bay leaves and garlic clove.

• Ladle paste into a hot jar to within 1/2 inch (1 cm) of top rim (headspace). Using nonmetallic utensil, remove air bubbles. Wipe jar rim removing any stickiness. Centre SNAP Lid on jar; apply screw band *securely & firmly until resistance is met – fingertip tight. Do not overtighten.* Place jar in canner; repeat for remaining paste.

• Cover canner; bring water to a boil. At altitudes up to 1,000 ft (305 m), process – *boil filled jars* – **45 minutes**. Remove jars without tilting. Cool upright, undisturbed 24 hours; DO NOT RETIGHTEN screw bands. After cooling check jar seals. *Sealed lids curve downward.* Remove screw bands; wipe and dry bands and jars. Store screw bands separately or replace loosely on jars, as desired. Label and store jars in a cool, dark place.

Yield – 9 x 250 ml jars

SASSY
SALSAS

Make your tastebuds mambo! Cook up a batch of salsa. Homemade salsas pack a fiesta of flavours and colours that store-bought can't touch. Today's salsas span a delicious spectrum of flavours and uses. Serve them as dips with chips, toppers for potatoes or as a tasty replacement of ketchup. But don't forget their marvelous potential as ingredients in recipes.

Turning garden-fresh produce into tantalizing salsas is quick and easy with Bernardin Salsa Mix. Ideal for novice cooks and home canners, this mix reduces the number of ingredients required as well as preparation and cooking time. When home canned, each of these recipes yields about 6 x 500 ml jars or 12 x 250 ml jars. These salsas can also be prepared, cooked and served fresh so they're great when you're expecting a crowd.

QUINTET OF QUICK 'N EASY SALSAS

• Place required number of clean mason jars in a boiling water canner; cover jars with water and heat water to a simmer (180°F/82°C). Set screw bands aside; heat SNAP Lids in hot water, NOT boiling (180°F/82°C). Keep jars and SNAP Lids hot until ready to use.

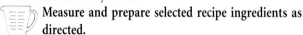 **Measure and prepare selected recipe ingredients as directed.**

▶▶▶ **In a large stainless steel saucepan, combine BERNARDIN Salsa Mix and cider vinegar (or lime juice & honey, as indicated).** Add remaining ingredients specified in selected recipe. Stirring continuously until well mixed, bring mixture to a full rolling boil; boil gently, uncovered, 5 minutes.

• Ladle hot salsa into a hot jar to within 1/2 inch (1 cm) of top rim (headspace). Using nonmetallic utensil, remove air bubbles. Wipe jar rim removing any stickiness. Centre SNAP Lid on jar; apply screw band *securely & firmly until resistance is met – fingertip tight. Do not overtighten.* Place jar in canner; repeat for remaining salsa.

• Cover canner; bring water to a boil. At altitudes up to 1,000 ft (305 m), process – *boil filled jars:* 250 ml jars – **15 minutes**; 500 ml jars – **20 minutes**. Remove jars without tilting. Cool upright, undisturbed 24 hours; DO NOT RETIGHTEN screw bands. After cooling check jar seals. *Sealed lids curve downward.* Remove screw bands; wipe and dry bands and jars. Store screw bands separately or replace loosely on jars, as desired. Label and store jars in a cool, dark place.

TOMATO SALSA

16 cups (4000 ml) coarsely chopped tomatoes, about 8 lb (3.6 kg), 30 medium
1 pkg (115 g) BERNARDIN Salsa Mix
1 1/3 cups (325 ml) cider vinegar

 Wash, seed and coarsely chop tomatoes; drain off excess liquid. Measure 16 cups (4000 ml). ◀◀◀

TOMATO CORN SALSA

12 cups (3000 ml) seeded, coarsely chopped tomatoes
8 cups (2000 ml) whole kernel corn
1 3/4 cups (425 ml) cider vinegar
1 pkg (115 g) BERNARDIN Salsa Mix

Wash, seed and coarsely chop tomatoes; drain off excess liquid. Measure 12 cups (3000 ml). If using fresh corn, blanch ears in boiling water 1 minute before cutting kernels off. Measure 8 cups (2000 ml). ◀◀◀

TOMATO & PEPPER SALSA

9 cups (2250 ml) coarsely chopped tomatoes, about 5 lb (2.3 kg), 20 medium
6 cups (1500 ml) chopped red or green peppers, about 2.5 lb (1.2 kg)
1 pkg (115 g) BERNARDIN Salsa Mix
1 1/3 cups (325 ml) cider vinegar

Wash, seed and coarsely chop tomatoes and peppers; drain off excess liquid. Measure 9 cups (2250 ml) tomatoes and 6 cups (1500 ml) peppers. ◀◀◀

TROPICAL SALSA

12 cups (3000 ml) chopped tomatoes, about 6 lb (2.8 kg), 24 medium
2 ripe mangoes
1 can (19 oz/540 ml) crushed pineapple, drained
1 pkg (115 g) BERNARDIN Salsa Mix
1/2 cup (125 ml) cider vinegar

Wash, core, seed and chop tomatoes; drain off excess liquid. Measure 12 cups (3000 ml). Peel, remove seeds and coarsely chop mangoes. ◀◀◀

EASY ORCHARD SALSA

10 cups (2500 ml) coarsely chopped, peeled peaches, about 6 1/2 lb (3 kg)
5 cups (1250 ml) chopped, peeled pears, about 2 3/4 lb (1.2 kg)
Grated peel and juice of 4 limes
4 tbsp (60 ml) liquid honey
1 pkg (115 g) BERNARDIN Salsa Mix

Peel, pit or core, chop & measure peaches and pears individually. Grate peel from limes and squeeze juice; measure 1/2 cup (125 ml) lime juice. ◀◀◀

SALSA FIESTA

• Place required number of clean mason jars in a boiling water canner; cover jars with water and heat water to a simmer (180°F/82°C). Set screw bands aside; heat SNAP Lids in hot water, NOT boiling (180°F/82°C). Keep jars and SNAP Lids hot until ready to use.

 Measure and prepare selected recipe as directed.

▶▶▶ **Ladle hot salsa into a hot jar to within 1/2 inch (1 cm) of top rim (headspace).** Using nonmetallic utensil, remove air bubbles. Wipe jar rim removing any stickiness. Centre SNAP Lid on jar; apply screw band *securely & firmly until resistance is met – fingertip tight. Do not overtighten.* Place jar in canner; repeat for remaining salsa.

• Cover canner; bring water to a boil. At altitudes up to 1,000 ft (305 m), process – *boil filled jars:* 250 ml jars – **15 minutes**; 500 ml jars – **20 minutes**. Remove jars without tilting. Cool upright, undisturbed 24 hours; DO NOT RETIGHTEN screw bands. After cooling check jar seals. *Sealed lids curve downward.* Remove screw bands; wipe and dry bands and jars. Store screw bands separately or replace loosely on jars, as desired. Label and store jars in a cool, dark place.

ROASTED TOMATO – CHIPOTLE SALSA

NOT ALL MARKETS STOCK THESE DRIED CHILIES, BUT THIS UNIQUE SALSA IS WELL WORTH THE EXTRA EFFORT REQUIRED TO FIND THE INGREDIENTS.

2 oz (56 g) dried chipotle chilies, about 12
1 1/2 oz (42 g) dried cascabel chilies, about 12
3 lb (1.4 kg) Italian plum tomatoes
1 lb (454 g) sweet green peppers, halved
1/2 lb (225 g) small cooking onions, peeled
1 head garlic, broken into pieces
2 tsp (10 ml) granulated sugar
1 tsp (5 ml) salt
1 cup (250 ml) vinegar

Grill or broil dried chilies, turning frequently, just until they start to char on all sides. Discard stems & seed pod. Place roasted chilies in bowl with 2 cups (500 ml) boiling water. Cover tightly with plastic wrap; let stand to steep.

• Grill or broil tomatoes, peppers, onions and garlic cloves 15 to 20 minutes, turning to roast all sides. Peel & chop tomatoes, peppers, onion and garlic; place in a large stainless steel saucepan. Purée chilies with soaking water; add purée to roasted vegetable mixture with sugar, salt and vinegar. Stirring frequently; bring to a boil; continue cooking 15 minutes. ◀◀◀

Yield: 8 x 250 ml jars or 4 x 500 ml jars

SUMMER SALSA

FRUIT ADDS A SWEET AND MELLOW FLAVOUR TO TRADITIONAL TOMATO SALSA. TRY THIS SALSA AS A CONDIMENT WITH YOUR MEAT, FISH OR GRILLED VEGETABLES.

4 cups (1000 ml) chopped tomatoes, about 2 lb (900 g)
2 cups (500 ml) *Each:* **chopped, peeled peaches & pears**
1 red pepper, finely chopped
1 cup (250 ml) chopped red onion
3-4 jalapeño peppers, finely chopped; *seeding optional*
1/2 cup (125 ml) finely chopped fresh cilantro
Grated peel and juice of 1 lemon
1/4 cup (50 ml) white balsamic vinegar
1 tbsp (15 ml) finely chopped fresh mint
1/2 cup (125 ml) liquid honey

Wash, seed and coarsely chop tomatoes; drain off excess liquid; measure 4 cups (1000 ml). Blanch, peel, pit/core and chop peaches and pears; measure 2 cups (500 ml) each. In a large stainless steel saucepan, combine tomatoes, peaches, pears, red pepper, onion and jalapeño peppers. Bring to a boil. Add cilantro, lemon zest and juice, balsamic vinegar, mint and honey; boil gently 5 minutes. ◀◀◀

Yield: 6 x 500 ml jars

FRESH VEGETABLE SALSA

ADD EXCITEMENT TO BAKED POTATOES WHILE KEEPING THE FAT PER SERVING TO A BARE MINIMUM – TOP POTATOES WITH THIS DELICIOUS SALSA INSTEAD OF SOUR CREAM.

7 cups (1750 ml) chopped tomatoes, about 6 lb (3.3 kg)
2 cups (500 ml) coarsely chopped onions
1 cup (250 ml) coarsely chopped green bell pepper
8 jalapeño peppers
3 cloves garlic, minced
1 can (156 ml) tomato paste
3/4 cup (175 ml) white vinegar
1/2 cup (125 ml) chopped cilantro, lightly packed
1/2 tsp (2 ml) ground cumin

Blanch, peel, seed and coarsely chop tomatoes. Measure 7 cups (1750 ml). Wearing rubber gloves remove seeds and finely chop jalapeños. Combine tomatoes, onions, green pepper, jalapeño pepper, garlic, tomato paste, vinegar, cilantro and cumin in a large stainless steel saucepan. Bring to a boil; boil gently, stirring occasionally, until salsa reaches desired consistency, about 30 minutes. ◀◀◀

Yield: 5 x 500 ml jars

PEPPER PEAR SALSA

A CARNIVAL OF COLOUR AND FLAVOUR. RED AND GREEN PEPPERS, SWEET JUICY PEARS AND A TANTALIZING BLEND OF SAVOURY SPICES CREATE A UNIQUE SALSA FOR DIPPING. IT'S EVEN BETTER SERVED AS A CONDIMENT WITH MEAT AND POULTRY.

1 cup (250 ml) white vinegar
2.2 lb (1 kg) firm, ripe pears
3 *Each:* green and red peppers, coarsely chopped
1 cup (250 ml) granulated sugar
2 tbsp (30 ml) pickling salt
2 tsp (10 ml) dry mustard
1 tsp (5 ml) turmeric
1/2 tsp (2 ml) *Each:* ground allspice and black pepper

Measure vinegar into a large stainless steel saucepan. Wash, core, peel and coarsely chop pears. Measure 8 cups (2000 ml) pears; stir into vinegar. Add red and green peppers, sugar, salt, mustard, turmeric, allspice and black pepper. Stirring constantly, bring mixture to a boil. Reduce heat; boil gently stirring occasionally until thickened, about 55 minutes. ◀◀◀
Yield: 3 x 500 ml or 6 x 250 ml jars

PEACH SALSA

TIRED OF TOMATO SALSA? TRY SOMETHING NEW! COMBINING THE MELLOW FLAVOUR OF PEACHES WITH HOT, SPICY INGREDIENTS YIELDS A UNIQUE, COLOURFUL CONDIMENT. SERVE IT WITH NACHOS OR GRILLED ENTRÉES.

6 cups (1500 ml) prepared peaches, 3 lb (1.4 kg)
1 1/4 cups (300 ml) chopped red onion
4 jalapeño peppers, finely chopped
1 red pepper, chopped
1/2 cup (125 ml) loosely packed finely chopped cilantro
1/2 cup (125 ml) white vinegar
2 tbsp (25 ml) liquid honey
1 clove garlic, finely chopped
1 1/2 tsp (7 ml) ground cumin
1/2 tsp (2 ml) cayenne pepper

Blanch, peel, pit and chop peaches; measure 6 cups (1500 ml). Combine peaches, onion, peppers, cilantro, vinegar, honey, garlic, cumin and cayenne pepper in a large stainless steel saucepan. Bring to a boil, stirring constantly to prevent scorching. Boil gently, stirring frequently, 5 minutes. Remove from heat. ◀◀◀
Yield: 8 x 250 ml jars

TOMATILLO SALSA

TOMATILLOS COMBINED WITH ONION, CHILIES AND CILANTRO CREATE AN AUTHENTIC TASTING MEXICAN SALSA. DON'T LIMIT THE USE OF THIS SALSA TO CORN CHIPS ONLY! USE IT AS A CONDIMENT FOR FAJITAS, BURRITOS AND QUESADILLAS.

5 1/2 cups (1375 ml) chopped tomatillos, 2 lb (900 g)
1 cup (250 ml) chopped onion
1 cup (250 ml) chopped hot green chili peppers
4 cloves garlic, minced
2 tbsp (25 ml) finely chopped cilantro
2 tsp (10 ml) cumin
1/2 tsp (2 ml) *Each:* salt & red pepper flakes
1 cup (250 ml) white vinegar
1/4 cup (50 ml) lime juice

Husk, core and chop tomatillos; measure 5 1/2 cups (1375 ml). Combine tomatillos, onion, green chili pepper, garlic, cilantro, cumin, salt, red pepper flakes, vinegar and lime juice in a large stainless steel saucepan. Bring mixture to a boil, stirring frequently. Boil gently until desired consistency is reached, about 10 minutes. ◀◀◀
Yield: 4 x 250 ml jars

SALSA VERDE

THIS SPICY GREEN TOMATO SALSA IS SURE TO PUT A TWIST ON TRADITIONAL SALSAS. USE A VARIETY OF HOT PEPPERS DEPENDING ON HOW MUCH 'HEAT' YOU CAN HANDLE. ENJOY IT WITH GRILLED MEATS AND FISH OR STRAIGHT FROM THE JAR WITH TORTILLA CHIPS.

7 cups (1750 ml) chopped green tomatoes, 3.5 lb (1.6 kg)
5-10 jalapeño or scotch bonnet peppers, finely chopped
2 cups (500 ml) finely chopped red onion, about 1 large
2 cloves garlic, minced
1/2 cup (125 ml) lime juice
1/2 cup (125 ml) chopped cilantro
2 tsp (10 ml) cumin
1 tsp (5 ml) oregano
1 tsp (5 ml) *Each:* salt and black pepper

Wash, core, seed and coarsely chop tomatoes; drain off excess liquid. Measure 7 cups (1750 ml) into a large stainless steel saucepan; add peppers, onion, garlic and lime juice. Bring to a boil. Stir in cilantro, cumin, oregano, salt and black pepper; simmer 5 minutes. Remove from heat. ◀◀◀
Yield: 6 x 250 ml jars

Yesteryear's forerunner to today's salsas, Chili Sauce is still a treasured home canning tradition for many. While tomatoes are the star ingredient in traditional chili sauces, recipes for this popular condiment have acquired new texture, flavour and ingredient definitions. To suit today's diverse tastes, these Chili Sauce recipes range from traditional to extraordinary.

CHILI SAUCE

 Prepare and cook sauce ingredients as directed in each recipe.

• While sauce is cooking, place required number of mason jars on a rack in a boiling water canner; cover jars with water and heat to a simmer (180°F/82°C). Set screw bands aside; heat SNAP Lids in hot water, NOT boiling (180°F/82°C). Keep jars and SNAP Lids hot until ready to use.

▶ ▶ ▶ **Ladle sauce into a hot jar to within 1/2 inch (1 cm) of top rim (headspace).** Using nonmetallic utensil, remove air bubbles. Wipe jar rim removing any stickiness. Centre SNAP Lid on jar; apply screw band *securely & firmly until resistance is met – fingertip tight. Do not overtighten.* Place jar in canner; repeat for remaining sauce.

• Cover canner; bring water to a boil. At altitudes up to 1,000 ft (305 m), process – *boil filled jars:* 500 ml jars – **20 minutes**; 250 ml jars – **15 minutes**. Remove jars without tilting. Cool upright, undisturbed 24 hours; DO NOT RETIGHTEN screw bands. After cooling check jar seals. *Sealed lids curve downward.* Remove screw bands; wipe and dry bands and jars. Store screw bands separately or replace loosely on jars, as desired. Label and store jars in a cool, dark place.

GRANDMA'S CHILI SAUCE

JUST LIKE GRANDMA USED TO MAKE! TRY THIS CLASSIC CHILI SAUCE TO ACCOMPANY ANY MEAL.

16 cups (4000 ml) peeled, cored & chopped tomatoes, about 8 lb (3.6 kg)
6 onions, chopped
6 green peppers, chopped
2 red peppers, chopped
2 cups (500 ml) white vinegar
1 cup (250 ml) lightly packed brown sugar
1 clove garlic, minced
1 tbsp (15 ml) fresh shredded horseradish, or drained bottled, *optional*
1 tbsp (15 ml) *Each:* celery salt, mustard seed and pickling salt
1 tsp (5 ml) *Each:* ground allspice, ground mace and ground cinnamon
1/4 tsp (1 ml) ground cloves

Combine prepared tomatoes, onions, green and red peppers, vinegar, brown sugar, garlic, horseradish (if using), celery salt, mustard seed, pickling salt, allspice, mace, cinnamon and cloves in a large stainless steel saucepan. Stirring frequently, bring to a boil. Boil gently, stirring occasionally to prevent scorching, until mixture reaches desired consistency, about 2 hours. ◀ ◀ ◀

Yield – about 7 x 500 ml jars

62

HOT 'N SWEET CHILI SAUCE

THIS SWEET AND SPICY CHILI SAUCE WILL ADD A DELIGHTFUL ZING TO BARBECUES.

6 cups (1500 ml) peeled, cored & chopped tomatoes, about 4.5 lb (2 kg)
2 small peaches, chopped
1 *Each:* apple, pear, onion & red pepper – chopped
6 to 8 hot peppers, finely chopped
1 1/2 cups (375 ml) white vinegar
1 1/2 cups (375 ml) granulated sugar
4 tsp (20 ml) pickling salt
1/2 cup (125 ml) sultana raisins
1/4 cup (50 ml) pickling spice

Combine tomatoes, apple, peaches, pear, onion, red pepper, hot pepper, vinegar, sugar, salt and raisins in a large stainless steel saucepan. Tie pickling spice in a large square of cheesecloth, creating a spice bag; add to tomatoes. Stirring frequently, bring mixture to a boil. Boil gently, stirring occasionally to prevent scorching, until mixture reaches desired consistency, about 1 1/2 hours. Discard spice bag. ◀◀◀
Yield – about 4 x 500 ml jars

GREEN CHILI SAUCE

WHEN WINTER IS KNOCKING AT YOUR DOOR, DON'T LET LATE TOMATOES GO TO WASTE. HARVEST THEM BEFORE A FROST AND MAKE A BATCH OF THIS TASTY SAUCE.

18 cups (4500 ml) cored & chopped green tomatoes, about 9 lb (4 kg)
3 onions, chopped
3 large celery stalks, chopped
1 green pepper, chopped
1 red pepper, chopped
1 hot red pepper, finely chopped
3 cups (750 ml) white vinegar
2 1/2 cups (675 ml) lightly packed brown sugar
4 1/2 tsp (25 ml) *Each:* pickling salt & pickling spice

Combine tomatoes, onions, celery, green, red and hot peppers, vinegar, brown sugar and salt in a large deep stainless steel saucepan. Tie pickling spice in a large square of cheesecloth, creating a spice bag; add to mixture. Stirring frequently, bring to a boil. Boil gently, stirring occasionally to prevent scorching, until mixture reaches desired consistency, about 3 hours. Discard spice bag. ◀◀◀
Yield – about 9 x 500 ml jars.

FIESTA FRUIT CHILI SAUCE

BERNARDIN SALSA MIX SHORTENS THE TRADITIONAL CHILI SAUCE PREPARATION/COOKING TIME AND YIELDS A VERSATILE, ZESTY CONDIMENT.

8 cups (2000 ml) chopped peeled & seeded plum tomatoes, 5 lb (2.3 kg)
2 cups (500 ml) chopped peeled peaches, about 1 1/4 lb (550 g)
2 cups (500 ml) chopped peeled pears, 1 lb (500 g)
2 cups (500 ml) chopped plums, about 1 1/4 lb (550 g)
1 cup (250 ml) apple cider vinegar
2 cups (500 ml) firmly packed light brown sugar
1 pkg (115 g) BERNARDIN Salsa Mix
12 inch (30 cm) cinnamon stick

Prepare, chop & measure tomatoes and each fruit individually. Combine tomatoes & fruits; set aside.
• Combine vinegar, sugar, Salsa Mix and cinnamon sticks in a large deep stainless steel saucepan. Bring to a full rolling boil, stirring until well mixed. While maintaining a boil, stir in tomato-fruit mixture one cup at a time. Stirring frequently, continue boiling 15 to 20 minutes or until sauce reaches desired consistency. Remove from heat; discard cinnamon sticks. ◀◀◀
Yield – about 6 x 500 ml jars

SINGAPORE CHILI SAUCE

SERVE THIS SWEET 'N HOT CONDIMENT WITH ASIAN OR WESTERN DISHES FROM SPRING ROLLS TO COLD ROAST MEAT. THIS SAUCE LOOKS LOVELY WHEN PURÉED – BEFORE PRESERVED OR JUST BEFORE SERVING.

4 cups (1 L) chopped fresh hot red peppers (Dutch or red Thai)
2 1/2 cups (625 ml) white vinegar
2 1/2 cups (625 ml) granulated sugar
1 1/2 cups (375 ml) sultana raisins
1/4 cup (50 ml) chopped garlic
1 tbsp (15 ml) grated gingerroot
2 tsp (10 ml) salt

Wearing rubber gloves, prepare red peppers, discarding stems and chop. (For a milder sauce, remove seeds and white membranes before chopping.)
• In a large stainless steel saucepan combine vinegar and sugar. Bring to a boil over high heat; stirring occasionally; reduce heat, boil gently 3 minutes. Add red peppers, sultanas, garlic, gingerroot and salt. Bring to boil; reduce heat, boil gently 5 minutes. ◀◀◀
Yield – about 6 x 250 ml jars

'LOVE APPLE' JELLY

8 cups (2000 ml) sliced tomatoes, about 3 lb (1.5 kg)
1/2 cup (125 ml) water
3 hot chili peppers
3/4 cups (175 ml) coarsely chopped fresh basil
3 1/4 cup (800 ml) granulated sugar
2 tbsp (30 ml) bottled lemon juice
1 pkg (57 g) BERNARDIN *Original Fruit Pectin*

• Combine tomatoes, 1/2 cup (125 ml) water, chilies and basil in a large stainless steel saucepan. Bring mixture to a boil; cover and boil gently, stirring occasionally, until tomatoes are soft, about 25 minutes.

• Pour prepared mixture into dampened Jelly Bag or cheese cloth-lined sieve suspended over a deep container. Let drip to collect juice. For quicker results, squeeze bag; juice maybe cloudy.

• Place 7 clean 125 ml mason jars on a rack in a boiling water canner; cover jars with water and heat to a simmer (180°F/82°C). Set screw bands aside; heat SNAP Lids in hot water, NOT boiling (180°F/82°C). Keep jars and SNAP Lids hot until ready to use.

• Measure sugar; set aside.

• Measure 1 3/4 cups (425 ml) juice into a large, deep stainless steel saucepan. Add lemon juice. Whisk in Fruit Pectin until dissolved.

• Stirring frequently, bring mixture to a boil over high heat. Add sugar. Stirring constantly, return mixture to a full rolling boil; boil hard 1 minute. Remove from heat; skim foam.

• Ladle jelly into a hot jar to within 1/4 inch (0.5 cm) of top rim (headspace). Using nonmetallic utensil, remove air bubbles. Wipe jar rim removing any stickiness. Centre SNAP Lid on jar; apply screw band ***securely & firmly*** *until resistance is met – fingertip tight. Do not overtighten.* Place jar in canner; repeat for remaining jelly.

• Cover canner; bring water to a boil. At altitudes up to 1,000 ft (305 m), process – *boil filled jars* – **10 minutes**. Remove jars without tilting. Cool upright, undisturbed 24 hours; DO NOT RETIGHTEN screw bands. After cooling check jar seals. *Sealed lids curve downward.* Remove screw bands; wipe and dry bands and jars. Store screw bands separately or replace loosely on jars, as desired. Label and store jars in a cool, dark place.

Yield – about 7 x 125 ml jars

Once thought to have aphrodisiac powers and christened "pommes d'amour" (love apples) by the French, versatile tomatoes also make a delicious amber-coloured jelly. Serve it as you do all sweet spreads or add to cheese and cracker trays. Try different herb combinations and intensities to add variety to this adaptable jelly.

PERFECT PICKLES

A sandwich without a pickle is like a kiss without a hug – incomplete! Pickles offer endless ways to compliment foods in a vast variety of flavours, colours and textures. From sparkling, crisp dills to pungent relish and chutney, pickling knows few boundaries.

PICKLING PLEASURES

Crisp, tangy cucumber dills may come immediately to mind when you hear pickles mentioned, but any fruit or vegetable preserved in a flavoured acid solution is classified as a pickle. This includes relish, chutney and a broad range of tantalizing condiments. Fermented foods, like sauerkraut, are also pickles.

Pickling employs one of two classic techniques:
• **FRESH PACK pickles** are the quickest and easiest pickles to make. Sometimes called "quick process" pickles, ingredients are preserved in a spicy vinegar solution without prior fermentation. Recipes for fresh pack pickles may require vegetables to be salted or iced and left for several hours or overnight but no fermentation takes place prior to canning. The standing time creates firmer-textured pickles as it helps reduce the vegetables' natural moisture content. After processing and before serving, store all Fresh Pack pickles 4 to 6 weeks to allow flavours time to mellow and blend. The flavour of relish, chutney and condiments also benefits from a 2 to 3 week resting time before serving.
• **FERMENTED pickles** require tender loving care, plus plenty of time and patience. When food is submerged in a salt-water "brine" and allowed to stand, it ferments or cures. Fermentation converts natural sugars in the food to lactic acid that, in turn, controls growth of undesirable microorganisms. Lactic acid also adds distinctive flavours and transforms low acid vegetables into high acid foods that can be safely processed in a boiling water canner.
Fermentation can require up to 6 weeks prior to the time the pickles are ready to eat and/or can be preserved in jars for shelf-stable storage. Dill, garlic, other herbs and spices can be incorporated into the pickling brine to add distinctive flavour profiles. Making fermented pickles is much more involved than Fresh Pack pickles, but many pickle connoisseurs argue that the superior flavour of the fermented product is well worth the extra effort.
Successful fermentation requires attention to details:
   • Containers – Use only large, deep glass, food-grade plastic, stainless steel or stone crock containers for fermenting foods. Select containers that are about 4 inches (10 cm) taller that the beginning quantity of food to be fermented.
   • Weighting – During fermentation, food must be submerged under the brine at all times. To keep vegetables submerged, place an undersized lid or glass pie plate on top of vegetables. The "lid" must fit down into the fermentation container yet cover as much of the food as possible. Weight the vegetables down into the brine by placing water-filled mason jars on the lid.
   • Temperature – Place fermentation container in a cool 70°-75°F (21°-24°C) location that will remain consistent throughout the fermentation process. Avoid temperature fluctuations!
   • Check container daily! Bubbles or scum formation is a sign of active fermentation. All scum that forms on top of the brine *must be skimmed off each day*. Left unattended, the scum can reduce the acidity of the brine and cause spoilage.
   • To determine when fermentation is complete, tap the container on the side with your hand. Bubbles rising to the surface indicate cucumbers are still fermenting. Secondly, cut a cucumber in half – an even consistent colour indicates fermentation is complete. Rings or white spots indicate that additional fermentation is required.
Regardless of the chosen pickling technique, all home canned jars of pickles, relish, chutney and condiments must be heat processed in a boiling water canner. Heat processing pickles does not cause them to become less crisp. The correct balance of ingredients together with top quality, fresh produce prepared according to a tested recipe are the keys to crisp, flavourful pickles.

Enhance the firm, crisp texture of Fresh Pack pickles with Bernardin Pickle Crisp™. It's simple! Add a small quantity of this powered natural mineral product to each packed jar of pickles just before ladling in the hot pickling liquid. Pickle Crisp™ is not a preservative and does not replace heat processing. Use it only as an ingredient in Fresh Pack pickle recipes. Pickle Crisp™ replaces old-fashioned firming agents, such as lime and alum, that are no longer recommended for homemade pickles. Modern research has shown that lime requires extreme caution in handling and can easily be very caustic. Alum has been shown to cause digestive problems for some people.

PICKLING POINTERS

In addition to top quality ingredients and accurate measures, pickling requires close attention to temperature control and maintenance details, especially when making fermented recipes.

INGREDIENTS – The best pickles are prepared with fruits and vegetables used within 24 hours of their harvest. This is particularly important when pickling cucumbers as they deteriorate rapidly at room temperature.

Use only pickling cucumbers when making cucumber pickles. Do not use waxed cucumbers since the brine cannot penetrate the wax coating. Other cucumber varieties may be used for certain relish and chutney recipes in which the vegetables are peeled and chopped. Cucumber blossom ends contain enzymes that can cause soft pickles. Slice off and discard the blossom end of all cucumbers.

Select tender vegetables and firm fruits for pickles. Unlike other home canned foods, some pickle recipes work better with slightly under ripe fruits and vegetables. i.e. pears, peaches, green tomatoes.

The best pickles demand top quality produce, but your choice of other ingredients is also important for pickling success.

VINEGAR acts as a preservative and gives pickles a tart taste. Unless a recipe specifies otherwise, use only commercial vinegar with a minimum 5% acidity. Never decrease the proportion of vinegar in a recipe. Doing so can upset the preservative balance and in turn the safety of the final product. "Pickling vinegar" has a 7% acidity and yields products with a more astringent flavour. Do not use vinegar of unknown acidity level – its food preservation ability is unknown and product safety can be affected. Do not dilute vinegar unless specified in a tested recipe.

White distilled vinegar provides a sharp, pungent, acid taste and will not darken or discolour produce. Use it whenever colour is important. *Cider, malt and balsamic vinegars* add subtle, distinct flavour accents but they also can discolour or darken produce. Rice vinegar also contributes noticeable flavour difference and does not influence colour. When using rice vinegar, always confirm that it meets the minimum 5% acidity rule.

SALT is another essential preservative component in pickling. Salt also adds flavour and crispness to pickles. In fermented recipes, salt draws juices and sugar from foods and forms lactic acid, a preservative. **Use only pickling salt.** *Kosher salt may also be used for pickles.* The iodine in table salt can cause pickles to darken. Table salt contains anti-caking agents that can cause a cloudy appearance in the product.

SUGAR tempers pickle recipes' tartness. Granulated white sugar is the most common choice for pickles. Chutney and specialty relishes occasionally utilize brown sugar or honey for added flavour and colour.

SPICES and **HERBS** transform ordinary vegetables and fruit into a tantalizing array of pickled specialties. Fresh, top quality spices and herbs are absolute necessities. Less than fresh herbs and spices will not deliver the desirable flavour level and may cause a musty tainted taste. Whole spices are preferred for whole pickles and many relish and chutney recipes as well. Powdered seasonings can cause pickling solutions to be cloudy. Tie whole spices in a spice bag to infuse flavour into pickling recipes without affecting the end product's texture and eating quality.

SOFT WATER makes the best pickles and is absolutely essential for "fermented pickles." Minerals in hard water reduce quality in pickles. When soft tap water is not available, soften the water you'll need using this technique: *Boil water in a stainless steel saucepan for 15 minutes. Cover and let stand 24 hours. After 24 hours, skim off scum that probably will have formed on top of the water. Carefully decant or ladle water into another container without disturbing sediment that collects at the bottom.*

EQUIPMENT – Due to pickles' acidic components, use only nonreactive utensils and cookware. Crocks, stainless steel pots and food-grade plastic containers work well for pickles that require salting, icing or fermentation.

Although these recipes require more time, pickle lovers believe the distinctive tangy flavours that result from fermentation are well worth the wait.

FERMENTED CUCUMBER PICKLES

• Thoroughly wash cucumbers, scrubbing lightly with a soft vegetable brush and removing all dirt and sand. Cut off and discard blossom ends.

 Following specific directions in each recipe, ferment cucumbers:

Place a weight on top of vegetables to keep them submerged under brine.

• ***Store container in a consistently cool 70°-75°F (21°-24°C) place in which temperature remains consistent throughout the fermentation process.***

• Daily, remove all scum that forms on top of the brine.

• Upon completion of fermentation, remove vegetables from brine and prepare pickling liquid as directed in individual recipes.

• Place required number of clean mason jars on a rack in a boiling water canner; cover jars with water and heat to a simmer (180°F/82°C). Set screw bands aside; heat SNAP Lids in hot water, NOT boiling (180°F/82°C). Keep jars and SNAP Lids hot until ready to use.

▶▶▶ **Pack fermented cucumbers into a hot jar to within 3/4 inch (2 cm) of top rim.** Add hot pickling liquid to cover vegetables to within 1/2 inch (1 cm) of top rim (headspace). Using nonmetallic utensil, remove air bubbles. Wipe jar rim removing any stickiness. Centre SNAP Lid on jar; apply screw band ***securely & firmly*** *until resistance is met – fingertip tight. Do not overtighten.* Place jar in canner; repeat for remaining vegetables and hot liquid.

• Cover canner; bring water to a boil. At altitudes up to 1,000 ft (305 m), process – *boil filled jars* – 500 ml jars – **10 minutes**; 1 L jars – **15 minutes**; 1.5 L jars – **20 minutes**. Remove jars without tilting. Cool upright, undisturbed 24 hours; DO NOT RETIGHTEN screw bands. After cooling check jar seals. *Sealed lids curve downward.* Remove screw bands; wipe and dry bands and jars. Store screw bands separately or replace loosely on jars, as desired. Label and store jars in a cool, dark place.

FERMENTED DILL PICKLES

10 lb (4.5 kg) medium pickling cucumbers
3/4 cup (175 ml) mixed pickling spices, divided
2-3 bunches fresh or dried dill, divided
1 1/2 cups (375 ml) pickling salt
2 cups (500 ml) vinegar
6 cloves garlic, *optional*

Place half of the pickling spices and dill in bottom of a large, deep nonreactive pickling container. Add pickling cucumbers to within 4 inches (10 cm) of top. Combine salt, vinegar and 32 cups (8000 ml) water. Add remaining dill, pickling spices and garlic, if using. Weight vegetables under brine and place container in cool place.

• Ferment 2 to 3 weeks, until cucumbers are well-flavoured and clear throughout. Skim scum daily.

• Lift pickles from brine. Strain brine, discarding spices; bring to a boil creating a pickling liquid. Pack fermented cucumbers into hot jars and fill with hot pickling liquid and heat process as directed in main recipe. ◀◀◀

Yield – about 6 x 1 L jars

SWEET ICICLE FERMENTED PICKLES

4 lb (1.8 kg) medium 4-6 inch (10-15 cm)
  pickling cucumbers
1 cup (250 ml) pickling salt
8 cups (2000 ml) water
1 1/2 tbsp (20 ml) mixed pickling spices
5 cups (1250 ml) granulated sugar
5 cups (1250 ml) vinegar

Cut prepared cucumbers lengthwise into quarters or smaller icicles. Place in clean pickling container. Dissolve salt in water and bring to a boil. Pour over cucumbers and weight under brine. Cover, let stand 1 week in cool place, checking daily.

• **8th day** – drain cucumbers discarding brine. Thoroughly rinse cucumbers and return to clean container. Cover with boiling water; let stand 24 hours.

• **9th day** – drain cucumbers discarding brine. Tie pickling spices in cheesecloth square, creating spice bag. Combine bag, sugar and vinegar in large stainless steel saucepan; bring to a boil. Pour over cucumbers; cover and let stand 24 hours.

• **10th day** – lift cucumbers from pickling liquid and reheat liquid to a boil. Return cucumbers to hot liquid and let stand.

• **11th, 12th & 13th days** – repeat reheating liquid step.

• **14th day** – discard spice bag. Remove cucumbers and heat liquid to boil. Pack pickles into hot jars, fill with hot liquid and heat process as directed in main recipe. ◀◀◀

Yield – 6 x 500 ml jars

SWEET FERMENTED GHERKINS

8 lb (3.6 kg) small 2-inch (2.5 cm) pickling
  cucumbers
1/2 cup (125 ml) pickling salt, divided
8 cups (2000 ml) granulated sugar, divided
6 cups (1500 ml) vinegar, divided
1/2 tsp (2 ml) ground turmeric
2 tsp (10 ml) celery seed
2 tsp (10 ml) whole mixed pickling spice
2 sticks cinnamon
1/2 tsp (2 ml) whole allspice

Place prepared cucumbers in a large, deep nonreactive pickling container. Dissolve 4 tbsp (60 ml) salt in 24 cups (6000 ml) boiling water; pour over cucumbers. Let stand overnight.

• **2nd day** – drain discarding brine. Dissolve remaining salt in 24 cups (6000 ml) boiling water; pour over cucumbers. Let stand overnight.

• **3rd day** – drain, discard brine and prick cucumbers in several places. Combine 3 cups (750 ml) each of sugar and vinegar in a large stainless steel saucepan with turmeric. Tie celery seed, pickling spice and cinnamon stick in cheesecloth creating a spice bag. Add bag to liquid and bring to a boil. Pour over cucumbers; weight and let stand 6 to 8 hours.

• **4th day** – reserving liquid, drain cucumbers. Add 2 cups (500 ml) sugar and 1 cup (250 ml) vinegar to reserved liquid. Bring to a boil & pour over cucumbers; weight and let stand 6 to 8 hours.

• Reserving liquid, drain cucumbers. Add 1 cup (250 ml) sugar to reserved liquid and bring to boil.

• Pack cucumbers into hot jars, fill with hot liquid and heat process as directed in main recipe. ◀◀◀

Yield – 7 x 500 ml jars

Sauerkraut sparks memories of farmers' markets and Oktoberfest. Neither event is complete without a kraut-topped Oktoberfest sausage. Freshly picked cabbage is essential for the best sauerkraut. i.e no more than 2 days old. For best flavour, use homemade sauerkraut within 6 months. Remember, sauerkraut is a fermented vegetable that requires consistent monitoring and attention to detail throughout a 3- to 6-week fermentation period.

SAUERKRAUT
(FERMENTED CABBAGE)

25 lb (11.3 kg) white cabbage, about 5 large heads
3/4 cup (175 ml) pickling salt

• Working with 5 lb (2 kg) cabbage at a time, discard outer leaves. Rinse heads under cold running water and drain. Quarter cabbage and remove cores. Shred or slice 1/16 inch (0.2 cm) thick. Remove any large pieces. Add 3 tbsp (45 ml) pickling salt to shredded cabbage; mix thoroughly and let stand a few minutes until cabbage begins to wilt and juices begin to flow. This allows packing with minimal breaking or bruising of shreds. Pack salted cabbage firmly and evenly into clean 5 gallon (20 L) crock, glass or stainless steel container.

• Repeat shredding, salting and packing 5 lb (2 kg) batches until all cabbage is in container. Be sure cabbage is at least 4 inches (10 cm) below rim of container. If liquid does not cover cabbage, add boiled, cooled brine (1 1/2 tbsp/20 ml pickling salt to 4 cups/1 L water). Weight cabbage to keep it 1 to 2 inches (2.5 to 5 cm) under the brine throughout fermentation. Place a clean dinner or glass pie plate on top of the cabbage inside the fermentation container. The plate must be slightly smaller than the container opening, yet large enough to cover most of the shredded cabbage. Fill 2 or 3 clean 1 L mason jars with water and close tightly with lids. Place jars on plate to weight cabbage. Cover the container with a clean, heavy bath towel to keep out airborne contaminants.

• Store at 70° to 75°F (21° to 24°C) for 3 to 4 weeks. At temperatures between 60° to 65°F (16° to 18°C), fermentation may take 5 to 6 weeks. At lower temperatures, kraut may not ferment; at higher temperatures, kraut may become soft.

• Check the kraut daily and skim off any scum that forms. Fermentation is complete when bubbling ceases.

• When kraut has fully fermented, store tightly covered in the refrigerator for several months or heat process as follows to preserve in mason jars:

• Place desired number of clean 500 ml or 1 L mason jars on a rack in a boiling water canner; cover jars with water and heat to a simmer (180°F/82°C). Set screw bands aside; heat SNAP Lids in hot water, NOT boiling (180°F/82°C). Keep jars and SNAP Lids hot until ready to use.

HOT PACK: Place sauerkraut in a large stainless steel saucepan; slowly bring to a boil, stirring frequently.

COLD PACK: Do not heat sauerkraut prior to filling jars.

• Pack sauerkraut into a hot jar to within 1/2 inch (1 cm) of top rim (headspace). Using nonmetallic utensil, remove air bubbles. Wipe jar rim removing any stickiness. Centre SNAP Lid on jar; apply screw band *securely & firmly* until resistance is met – *fingertip tight. Do not overtighten.* Place jar in canner; repeat for remaining sauerkraut.

• Cover canner; bring water to a boil. At altitudes up to 1,000 ft (305 m), process – *boil filled jars* – **for the time indicated below.**

Jar size	Hot Pack Processing time	Cold Pack Processing time
500 ml	10 minutes	20 minutes
1 L	15 minutes	25 minutes

• Remove jars without tilting. Cool upright, undisturbed 24 hours; DO NOT RETIGHTEN screw bands. After cooling check jar seals. *Sealed lids curve downward.* Remove screw bands; wipe and dry bands and jars. Store screw bands separately or replace loosely on jars, as desired. Label and store jars in a cool, dark place.

Yield – about 18 x 500 ml or 9 x 1 L jars.

VEGETABLE ANTIPASTO

1 1/2 cups (375 ml) coarsely chopped carrots
2 1/2 cups (625 ml) green beans, cut into 1/2-inch (1 cm)
  pieces
2 1/2 cups (625 ml) cauliflower florets
2 cups (500 ml) coarsely chopped onion
2 cups (500 ml) coarsely chopped green pepper
2 cups (500 ml) coarsely chopped red pepper
1 1/2 cups (375 ml) coarsely chopped celery
2 cups (500 ml) coarsely chopped, unpeeled zucchini or
  peeled eggplant
2 cups (500 ml) lightly packed brown sugar
3 tbsp (45 ml) pickling salt
2 cups (500 ml) red wine vinegar
3 cans (each 5 1/2 oz/156 ml) tomato paste
1/4 cup (50 ml) Worcestershire sauce
2 tbsp (25 ml) hot pepper sauce
4 garlic cloves, minced
3 tbsp (45 ml) dried basil
1 tbsp (15 ml) ground mustard

• Place 7 clean 500 ml mason jars on a rack in a boiling water canner; cover jars with water and heat to a simmer (180°F/82°C). Set screw bands aside; heat SNAP Lids in hot water, NOT boiling (180°F/82°C). Keep jars and SNAP Lids hot until ready to use.
• Prepare, measure vegetables and set aside keeping carrots separate. If using, prepare eggplant last due to rapid browning.
• In a large, deep stainless steel saucepan, combine sugar, salt, vinegar, tomato paste, Worcestershire and hot pepper sauces and garlic. Stirring frequently, bring to a boil over medium-high heat. Stir in carrots; boil 2 minutes.
• Add remaining vegetables, basil and mustard. Stirring frequently, bring mixture to a boil over medium-high heat; boil gently for 5 minutes. Remove from heat.
• Ladle antipasto into a hot jar to within 1/2 inch (1 cm) of top rim (headspace). Using nonmetallic utensil, remove air bubbles. Wipe jar rim removing any stickiness. Centre SNAP Lid on jar; apply screw band *securely & firmly until resistance is met – fingertip tight. Do not overtighten.* Place jar in canner; repeat for remaining antipasto.
• Cover canner; bring water to a boil. At altitudes up to 1,000 ft (305 m), process – *boil filled jars* – **25 minutes**. Remove jars without tilting. Cool upright, undisturbed 24 hours; DO NOT RETIGHTEN screw bands. After cooling check jar seals. *Sealed lids curve downward.* Remove screw bands; wipe and dry bands and jars. Store screw bands separately or replace loosely on jars, as desired. Label and store jars in a cool, dark place.   **Yield – about 7 x 500 ml jars.**

Because antipasto is sold commercially, many people want to preserve their "own antipasto recipe" at home. Unfortunately, many traditional antipasto recipes cannot be home canned safely and successfully. The use of low acid ingredients – olives, fish, artichokes & other vegetables – in traditional antipastos require such homemade recipes to be processed in a pressure canner for extended time periods. (This holds true even if the ingredient originated as a commercially canned product.) Due to the extended exposure to high temperatures, pressure canned homemade antipasto is unacceptable in both texture and taste.

This recipe has been specially formulated to yield well-balanced flavour and varied texture. Vinegar is added to "pickle" the low acid ingredients, allowing the product to be processed safely in a boiling water canner. Do NOT alter ingredients or measures.

To create a traditional antipasto – preserve salmon or other seafood separately in a pressure canner. When ready to serve antipasto, mix a jar of Vegetable Antipasto with a jar of salmon and add your personal finishing touches – mushrooms, olive oil, olives, artichokes. You'll have tantalizing fresh antipasto each time it's served!

"Icing" the cucumbers in a cold saltwater solution prior to pickling enhances their crispness. Select uniformly shaped, firm cucumbers about 4-6 inches (10-15 cm) long. *Use odd-shaped and more mature cucumbers for relishes and sliced pickles.* For best flavour, store fresh pack pickles 4 to 6 weeks to allow flavours to develop before serving. A bushel of pickling cucumbers weighs 48 lb (21.7 kg) and yields about 16 to 24 L jars of pickles.

FRESH PACK
DILL PICKLES

Ingredient quantities are approximate. Variations in sizes of pickling cucumbers & jar size dictate quantity of pickles that can be placed in each jar. This in turn affects quantity of liquid required.

	500 ml jars x 7	1 L jars x 7	or 1.5 L jars x 5
OVERNIGHT ICING			
Pickling cucumbers	8 lb/3.6 kg	14 lb/6.3 kg	15 lb/6.8 kg
Ice	16 cups/4 L	16 cups/4 L	16 cups/4 L
Water	4 cups/1 L	8 cups/2 L	12 cups/3 L
Pickling salt	1/2 cup/125 ml	1 cup/250 ml	1 cup/250 ml
PICKLING LIQUID			
Water	8 cups/2 L	16 cups/4 L	16 cups/4 L
White vinegar (5%)	6 cups/1.5 L	12 cups/3 L	12 cups/3 L
Pickling salt	3/4 cup/175 ml	1 1/2 cups/375 ml	2 cups/500 ml
Granulated sugar	1/4 cup/50 ml	1/2 cup/125 ml	1/2 cup/125 ml
Whole mixed pickling spice	2 tbsp/30 ml	4 tbsp/60 ml	4 tbsp/60 ml
QUANTITY TO PACK PER JAR:			
Whole mustard seed	1 tsp/5 ml	2 tsp/10 ml	1 tbsp/15 ml
Fresh dill heads	1 1/2 heads	2-3 heads	4-5 heads
or	or	or	or
Dill seed or dill weed	1 tbsp/15 ml	2 tbsp/30 ml	3 tbsp/45 ml
Peeled cloves	1	2-3	3-4
garlic, *optional*			
Bernardin Pickle Crisp™, *optional*	3/4 tsp/4 ml	1 1/2 tsp/7 ml	2 tsp/10 ml

• Wash cucumbers, scrubbing lightly with a soft vegetable brush. Rinse well in cool running water. Cut 1/8 inch (3 mm) slice off blossom end (opposite stem end) and discard. Layer cucumbers and ice in a large, deep glass or stainless steel container. Dissolve pickling salt in quantity of water listed in "overnight icing"; pour over cucumbers. Add cold water to just cover cucumbers. Fill a plastic bag with water and place over ice & cucumbers to keep vegetables submerged. Refrigerate (or place in cool place) overnight (minimum 12 hours).

Preserving Day
• Place required number of clean mason jars on a rack in a boiling water canner; cover jars with water and heat to a simmer (180°F/82°C). Set screw bands aside; heat SNAP Lids in hot water, NOT boiling (180°F/82°C). Keep jars and SNAP Lids hot until ready to use.

• Prepare PICKLING LIQUID. In a large stainless steel saucepan, combine water, vinegar, pickling salt and sugar in quantities for the size jars you are preparing. Tie pickling spice in a large square of cheesecloth, creating a spice bag; add to saucepan and bring to a boil; boil gently 15 minutes.
• Drain cucumbers, discarding soaking solution.
• Remove hot jars from canner and fill, one at a time. In each jar, place the quantity of dill, mustard seed and garlic indicated for the size mason jar you are using. Pack cucumbers in the jar to within 3/4 inch (2 cm) of top rim.
• Add hot pickling liquid to cover cucumbers to within 1/2 inch (1 cm) of top rim (headspace). Using nonmetallic utensil, remove air bubbles. Wipe jar rim removing any stickiness. Centre SNAP Lid on jar; apply screw band *securely & firmly until resistance is met – fingertip tight. Do not overtighten.* Place jar in canner; repeat for remaining herbs, cucumber and hot pickling liquid.
• Cover canner; bring water to a boil. At altitudes up to 1,000 ft (305 m), process – *boil filled jars –*

Jar size	Processing time
500 ml	10 minutes
1 L	15 minutes
1.5 L	20 minutes

When processing time is complete, turn off heat and allow boil to subside. Remove jars without tilting. Cool upright, undisturbed 24 hours; DO NOT RETIGHTEN screw bands. After cooling check jar seals. *Sealed lids curve downward.* Remove screw bands; wipe and dry bands and jars. Store screw bands separately or replace loosely on jars, as desired. Label and store jars in a cool, dark place.

FRESH PACK CUCUMBER PICKLES

• Thoroughly wash cucumbers, scrubbing lightly with a soft vegetable brush and removing all dirt and sand. Discard blossom ends. Prepare as individual recipe directs.

• Place required number of mason jars on a rack in a boiling water canner; cover jars with water and heat to a simmer (180°F/82°C). Set screw bands aside; heat SNAP Lids in hot water, NOT boiling (180°F/82°C). Keep jars and SNAP Lids hot until ready to use.

 Prepare remaining ingredients and pickling liquid as individual recipe directs.

▶▶▶ **Pack cucumbers into a hot jar to within 3/4 inch (2 cm) of top rim.** Add hot pickling liquid to cover vegetables to within 1/2 inch (1 cm) of top rim (headspace). Using nonmetallic utensil, remove air bubbles. Wipe jar rim removing any stickiness. Centre SNAP Lid on jar; apply screw band *securely & firmly* until resistance is met – *fingertip tight. Do not overtighten.* Place jar in canner; repeat for remaining vegetables and hot liquid.

• Cover canner; bring water to a boil. At altitudes up to 1,000 ft (305 m), process – *boil filled jars* – **10 minutes**. Remove jars without tilting. Cool upright, undisturbed 24 hours; DO NOT RETIGHTEN screw bands. After cooling check jar seals. *Sealed lids curve downward.* Remove screw bands; wipe and dry bands and jars. Store screw bands separately or replace loosely on jars, as desired. Label and store jars in a cool, dark place.

ZESTY BREAD 'N BUTTER PICKLES

6 1/2 lb (3 kg) pickling cucumbers
1 lb (454 g) onions, sliced 1/4 inch (0.5 cm) thick
1/3 cup (75 ml) pickling salt
5 cups (1250 ml) white vinegar
1 1/4 cups (300 ml) granulated sugar
1/2 cup (125 ml) pickling spice
2 tbsp (25 ml) celery seed
2 tsp (10 ml) ground ginger
1 tsp (5 ml) ground turmeric

Slice unpeeled washed cucumbers 1/4 inch (0.5 cm) thick, discard ends. In a large glass or stainless steel container, layer cucumbers and onions, lightly sprinkling each layer with salt. Cover and let stand 15 minutes.

• Combine vinegar, sugar, pickling spice, celery seed, ginger and turmeric in a large stainless steel saucepan. Cover and bring to a boil; reduce heat and boil gently 15 minutes.

• Drain vegetables, add to pickling liquid; mix well. Return mixture to a boil. ◀◀◀

Yield – 7 x 500 ml jars

DILL SLICES

4 lb (1.8 kg) medium pickling cucumbers
4 cups (1000 ml) cider vinegar
4 cups (1000 ml) water
3/4 cup (175 ml) granulated sugar
1/2 cup (125 ml) pickling salt
3 tbsp (45 ml) fresh mixed pickling spices
5 bay leaves
5 garlic cloves
2 1/2 tsp (12 ml) mustard seed
5 heads fresh dill or 5 tsp (25 ml) dried dill seed

Cut cucumbers lengthwise into 1/4 inch (0.5 cm) slices. Combine vinegar, water, sugar and salt in a large stainless steel saucepan. Tie pickling spices in cheesecloth creating a spice bag; add spice bag to vinegar mixture and simmer 15 minutes.

• In each hot jar, place 1 bay leaf, 1 garlic clove, 1/2 tsp (2 ml) mustard seed and 1 head of fresh dill or 1 tsp (5 ml) dried dill seed. Pack cucumber slices into jars. ◀◀◀

Yield – about 5 x 500 ml jars

LEMON CUCUMBER PICKLES

IF YOU FIND TRADITIONAL PICKLES TOO ASTRINGENT, TRY THIS REFRESHING, LIGHT TASTING ALTERNATIVE. LEMON JUICE PROVIDES THE UNIQUE FLAVOUR WHILE A TOUCH OF SUGAR TAKES THE BITE OUT OF THE VINEGAR.

8 large cucumbers, peeled, sliced
4 sweet red peppers, seeded & sliced
2 tbsp (30 ml) pickling salt
1 1/3 cups (325 ml) white vinegar
1 1/4 cups (300 ml) granulated sugar
3/4 cup (175 ml) fresh lemon juice
7 small bay leaves
1 tbsp (15 ml) peppercorns
1 tsp (5 ml) whole allspice
1 lemon, sliced
6 cloves garlic, peeled

Cut cucumbers into 1/2 inch (1 cm) chunks or 1/4 inch (0.5 cm) slices; measure 14 cups (3500 ml). Combine cucumbers, peppers and salt in a large glass bowl; cover with ice water. Let stand 3 hours.

• In a large stainless steel saucepan, combine vinegar, sugar and lemon juice. Tie 1 bay leaf, peppercorns and allspice in a large square of cheesecloth, creating a spice bag; add to saucepan. Bring to a boil; boil gently 7 minutes. Drain vegetables; add to pickling liquid in saucepan; return to a full boil. Discard spice bag.

• Place 1 bay leaf, 1 lemon slice and 1 clove garlic in each hot jar. Pack cucumbers and pepper into jars. ◀◀◀

Yield – about 6 x 500 ml jars

SAVOURY PICKLES

• Place required number of mason jars on a rack in a boiling water canner; cover jars with water and heat to a simmer (180°F/82°C). Set screw bands aside; heat SNAP Lids in hot water, NOT boiling (180°F/82°C). Keep jars and SNAP Lids hot until ready to use.

 Prepare vegetables and pickling liquid as directed in selected recipe.

▶▶▶ **Pack prepared vegetables into a hot jar to within 3/4 inch (2 cm) of top rim.** Add hot liquid to cover vegetables to within 1/2 inch (1 cm) of top rim (headspace). Using nonmetallic utensil, remove air bubbles. Wipe jar rim removing any stickiness. Centre SNAP Lid on jar; apply screw band *securely & firmly until resistance is met – fingertip tight. Do not overtighten.* Place jar in canner; repeat for remaining ingredients.

• Cover canner; bring water to a boil. At altitudes up to 1,000 ft (305 m), process – *boil filled jars* – **10 minutes**. Remove jars without tilting. Cool upright, undisturbed 24 hours; DO NOT RETIGHTEN screw bands. After cooling check jar seals. *Sealed lids curve downward.* Remove screw bands; wipe and dry bands and jars. Store screw bands separately or replace loosely on jars, as desired. Label and store jars in a cool, dark place.

PICKLED HOT PEPPERS

SPICE UP YOUR LIFE WITH THIS HOT PEPPER MIX. HANDLE HOT PEPPERS CAREFULLY; WEAR RUBBER GLOVES TO PREVENT BURNS.

1 1/2 lb (680 g) banana peppers
1 lb (450 g) jalapeño peppers
1/4 lb (125 g) serrano peppers
6 cups (1500 ml) vinegar
2 cups (500 ml) water
3 cloves garlic, crushed

Wash peppers. Leave whole or cut into 1-inch (2.5 cm) pieces. Pierce whole peppers 2-3 times with fork.

• Combine vinegar, water and garlic in large stainless steel saucepan. Bring to a boil; reduce heat and simmer 5 minutes. Discard garlic. ◀◀◀

Yield – about 5 x 500 ml jars

PICKLED ONIONS

SERVE PICKLED ONIONS AS A CONDIMENT WITH ANY MEAT. SERVE IN A SALAD OR WITH CHEESE FOR A PLOWMAN'S LUNCH.

4 1/2 lb (2 kg) small pickling or pearl onions
4 tbsp + 2 tsp (60 ml + 10 ml) pickling salt
2 tsp (10 ml) black peppercorns
1 1/2 tsp (7 ml) whole allspice
1 tsp (5 ml) mustard seed
4 1/2 cups (1125 ml) malt or white vinegar
1 cup (250 ml) granulated sugar
5-10 small hot red peppers, *optional*
5-10 bay leaves

To soften and loosen skins, blanch onions in boiling water 1 minute. Immediately immerse in cold water, drain, trim off root end and slip skins off. Combine onions and 4 tbsp (60 ml) pickling salt in, stainless steel container. Cover and let stand overnight, stirring once or twice.

Preserving day: Drain salted onions, rinse thoroughly in cold running water; drain, pat dry with a towel. Tie peppercorns, allspice and mustard seed in a large square of cheesecloth, creating a spice bag. Combine vinegar, sugar and 2 teaspoons (10 ml) salt in a large stainless steel saucepan; add spice bag; bring to a boil; boil 2 minutes. Add onions and return mixture to a boil. Discard spice bag. If using hot peppers, thoroughly wash them in hot water.

• Place 1 hot pepper and 1 bay leaf in each hot jar. Pack onions in jar. ◀◀◀

Yield – 5 x 500 ml jars

PICKLED GARLIC

TOSS PICKLED GARLIC INTO ITALIAN SPAG-
HETTI SAUCE, SERVE IT IN SANDWICHES, USE
AS AN ANTIPASTO OR AS A GARNISH FOR
SALADS.

12 large heads garlic, about 1 3/4 lb (838 g)
2 1/2 cups (625 ml) white vinegar
1 cup (250 ml) dry white wine
1 tbsp (15 ml) pickling salt
1 tbsp (15 ml) granulated sugar
1 tbsp (15 ml) dried oregano
5 dried whole chili peppers, *optional*

Separate garlic bulbs into cloves. To soften and
loosen skins, blanch garlic cloves in rapidly
boiling water 30 seconds. Immediately immerse in
cold water, drain and peel cloves.

• In a large stainless steel saucepan, combine
vinegar, wine, pickling salt, sugar, and oregano.
Bring to a boil; boil gently 1 minute; remove from
heat. Add peeled garlic cloves to hot vinegar
mixture. Stir constantly 1 minute. ◀◀◀

Yield – about 5 x 250 or 236 ml jars

ZANY ZUCCHINI PICKLES

THESE ZESTY PICKLES ARE A DELICIOUS
ANSWER TO AN OVER PRODUCTIVE ZUC-
CHINI CROP.

14 cups (3500 ml) prepared zucchini, 4 1/2 lb (2 kg)
1/2 cup (125 ml) pickling salt
6 cups (1500 ml) white vinegar
4 cups (1000 ml) granulated sugar
4 tsp (20 ml) mustard seed
2 tsp (10 ml) celery seed
2 tsp (10 ml) ground turmeric

Wash zucchini; do not peel. Slice into 1/4 inch
(0.5 cm) diagonal slices. Layer zucchini slices
and salt in a glass or stainless steel container; cover
with cold water and let stand 2 hours. Drain; rinse
thoroughly with cold running water. Drain well
and pat dry.

• Combine vinegar, sugar, mustard, celery seeds
and turmeric in a large stainless steel saucepan.
Bring to a boil; boil gently 5 minutes. Remove from
heat; stir in zucchini and let stand 1 hour. Return to
a boil before packing into jars. ◀◀◀

Yield – about 6 x 500 ml jars

AUBERGINE PICKLES

CHINESE EGGPLANT WORKS BEST IN THIS
RECIPE, HOWEVER THE LARGER, MORE
COMMON EGGPLANT MAY ALSO BE USED.

5 lb (2.25 kg) eggplant (aubergine)
Cold water
1 1/2 cups (375 ml) white vinegar
1/2 cup (125 ml) balsamic vinegar
3 tbsp (45 ml) granulated sugar
1 tbsp (15 ml) oregano leaves
2 tsp (10 ml) pickling salt
6 cloves garlic

Bring a large pot of water to a boil. Working
quickly to prevent browning, remove ends and
peel eggplant. Cut into 3-inch (8 cm) sticks, 3/4 inch
(2 cm) thick. Drop eggplant into boiling water; boil
gently 10 minutes, pressing eggplant under the
water frequently to remove air. Carefully drain
eggplant; cover with cold water, drain thoroughly.

• Combine vinegars, sugar, oregano and salt with
4 1/2 cups (1125 ml) water in a large stainless steel
saucepan. Cover and bring to a boil. Add drained
eggplant and return to boil.

• Place 1 clove garlic in each hot jar. Fill jar with
eggplant. ◀◀◀

Yield – about 6 x 500 ml jars

Choose from a variety of vegetables, or combine your favourites to make quick and delicious homemade pickles using BERNARDIN Dill Pickle Mix.

QUICK 'N EASY PICKLED VEGETABLES

Asparagus, Carrots, Cauliflower, Cucumbers, Green Beans,
   Pickling Onions and/or Zucchini
1 pouch (85 g) BERNARDIN Dill Pickle Mix
4 1/2 cups (1125 ml) white vinegar
3 cups (750 ml) water

• Place 6 clean 500 ml mason jars on a rack in a boiling water canner; cover jars with water and heat to a simmer (180°F/82°C). Set screw bands aside; heat SNAP Lids in hot water, NOT boiling (180°F/82°C). Keep jars and SNAP Lids hot until ready to use.
• Wash produce thoroughly, removing all surface dirt/sand. Remove tough ends and cut into suitable sized pieces for pickles.
• In a large stainless steel saucepan, combine BERNARDIN Dill Pickle Mix, vinegar and water. Bring to a boil; boil 1 minute. Remove from heat.
• Pack prepared vegetables into a hot jar to within 3/4 inch (2 cm) of top rim. Add hot liquid to cover vegetables to within 1/2 inch (1 cm) of top rim (headspace). Using nonmetallic utensil, remove air bubbles. Wipe jar rim removing any stickiness. Centre SNAP Lid on jar; apply screw band *securely & firmly until resistance is met – fingertip tight. Do not overtighten.* Place jar in canner; repeat for remaining vegetables and hot liquid.
• Cover canner; bring water to a boil. At altitudes up to 1,000 ft (305 m), process – *boil filled jars* – **10 minutes**. Remove jars without tilting. Cool upright, undisturbed 24 hours; DO NOT RETIGHTEN screw bands. After cooling check jar seals. *Sealed lids curve downward.* Remove screw bands; wipe and dry bands and jars. Store screw bands separately or replace loosely on jars, as desired. Label and store jars in a cool, dark place.

Yield – about 6 x 500 ml jars

Pickled beets are a staple on most pantry shelves. Make them to suit your family's tastes with your choice of these three spice blend options.

PICKLED BEETS

10 cups (2500 ml) prepared beets
2 1/2 cups (625 ml) white vinegar
1 cup (250 ml) water
1 cup (250 ml) granulated sugar
Spice mixture – choice of:
TRADITIONAL PICKLED BEETS
   3 tbsp (45 ml) pickling spice
SWEET SPICED PICKLED BEETS
   2 cinnamon sticks, halved and 10 whole cloves
CARAWAY PICKLED BEETS
   2 tbsp (25 ml) caraway seeds and 2 tsp (10 ml)
   black peppercorns

• Scrub beets, leaving root and 2 inches (5 cm) of stem intact to prevent bleeding. Sort beets by size and place beets in saucepan; cover with water. Boil similar sized beets until tender. Drain, discard liquid and slip off the skins removing tap root and stems. Leave baby beets whole, slice or quarter larger beets.
• Place required number of clean 500 ml mason jars on a rack in a boiling water canner; cover jars with water and heat to a simmer (180°F/82°C). Set screw bands aside; heat SNAP Lids in hot water, NOT boiling (180°F/82°C). Keep jars and SNAP Lids hot until ready to use.

Tie chosen spice mixture in a square of cheesecloth, creating a spice bag. Combine with vinegar, water and sugar in a stainless steel saucepan. Bring to a boil; cover and boil gently 15 minutes. Discard spice bag.

▶▶▶ Pack prepared beets into a hot jar to within 3/4 inch (2 cm) of top rim. Add hot pickling liquid to cover beets to within 1/2 inch (1 cm) of top rim (headspace). Using nonmetallic utensil, remove air bubbles. Wipe jar rim removing any stickiness. Centre SNAP Lid on jar; apply screw band *securely & firmly* until resistance is met – *fingertip tight. Do not overtighten.* Place jar in canner; repeat for remaining beets and hot liquid.
• Cover canner; bring water to a boil. At altitudes up to 1,000 ft (305 m), process – *boil filled jars* – **30 minutes**. Remove jars without tilting. Cool upright, undisturbed 24 hours; DO NOT RETIGHTEN screw bands. After cooling check jar seals. *Sealed lids curve downward.* Remove screw bands; wipe and dry bands and jars. Store screw bands separately or replace loosely on jars, as desired. Label and store jars in a cool, dark place.
Yield – about 6 x 500 ml jars

BEET & ONION PICKLES

8 cups (2000 ml) prepared beets, about 4 lb (1.8 kg)
3 cups (750 ml) sliced onions or peeled pearl
   onions
2 1/2 cups (625 ml) cider vinegar
2 cups (500 ml) granulated sugar
1 1/2 cups (375 ml) water
1 tbsp (15 ml) mustard seed
1 tsp (5 ml) *Each:* salt, whole allspice and cloves
6 inch (15 cm) cinnamon stick

• Prepare beets, jars and lids as directed in Pickled Beets.

Combine onions, vinegar, sugar, water, mustard seed, salt, allspice, cloves and cinnamon sticks in a large stainless steel saucepan. Bring to a boil; boil gently 5 minutes. Add beets and return to a full boil. Remove from heat. Discard cinnamon sticks. ◀◀◀
• Pack hot beets and liquid into hot jars and heat process as directed in Pickled Beets.
Yield – about 5 x 500 ml jars

Tangy sweet pickles make eye-pleasing, deliciously edible garnishes.

SWEET VARIETY PICKLES

• Place required number of mason jars on a rack in a boiling water canner; cover jars with water and heat to a simmer (180°F/82°C). Set screw bands aside; heat SNAP Lids in hot water, NOT boiling (180°F/82°C). Keep jars and SNAP Lids hot until ready to use.

Prepare fruit and pickling liquid as directed in selected recipe.

Pack prepared fruit or vegetables into a hot jar to within 3/4 inch (2 cm) of top rim. Add hot liquid to cover fruit to within 1/2 inch (1 cm) of top rim (headspace). Using nonmetallic utensil, remove air bubbles. Wipe jar rim removing any stickiness. Centre SNAP Lid on jar; apply screw band *securely & firmly until resistance is met – fingertip tight. Do not overtighten.* Place jar in canner; repeat for remaining ingredients and hot liquid.

• Cover canner; bring water to a boil. At altitudes up to 1,000 ft (305 m), process – *boil filled jars* – **20 minutes.** Remove jars without tilting. Cool upright, undisturbed 24 hours; DO NOT RETIGHTEN screw bands. After cooling check jar seals. *Sealed lids curve downward.* Remove screw bands; wipe and dry bands and jars. Store screw bands separately or replace loosely on jars, as desired. Label and store jars in a cool, dark place.

PEARS EXOTICA

ZESTY AND REFRESHING PEARS TO GARNISH ENTRÉES OR SERVE AS A SWEET WITH CHEESE.

1 large lemon
8 1/2 cups (2125 ml) water, divided
6 1/2 lb (2.9 kg) pears, about 12 medium
1 1/4 cups (300 ml) granulated sugar
1/2 cup (125 ml) white vinegar
4 bay leaves
12 pink peppercorns
12 green peppercorns

With a vegetable peeler, remove yellow peel from lemon in a continuous spiral; cut peel into 4 pieces; set aside. Squeeze lemon juice into a large bowl and add 4 cups (1000 ml) water. Peel, core and quarter pears, placing them in lemon juice solution to prevent discolouration.

• In a large stainless steel saucepan, combine sugar, vinegar, remaining 4 1/2 cups (1125 ml) water and lemon peel; bring to a boil. Thoroughly drain pears; add to boiling syrup; return to a boil; remove from heat.

• Place 1 strip lemon peel, 1 bay leaf, 3 pink and 3 green peppercorns in each jar. Pack pears and hot liquid as directed in main recipe. ◀◀◀

Yield – about 4 x 500 ml jars

PICKLED PLUMS

LET THIS RICH, DARK SPICY PICKLE AGE FOR AT LEAST TWO WEEKS BEFORE USING. SERVE WITH GRILLED MEATS. SAVE THE SYRUP TO BASTE SPARERIBS.

5 lb (2.3 kg) firm blue plums, washed
5 cups (1250 ml) firmly packed brown sugar
2 cups (500 ml) cider vinegar
1/2 cup (125 ml) water
3 inch (7.5 cm) piece fresh gingerroot
8 inch (20 cm) cinnamon stick
1 tsp (5 ml) whole cloves
2 dried whole chili peppers
1 small piece nutmeg, cracked
Peel of 1 orange

In a large shallow stainless steel saucepan, combine sugar, vinegar and water. Peel gingerroot and cut into small pieces. Break cinnamon stick into pieces. Tie gingerroot, cinnamon, cloves, chili peppers and nutmeg in a large square of cheesecloth, creating a spice bag. Add to pan. With vegetable peeler, remove peel from orange in continuous spiral. Add to pan. Bring mixture to a boil; boil gently 10 minutes.

• Prick plums all over with a toothpick; place in oven-proof dish. Add boiled syrup, cover and cook in 275°F (130°C) oven 30 minutes or until plums are tender but firm. Discard spice bag and orange rind. ◀◀◀

Yield – about 6 x 500 ml jars

SWEET PUMPKIN PICKLES

WITH WARM SPICES AND A GOLDEN ORANGE COLOUR, THESE PICKLES LOOK AS GOOD AS THEY TASTE.

6 lb (2.7 kg) pumpkin or butternut squash
Peel and pulp of 1 medium lemon
6 cups (1500 ml) granulated sugar
4 cups (1000 ml) white vinegar
8 inches (20 cm) cinnamon sticks, halved
12 whole allspice berries
10 whole cloves

Halve, seed and peel pumpkin; cut into 3/4 inch (2 cm) cubes; set aside.

• With vegetable peeler, remove thin yellow peel from lemon; place in a large stainless steel saucepan. Using a sharp knife, remove remaining white pith from lemon; discard. Separate segments from membrane and coarsely chop. Squeeze juice from membrane; add juice and pulp to peel in saucepan; discard membrane and seeds.

• Add sugar and vinegar to lemon mixture. Tie cinnamon, allspice and cloves in a square of cheesecloth, creating a spice bag; add to mixture. Bring to a boil; cover and boil gently 10 minutes. Add prepared pumpkin and boil 3 minutes longer. Remove spice bag and take off heat. ◀◀◀

Yield – about 6 x 500 ml jars

CINNAMON WATERMELON RIND PICKLES

USE YOUR MELON! TRIM THE RIND FROM WATERMELON BEFORE SERVING THE JUICY RED PULP.

16 cups (4000 ml) watermelon rind cubes,
1 cup (250 ml) pickling salt
6 cups (1500 ml) granulated sugar
4 cups (1000 ml) white vinegar
16 inches (40 cm) cinnamon sticks, broken in half

Remove dark green peel from watermelon rind. Cut rind into 1 x 2 inch (2.5 x 5 cm) cubes; measure 16 cups (4000 ml). Layer rind and salt in a large glass or stainless steel container; cover with cold water and place a weight on top to prevent rind from floating. Refrigerate overnight.

• Drain; rinse twice in cold water and drain thoroughly. Place rind in a stainless steel saucepan; add 4 cups (1000 ml) cold water. Bring to a boil; cook until fork tender, about 10 minutes; drain.

• Combine sugar, vinegar and cinnamon sticks in a large stainless steel saucepan. Bring to a boil; boil gently 5 minutes. Add drained rind to boiling liquid; boil gently 1 hour. Discard cinnamon sticks. ◀◀◀

Yield – about 6 x 500 ml jars

CANTALOUPE PICKLES

CINNAMON, CLOVES AND ALLSPICE ADD A DASH OF SPICE TO THESE COLOURFUL CUBES. FOR BEST RESULTS, CHOOSE A MELON THAT'S JUST RIPE.

13 cups (3250 ml) prepared just-ripe, firm cantaloupe
3 cups (750 ml) white vinegar
2 cups (500 ml) water
4 inches (10 cm) cinnamon stick
2 whole cloves
1 tsp (5 ml) allspice
4 1/2 cups (1125 ml) granulated sugar

Peel cantaloupe and remove seeds. Cut melon into 1 inch (2.5 cm) cubes; measure 13 cups (3250 ml).

• Combine vinegar and water in a large stainless steel saucepan. Tie cinnamon stick, cloves and allspice in a square of cheesecloth, creating a spice bag; add to vinegar mixture and bring to a boil. Boil gently 5 minutes; remove from heat. Stir melon into vinegar-spice mixture; let stand 30 minutes.

• Add sugar to cantaloupe mixture. Bring to a boil, stirring occasionally; reduce heat and boil gently until melon becomes transparent, about 45 minutes. Discard spice bag. ◀◀◀

Yield – about 6 x 500 ml jars

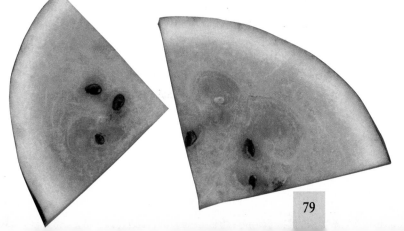

Extend distinctive grilled flavour into the winter. Toss these roasted peppers with spaghetti sauce, serve them in sandwiches, use on an antipasto platter or as a garnish for salads.

PICKLED ROASTED RED PEPPERS

20 medium sweet red peppers, 8 lb (3.6 kg)
4 large cloves garlic
1 1/2 cups (375 ml) white vinegar
1 1/2 cups (375 ml) apple cider vinegar
1 1/2 cups (375 ml) dry white wine
1/2 cup (125 ml) water
1 cup (250 ml) onion, coarsely chopped
1/2 cup (125 ml) granulated sugar
2 tbsp (30 ml) dried oregano leaves
4 tsp (20 ml) pickling salt

• Roast peppers and garlic over hot coals or under broiler until charred. Place peppers in a paper bag until cool enough to handle. Squeeze roasted garlic cloves to remove from peel; mash and set aside. When peppers are cooled, remove skins; core and seed. Cut lengthwise into serving-sized pieces.

• Place 4 clean 500 ml mason jars on a rack in a boiling water canner; cover jars with water and heat to a simmer (180°F/82°C). Set screw bands aside; heat SNAP Lids in hot water, NOT boiling (180°F/82°C). Keep jars and SNAP Lids hot until ready to use.

• Combine garlic, white and cider vinegars, wine, water, onion, sugar, oregano and pickling salt in a large stainless steel saucepan. Bring to a boil; boil gently 5 minutes and remove from heat.

• Pack roasted peppers into a hot jar to within 3/4 inch (2 cm) of top rim. Add hot liquid to cover peppers to within 1/2 inch (1 cm) of top rim (headspace). Using nonmetallic utensil, remove air bubbles. Wipe jar rim removing any stickiness. Centre SNAP Lid on jar; apply screw band *securely & firmly until resistance is met – fingertip tight. Do not overtighten.* Place jar in canner; repeat for remaining peppers and hot liquid.

• Cover canner; bring water to a boil. At altitudes up to 1,000 ft (305 m), process – *boil filled jars* – **15 minutes**. Remove jars without tilting. Cool upright, undisturbed 24 hours; DO NOT RETIGHTEN screw bands. After cooling check jar seals. *Sealed lids curve downward.* Remove screw bands; wipe and dry bands and jars. Store screw bands separately or replace loosely on jars, as desired. Label and store jars in a cool, dark place.

Yield – 4 x 500 ml jars

CHUNKY MUSTARD PICKLES

A DELICIOUS ANSWER TO BUMPER CROPS OF CUCUMBERS OR ZUCCHINI. SERVED IN A CUT-GLASS DISH, THESE PICKLES ADD COLOUR AND FLAVOUR TO ANY MEAL.

14 cups (3500 ml) prepared cucumbers, or zucchini
6 cups (1500 ml) finely chopped onion
1/4 cup (50 ml) pickling salt
3 cups (750 ml) granulated sugar
1/2 cup (125 ml) all purpose flour
1/4 cup (50 ml) dry mustard
1 tbsp (15 ml) ground ginger
1 tsp (5 ml) ground turmeric
1/2 cup (125 ml) water
2 cups (500 ml) white vinegar
1 large sweet red pepper, finely chopped

• Peel cucumbers. (If using zucchini, do not peel.) Cut vegetables in half lengthwise; using spoon, remove seeds. Cut vegetables into 1/2 inch (1 cm) cubes. In a large glass or stainless steel container, combine vegetables and onions; sprinkle with salt. Let stand 1 hour. Drain.
• Place 7 clean 500 ml mason jars in a boiling water canner; cover jars with water and heat to a simmer (180°F/82°C). Set screw bands aside; heat SNAP Lids in hot water, NOT boiling (180°F/82°C). Keep jars and SNAP Lids hot until ready to use.
• In a large stainless steel saucepan, combine sugar, flour, dry mustard, ginger and turmeric. Gradually blend in water and vinegar; bring to a boil, stirring constantly. Cook until thickened, about 5 minutes. Add drained cucumber-onion mixture and red pepper; return to a boil, stirring constantly.
• Ladle hot mixture into a hot jar to within 1/2 inch (1 cm) of top rim (headspace). Using nonmetallic utensil, remove air bubbles. Wipe jar rim removing any stickiness. Centre SNAP Lid on jar; apply screw band *securely & firmly* until resistance is met – *fingertip tight. Do not overtighten.* Place jar in canner; repeat for remaining cucumber mixture.
• Cover canner; bring water to a boil. At altitudes up to 1,000 ft (305 m), process – *boil filled jars* – **15 minutes**. Remove jars without tilting. Cool upright, undisturbed 24 hours; DO NOT RETIGHTEN screw bands. After cooling check jar seals. *Sealed lids curve downward.* Remove screw bands; wipe and dry bands and jars. Store screw bands separately or replace loosely on jars, as desired. Label and store jars in a cool, dark place.

Yield – 7 x 500 ml jars

MUSTARD BEANS

SERVE AS A CONDIMENT OR ADD TO POTATO OR PASTA SALADS.

11 cups (2750 ml) prepared green or yellow beans
1 large sweet red pepper, finely chopped
SAUCE:
    3 cups (750 ml) granulated sugar
    1/2 cup (125 ml) all purpose flour
    1/4 cup (50 ml) dry mustard
    1/4 cup (50 ml) pickling salt
    1 tbsp (15 ml) ground ginger
    1 tsp (5 ml) ground turmeric
    2 1/2 cups (625 ml) white vinegar
    1/2 cup (125 ml) water
    4 cups (1000 ml) chopped onion

• Prepare jars and lids as directed for Chunky Mustard Pickles.
• Wash and trim beans. Cut into 1 1/2 inch (4 cm) pieces; set aside.
• Combine sauce ingredients in large stainless steel saucepan; cook until thickened. Add prepared beans and red pepper; return to a boil, stirring constantly.
• Fill jars and heat process as directed for Chunky Mustard Pickles.

Yield – 7 x 500 ml jars

MARROW 'N ONION MUSTARD PICKLES

MARROW IS A GREEN & YELLOW-HUED MEMBER OF THE SUMMER SQUASH FAMILY.

12 cups (3000 ml) prepared vegetable marrow
1/4 cup (50 ml) pickling salt
8 cups (2000 ml) small pickling or pearl onions
SAUCE:
    1 3/4 cups (425 ml) granulated sugar
    1/3 cup (75 ml) all purpose flour
    1/3 cup (75 ml) mustard seed
    1 1/2 tsp (7 ml) celery seed
    1 1/2 tsp (7 ml) ground turmeric
    1/2 cup (125 ml) water
    2 cups (500 ml) white vinegar
    2 large hot red peppers, seeded & chopped

• Prepare jars and lids as directed for Chunky Mustard Pickles.
• Peel vegetable marrow. Cut marrow in half; scrape out seeds and membrane. Cut into 3/4 inch (2 cm) cubes. Layer cubes with pickling salt in a large glass or stainless steel container. Let stand 4 hours. Drain well. Blanch onions in boiling water; drain and peel.
• Combine sauce ingredients in large stainless steel saucepan; cook until thickened. Add drained vegetable marrow and onions; return to a full boil.
• Fill jars and heat process as directed for Chunky Mustard Pickles.

Yield – about 6 x 500 ml jars

For best flavour, let jars of relish stand two weeks for the flavours to blend before serving.

RELISH

- Place required number of mason jars on a rack in a boiling water canner; cover jars with water and heat to a simmer (180°F/82°C). Set screw bands aside; heat SNAP Lids in hot water, NOT boiling (180°F/82°C). Keep jars and SNAP Lids hot until ready to use.

Prepare and cook selected Relish as directed in individual recipe.

▶ ▶ ▶ **Ladle relish into a hot jar to within 1/2 inch (1 cm) of top rim (headspace).** Using nonmetallic utensil, remove air bubbles. Wipe jar rim removing any stickiness. Centre SNAP Lid on jar; apply screw band *securely & firmly until resistance is met – fingertip tight. Do not overtighten.* Place jar in canner; repeat for remaining relish.

- Cover canner; bring water to a boil. At altitudes up to 1,000 ft (305 m), process – *boil filled jars* – 500 ml jars – **15 minutes**; 250 ml jars – **10 minutes**. Remove jars without tilting. Cool upright, undisturbed 24 hours; DO NOT RETIGHTEN screw bands. After cooling check jar seals. *Sealed lids curve downward.* Remove screw bands; wipe and dry bands and jars. Store screw bands separately or replace loosely on jars, as desired. Label and store jars in a cool, dark place.

SWEET & SOUR PEPPER RELISH

IF YOU WANT A FIERY RELISH, USE HOT RED OR BANANA PEPPERS.

4 cups (1000 ml) finely chopped green peppers
1 cup (250 ml) finely chopped banana peppers
1 hot red pepper, chopped, *optional*
3 cups (750 ml) chopped, peeled tart apples
2 cups (500 ml) chopped cabbage
2 tbsp (30 ml) pickling salt
3 cups (750 ml) cider vinegar
3 cups (750 ml) granulated sugar
1 tsp (5 ml) mustard seed

In a large bowl, combine prepared green and banana peppers, red pepper, if using, apples, cabbage and salt. Let stand 2 hours; drain well.
- Combine vinegar, sugar and mustard seed in a large stainless steel saucepan. Bring to a boil; reduce heat. Add drained pepper mixture and boil gently 10 minutes. ◀ ◀ ◀
Yield – about 7 x 250 or 236 ml jars

CUCUMBER RELISH

THIS BEAUTIFUL RELISH COMPLEMENTS ANY HOT SUMMER BARBECUE.

7 cups (1750 ml) peeled, finely chopped cucumbers
4 cups (1000 ml) *Each:* finely chopped green & red peppers
2 cups (500 ml) finely chopped celery
1 cup (250 ml) finely chopped onion
1/2 cup (125 ml) pickling salt
2 1/4 cups (550 ml) granulated sugar
3 cups (750 ml) white vinegar
3 tbsp (45 ml) *Each:* celery seed and mustard seed

Combine prepared measured cucumbers, peppers, celery, onions and pickling salt in a large glass or stainless steel bowl. Cover and let stand 4 hours.
- Drain vegetable mixture through cheesecloth-lined sieve. Rinse with water, drain again squeezing out excess liquid.
- Combine sugar, vinegar, celery seed and mustard seed in a large stainless steel saucepan. Mix well; bring to a boil. Add vegetables. Stirring frequently, return to a boil and boil gently 10 minutes. ◀ ◀ ◀
Yield – about 6 x 500 ml jars

RED ROOT RELISH

ENJOY THIS ZESTY RELISH IN PLACE OF HORSE-RADISH. FOR A FINER TEXTURED PRODUCT, SHRED BEETS.

4 cups (1000 ml) prepared beets
4 cups (1000 ml) finely chopped cabbage
3 cups (750 ml) white vinegar
1 1/2 cups (375 ml) granulated sugar
1 cup (250 ml) finely chopped onion
1 cup (250 ml) finely chopped red pepper
1 tbsp (15 ml) prepared horseradish
1 tbsp (15 ml) pickling salt

Scrub beets, leaving root and 2 inches (5 cm) of stem intact to prevent bleeding. Cover beets with water; boil until tender. Drain, discard liquid and slip off the skins removing tap root and stems. Dice beets; measure 4 cups (1000 ml).

• Combine beets, cabbage, vinegar, sugar, onion, pepper, horseradish and salt in a large stainless steel saucepan. Bring to a boil; boil gently 10 minutes. ◀◀◀

Yield – about 5 x 500 ml jars

HOMESTYLE CORN RELISH

8 cups (2000 ml) corn kernels
4 cups (1000 ml) diced red & green peppers
1 3/4 cups (425 ml) diced celery
1 cup (250 ml) finely chopped onion
4 cups (1000 ml) white vinegar
1 1/4 cups (300 ml) granulated sugar
2 tbsp (30 ml) *Each:* pickling salt & dry mustard
2 tsp (10 ml) celery seed
1-2 tsp (5-10 ml) turmeric
2 tbsp (30 ml) all purpose flour or ClearJel®
 (see pg 43)
1/4 cup (50 ml) water

If using fresh corn, blanch ears in boiling water 5 minutes before removing kernels. Measure corn, peppers, celery and onion; set aside.

• Combine vinegar, sugar and salt in a large stainless steel saucepan. Bring to a rolling boil. Maintaining the boil, gradually stir in vegetables. Stir in mustard, celery seed and turmeric. Combine flour and water making a paste; stir into vegetables. Boil gently, stirring frequently, 5 minutes or until relish reaches desired consistency. ◀◀◀

Yield – 6 x 500 ml jars

FENNEL RELISH

1 large head fennel, bulb and feathery leaves
2 1/2 cups (625 ml) firmly packed, finely chopped
 onions
1/4 cup (50 ml) pickled capers
1 cup (250 ml) cider vinegar
1/2 cup (125 ml) water
1/3 cup (75 ml) firmly packed brown sugar
2 tbsp (25 ml) all purpose flour
1 tbsp (15 ml) ground mustard
1 tsp (5 ml) finely grated lemon peel
1 tsp (5 ml) fennel seed
1 tsp (5 ml) pickling salt
1/4 tsp (1 ml) fresh cracked black pepper

Remove feathery leaves from fennel; finely chop enough to measure 2 tbsp (25 ml) lightly packed; set aside. Remove stalks and core from fennel bulb and discard. Pulse fennel in food processor (do not purée). Measure 3 cups (750 ml) firmly packed and set aside.

• Combine onions, capers, vinegar, water, brown sugar, flour, mustard, lemon peel, fennel seed, salt and pepper in a large stainless steel sauce pan. Bring mixture to a boil and boil gently, covered, 4 minutes. Add fennel pulp and chopped leaves; return to a full boil. ◀◀◀

Yield – about 5 x 250 or 236 ml jars

Re-establish a delicious tradition! Preserving a cherished family recipe is a rewarding cross-generational activity. When an Ontario grandmother retired from home canning several years ago, her granddaughter convinced her to share the recipe with Bernardin so that the family could once again enjoy this golden condiment.

RELISH

Preserving Day:

• Prepare vegetables in selected recipe as directed; cover and let stand as directed.

• Place required number of mason jars on a rack in a boiling water canner; cover jars with water and heat to a simmer (180°F/82°C). Set screw bands aside; heat SNAP Lids in hot water, NOT boiling (180°F/82°C). Keep jars and SNAP Lids hot until ready to use.

 Prepare and cook selected Relish as directed in individual recipe.

▶▶▶ **Ladle relish into a hot jar to within 1/2 inch (1 cm) of top rim (headspace).** Using nonmetallic utensil, remove air bubbles. Wipe jar rim removing any stickiness. Centre SNAP Lid on jar; apply screw band *securely & firmly* *until resistance is met – fingertip tight. Do not overtighten.* Place jar in canner; repeat for remaining relish.

• Cover canner; bring water to a boil. At altitudes up to 1,000 ft (305 m), process – *boil filled jars* – 500 ml jars – **15 minutes**; 250 ml jars – **10 minutes**. Remove jars without tilting. Cool upright, undisturbed 24 hours; DO NOT RETIGHTEN screw bands. After cooling check jar seals. *Sealed lids curve downward.* Remove screw bands; wipe and dry bands and jars. Store screw bands separately or replace loosely on jars, as desired. Label and store jars in a cool, dark place.

GRANDMA'S GOLDEN RELISH

GRANDMA'S GOLDEN RELISH DELIVERS A HOMEMADE GOODNESS THAT STORE-BOUGHT CAN'T MATCH.

12 cups (3000 ml) chopped peeled & seeded cucumbers
4 cups (1000 ml) chopped onion, about 1.8 kg
2 cups (500 ml) chopped, seeded sweet red pepper
2 cups (500 ml) chopped, seeded green pepper
1/2 cup (125 ml) pickling salt
6 cups (1500 ml) granulated sugar
5 tbsp (75 ml) ClearJel® *(see pg 43)*
4 tbsp (60 ml) dry mustard
1 tbsp (15 ml) *Each:* celery seed, mustard seed & ground turmeric
4 cups (1000 ml) white vinegar

• In a large glass or stainless steel container, combine cucumbers, onions, red and green peppers with salt. Cover and let stand in cool place overnight.

 Preserving Day: Prepare required number of jars and lids.

• In a large, deep stainless steel saucepan, combine sugar, ClearJel, spices and vinegar. Bring to a boil, stirring until thickened. Thoroughly drain vegetables, squeezing out excess moisture. Stir vegetables into liquid, return mixture to a boil that cannot be stirred down. ◀◀◀

Yield – 8 to 9 x 500 ml jars

GREEN TOMATO HOT DOG RELISH

USE THIS RELISH FOR HOT DOGS, SANDWICH SPREADS AND DIPPING SAUCES FOR FISH.

6 cups (1500 ml) finely chopped green tomatoes
2 onions, finely chopped
1/4 cup (50 ml) pickling salt
2 green peppers, chopped
1 red pepper, chopped
2 cups (500 ml) white vinegar
1 clove garlic, minced
1 1/2 cup (375 ml) brown sugar
1 tbsp (15 ml) dry mustard
1 tsp (5 ml) *Each:* whole cloves & celery seed
1/2 tsp (2 ml) *Each:* salt & ground ginger
4 inches (10 cm) cinnamon stick

• In a large stainless steel saucepan combine green tomatoes, onions, green and red peppers with pickling salt. Cover and let stand 12 hours in a cool place. Drain thoroughly.

Preserving Day: Drain & rinse vegetables, pressing out excess moisture; set aside. Prepare required number of jars and lids.

• In a large stainless steel saucepan combine vinegar, garlic, brown sugar, mustard, salt, and ginger. Tie cloves, cinnamon stick and celery seed in a square of cheesecloth, creating a spice bag; add to saucepan. Mix well; bring to a boil. Add drained tomato-onion mixture and peppers; simmer 1 hour, stirring frequently, until tomatoes are transparent. Discard spice bag. ◀◀◀

Yield – about 6 x 250 ml jars

ZESTY ZUCCHINI RELISH

HORSERADISH AND HOT PEPPERS GIVE THIS RELISH ITS "ZEST".

12 cups (3000 ml) finely chopped zucchini, about 14 medium
4 cups (1000 ml) chopped onions, about 5 medium
2 large sweet red peppers, chopped
1 large sweet green pepper, chopped
1/3 cup (75 ml) pickling salt
2 1/2 cups (675 ml) granulated sugar
1 tbsp (15 ml) *Each:* ground nutmeg & turmeric
2 1/2 cups (625 ml) white vinegar
4 tbsp (60 ml) prepared horseradish
1 large hot pepper including seeds, chopped

• In a large stainless steel saucepan combine zucchini, onions, red & green peppers with pickling salt. Cover and let stand 12 hours in a cool place.

Preserving Day: Drain & rinse vegetables, pressing out excess moisture; set aside. Prepare required number of jars and lids.

• Place vegetables in a large stainless steel saucepan. Stir in sugar, nutmeg, turmeric, vinegar, horseradish and hot pepper; bring to a boil. Reduce heat and boil gently until thick, about 45 minutes. ◀◀◀

Yield – about 6 x 500 ml jars

Serve these zesty sauces as condiments, use them to baste barbecued meats, in dips or add to any recipe that requires a sweet, tangy accent.

CONDIMENTS

• Place required number of clean mason jars on a rack in a boiling water canner; cover jars with water, bring to a rolling boil. Set screw bands aside; heat SNAP Lids in hot water, NOT boiling (180°F/82°C). Keep jars and SNAP Lids hot until ready to use.

Prepare ingredients as indicated in individual recipes. Cook as directed.

▶▶▶ **Ladle hot condiment into a hot jar to within 1/2 inch (1 cm) of top rim (headspace).** Using nonmetallic utensil, remove air bubbles. Wipe jar rim removing any stickiness. Centre SNAP Lid on jar; apply screw band *securely & firmly until resistance is met – fingertip tight. Do not overtighten.* Place jar in canner; repeat for remaining

• Cover canner; bring water to a boil. At altitudes up to 1,000 ft (305 m), process – *boil filled jars* – **15 minutes.** Remove jars without tilting. Cool upright, undisturbed 24 hours; DO NOT RETIGHTEN screw bands. After cooling check jar seals. *Sealed lids curve downward.* Remove screw bands; wipe and dry bands and jars. Store screw bands separately or replace loosely on jars, as desired. Label and store jars in a cool, dark place.

TOMATO KETCHUP

MUCH BETTER THAN STORE BOUGHT! THIS KETCHUP IS ALSO LOWER IN SUGAR AND SALT THAN COMMERCIAL BRANDS.

24 lb (11 kg) tomatoes, peeled, cored & quartered
3 cups (750 ml) chopped onion
1 tsp (5 ml) cayenne pepper
4 tsp (20 ml) whole cloves
8 inch (20 cm) cinnamon stick, crushed
1 1/2 tsp (7 ml) whole allspice berries
3 tbsp (45 ml) celery seed
3 cups (750 ml) cider vinegar
1 1/2 cup (375 ml) granulated sugar
1/4 cup (50 ml) pickling salt

Combine tomatoes, onion and cayenne pepper in large stainless steel saucepan. Bring to a boil; reduce heat and simmer 20 minutes, uncovered.

• Tie cloves, cinnamon, allspice and celery seed in a large square of cheesecloth, creating a spice bag. In a separate stainless steel saucepan, bring vinegar and spice bag to a boil. Cover, turn off heat and let stand while tomatoes cook. Discard spice bag and add spiced vinegar to tomato mixture; boil 30 minutes.

• Purée mixture in small batches and return mixture to saucepan. Add sugar and salt. Stirring frequently, boil gently until volume is reduced by half, or until mixture mounds on spoon. ◀◀◀

Yield – 7 x 500 ml jars

RED HOT SAUCE

8 cups (2000 ml) chopped, peeled tomatoes
1 1/2 cups (375 ml) chopped, seeded hot peppers
4 cups (1000 ml) vinegar, divided
1 cup (250 ml) granulated sugar
1 tbsp (15 ml) pickling salt
2 tbsp (30 ml) pickling spice

In stainless steel saucepan, combine tomatoes, peppers and 2 cups (500 ml) vinegar. Cook until soft; purée. Return to saucepan with sugar, salt and pickling spices tied in cheesecloth bag.

• Stirring frequently stir until thickened; add remaining vinegar and cook to desired consistency. ◀◀◀

Yield – 4 x 250 ml jars

FRUIT OF THE VINE KETCHUP

A DELICIOUS BLEND OF TOMATOES AND FRUIT GIVES THIS KETCHUP A UNIQUE TASTE.

4 cups (1000 ml) *Each:* peeled & chopped tomatoes & peaches
2 cups (500 ml) chopped apples
1 cup (250 ml) finely chopped onion
3 cloves garlic, minced
1 cup (250 ml) liquid honey
1/2 cup (125 ml) white vinegar
2 tsp (10 ml) dry mustard
1 tsp (5 ml) *Each:* salt, pepper, and ground cloves
1/2 tsp (2 ml) ground allspice
1/4 tsp (1 ml) cayenne pepper

Combine prepared tomatoes, peaches and apples in a large stainless steel saucepan. Heat gently, mashing fruit until juices flow. Add onion and garlic. Bring to a boil, cover and boil gently 10 minutes.

• Purée mixture in small batches; measure 5 cups (1250 ml) and return mixture to saucepan. Add honey, vinegar, mustard, salt, pepper, cloves, allspice and cayenne pepper. Bring to a boil; boil gently, stirring occasionally, uncovered, 45 minutes or until desired consistency is reached. ◄◄◄

Yield – 4 x 500 ml jars

CRANBERRY KETCHUP

THIS TASTY KETCHUP IS SIMILAR IN FLAVOUR TO COMMERCIAL HP SAUCE.

11 cups (2750 ml) cranberries
2 cups (500 ml) finely chopped onion
3-5 cloves garlic, finely chopped
1 1/2 cups (375 ml) water
1 cup (250 ml) vinegar
3 cups (750 ml) lightly packed brown sugar
2 tsp (10 ml) dry mustard
1 tsp (5 ml) *Each:* ground cloves, salt, pepper
1/2 tsp (2 ml) *Each:* ground allspice, cayenne pepper

Combine cranberries, onion, garlic and water in a large stainless steel saucepan. Bring to a boil; boil gently 10 minutes until cranberries are soft.

• Purée mixture in small batches and return mixture to saucepan. Add vinegar, brown sugar and spices. Stirring frequently, boil gently until mixture reduces and thickens, 30 to 45 minutes. ◄◄◄

Yield – about 4 x 250 or 236 ml jars

STEAK & BURGER SAUCE

USE THIS FRUITY SAUCE TO BASTE GRILLED MEATS; OR SERVE IT WITH HEARTY CHEESE AND ONION SANDWICHES FOR A 'PUB' STYLE LUNCH.

4 cups (1000 ml) *Each:* peeled, pitted & chopped plums and peaches
2 cups (500 ml) chopped apple
3 hot banana peppers, seeded and chopped
2 tbsp (25 ml) peeled and grated fresh gingerroot
2 tbsp (25 ml) minced garlic
1 1/2 cups (375 ml) cider vinegar
3 cups (750 ml) sugar
1 tbsp (15 ml) ground cinnamon
1 tbsp (15 ml) dry hot mustard
1 tsp (5 ml) ground cloves
1/2 tsp (2 ml) allspice
2 tbsp (25 ml) mixed pickling spice

Combine plums, peaches, apple, peppers, gingerroot, garlic and vinegar in a large stainless steel saucepan. Bring to a boil; reduce heat and boil gently 8 to 10 minutes or until fruit is tender. Purée mixture in small batches and return mixture to saucepan.

• Stir in sugar, cinnamon, mustard, cloves and all-spice. Tie pickling spice in a large square of cheese-cloth, creating a spice bag; add to pan. Bring to a boil; reduce heat and cook 35 to 45 minutes, stirring frequently until consistency is thick but slightly thinner than ketchup. Discard spice bag. ◄◄◄

Yield – 5 x 250 or 236 ml jars

THAI HOT AND SWEET DIPPING SAUCE

EXCELLENT FOR COLD THAI RICE PAPER ROLLS, THIS SAUCE IS ALSO DELICIOUS WITH ANY TYPE OF DEEP-FRIED ORIENTAL APPETIZERS.

1/2 cup (125 ml) chopped garlic
1 tbsp (15 ml) pickling salt
6 cups (1500 ml) cider vinegar
6 cups (1500 ml) granulated sugar
1/2 cup (125 ml) dried chili flakes

In small bowl, mix garlic and salt; let stand 5 minutes.

• Meanwhile, in a large, stainless steel saucepan, bring cider vinegar to a boil, over high heat. Add sugar, cook and stir until dissolved. Reduce heat; simmer 5 minutes. Stir in garlic-salt mixture and chili flakes. Remove from heat. ◄◄◄

Yield – about 9 x 250 ml jars

Spend a casual afternoon with friends making chutney. Catch up on all the latest news, while you chop the vegetables and let these rich flavours fill your kitchen.

CHUTNEY

• Place required number of clean mason jars on a rack in a boiling water canner; cover jars with water and heat to a simmer (180°F/82°C). Set screw bands aside; heat SNAP Lids in hot water, NOT boiling (180°F/82°C). Keep jars and SNAP Lids hot until ready to use.

Prepare, measure and cook ingredients specified in individual recipe. Remove from heat.

▶▶▶ **Ladle hot chutney into a hot jar to within 1/2 inch (1 cm) of top rim (headspace).** Using nonmetallic utensil, remove air bubbles. Wipe jar rim removing any stickiness. Centre SNAP Lid on jar; apply screw band *securely & firmly until resistance is met – fingertip tight. Do not overtighten.* Place jar in canner; repeat for remaining chutney.

• Cover canner; bring water to a boil. At altitudes up to 1,000 ft (305 m), process – *boil filled jars* – **15 minutes.** Remove jars without tilting. Cool upright, undisturbed 24 hours; DO NOT RETIGHTEN screw bands. After cooling check jar seals. *Sealed lids curve downward.* Remove screw bands; wipe and dry bands and jars. Store screw bands separately or replace loosely on jars, as desired. Label and store jars in a cool, dark place.

GREEN TOMATO CHUTNEY

16 cups (4000 ml) peeled & sliced green tomatoes
1/2 cup (125 ml) pickling salt
3 onions, chopped
16 cups (4000 ml) chopped apples
3 green peppers, seeded & chopped
4 cups (1000 ml) vinegar
3 tbsp (45 ml) pickling spice
6 cups (1500 ml) lightly packed light brown sugar
1 tsp (5 ml) chili powder

In a large glass or stainless steel container, layer tomatoes and pickling salt; add enough cold water to cover; refrigerate overnight.

• **Preserving Day:** Drain and rinse tomatoes, pressing out excess moisture. In a large stainless steel saucepan, combine tomatoes with onions, apples, green peppers and vinegar; bring to a boil; boil 30 minutes. Tie pickling spice in a large square of cheesecloth, creating a spice bag; add to mixture in saucepan. Add sugar. Stir frequently to prevent scorching, boil gently until thickened, 1 to 2 hours. Discard spice bag. ◀◀◀

Yield – about 7 x 500 ml jars

TAMARIND CHUTNEY

22 oz (625 g) dried tamarind block
2 tbsp (25 ml) cumin seeds
3 cups (750 ml) granulated sugar
1 cup (250 ml) sultana raisins, rinsed
4 tsp (20 ml) grated fresh gingerroot
2 1/2 tsp (12 ml) pickling salt
1/4 tsp (1 ml) freshly ground black pepper
1 tsp (5 ml) cayenne

In a medium bowl, break dried tamarind into chunks and soak in 4 cups (1000 ml) warm water 20 minutes. With your fingers, squeeze and break up tamarind under the water. Pour through a sieve into a non-metallic bowl, pressing tamarind with back of a spoon to extract all the liquid. Scrape bottom of sieve to remove pulp clinging to it. Measure 3 cups (750 ml) tamarind pulp.

• Meanwhile, roast cumin seeds in a dry frying pan. Heat, on high, shaking seeds and roasting for about 2 minutes or until seeds are golden brown and begin to smoke. Transfer to small bowl to cool. Grind seeds in coffee or spice mill or food processor.

• In a large stainless steel saucepan, combine tamarind pulp, ground roasted cumin, sugar, raisins, ginger, salt, black pepper and cayenne; stirring constantly bring to a full rolling boil. ◀◀◀

Yield – about 5 x 250 ml jars

Note: This chutney may separate during storage; simply shake jar before opening.

GOLDEN GOSSIP CHUTNEY

4 cups (1000 ml) grated carrots, about 1 lb (454 g)
2 1/2 cups (625 ml) granulated sugar
2 1/4 cups (550 ml) water
5 inch (12.5 cm) cinnamon stick
1/2 tsp (2 ml) cayenne pepper
2 tbsp (25 ml) mustard seed
2 tsp (10 ml) whole cloves
3 tbsp (45 ml) finely chopped gingerroot
3 cloves garlic, finely chopped
1 1/2 cups (375 ml) coarsely chopped, pitted dates
3 cups (750 ml) grated, peeled apples
1 1/2 cups (375 ml) malt vinegar
3/4 lb (340 g) onions, finely chopped
1 tbsp (15 ml) tomato paste
2 small red peppers, finely chopped
1/4 cup (50 ml) bottled lemon juice

In a large stainless steel saucepan, combine carrots, sugar, water, cinnamon stick and cayenne pepper. Tie mustard seed and cloves in a large square of cheesecloth, creating a spice bag; add to carrots. Stirring to prevent scorching, bring mixture to a boil.

• Stir in gingerroot, garlic and dates to simmering mixture. Cover, continue boiling gently, adding apples and onions as they are prepared. Stir in vinegar and tomato paste; cook until thickened to desired consistency. Add red pepper and lemon juice, cook 10 minutes longer. Discard spice bag. ◀◀◀
Yield – about 9 x 250 or 236 ml jars

SPICED PEACH CHUTNEY

6 1/2 lb (3 kg) peaches, peeled, seeded and chopped
2 cups (500 ml) malt vinegar
2 cups (500 ml) lightly packed brown sugar
4 oz (100 g) fresh gingerroot, chopped
2 medium onions, finely chopped
2 green peppers, seeded & finely chopped
1 hot banana pepper, seeded & finely chopped
1 cup (250 ml) *Each:* dark raisins, golden raisins
  & mixed glace peel
1 tbsp (15 ml) pickling salt
Spices Mixture – choose one:
Island: 1 tsp (5 ml) ground cinnamon, 1/2 tsp (2 ml) ground nutmeg, 1/4 tsp (1 ml) ground cloves, *OR*

Calcutta (Traditional) – Tie in spice bag: 2 tsp (10 ml) curry powder, 2 tbsp (25 ml) celery seed, 1 tbsp (15 ml) mustard seed.

Combine peaches and vinegar in a large stainless steel saucepan. Stir in sugar. Bring to a boil and cook until peaches are tender.

• Tie gingerroot in a large square of cheesecloth, creating a spice bag. Add spice bag, onions, green and banana peppers, dark and golden raisins, mixed peel, salt and chosen Spice Mixture to peaches. Return mixture to a boil. Stirring frequently, simmer until thick, about 45 minutes. Discard spice bag(s). ◀◀◀
Yield – about 6 x 500 ml jars

MANGO CHUTNEY

4 cups (1000 ml) chopped, peeled, pitted mangos,
  5-6 medium
1 cup (250 ml) coarsely chopped yellow onion
3/4 cup (175 ml) golden raisins
1/2 cup (125 ml) *Each:* peeled, seeded and
  chopped lime & orange
1/4 cup (50 ml) peeled, seeded and chopped lemon
3 cloves garlic, minced
1 cup (250 ml) dark brown sugar
1 cup (250 ml) apple cider vinegar
1/2 cup (125 ml) *Each:* grated gingerroot, molasses
1 tbsp (15 ml) mustard seed
1 tsp (5 ml) *Each:* dried red pepper flakes,
  ground cinnamon
1/4 tsp (1 ml) *Each:* ground cloves, ground allspice
2 tbsp (25 ml) finely chopped fresh cilantro

Combine mango, onion, raisins, lime, orange, lemon, garlic, brown sugar, vinegar, gingerroot, molasses, mustard seed, red pepper flakes, cinnamon, cloves and allspice in a large stainless steel saucepan. Bring to a boil, stirring constantly. Boil gently, stirring occasionally, 20 minutes. Add cilantro and continue to cook 10 minutes. ◀◀◀
Yield – about 6 x 250 or 236 ml jars

Special dietary requirements? There's no need to eliminate pickles from your food choices. Home canned recipes offer tasty alternatives. With substantially less salt than most pickling recipes, these reduced sodium recipes use spices and a slightly sweeter profile to create flavourful pickles. The light recipes use a granular sugar replacement, measured in the same manner as sugar.

SPECIAL DIET PICKLES

• Place required number of mason jars on a rack in a boiling water canner; cover jars with water and heat to a simmer (180°F/82°C). Set screw bands aside; heat SNAP Lids in hot water, NOT boiling (180°F/82°C). Keep jars and SNAP Lids hot until ready to use.

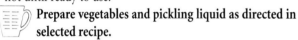 **Prepare vegetables and pickling liquid as directed in selected recipe.**

▶▶▶ Pack vegetables into a hot jar to within 3/4 inch (2 cm) of top rim. Add hot pickling liquid to cover vegetables to within 1/2 inch (1 cm) of top rim (headspace). Using nonmetallic utensil, remove air bubbles. Wipe jar rim removing any stickiness. Centre SNAP Lid on jar; apply screw band *securely & firmly until resistance is met – fingertip tight. Do not overtighten.* Place jar in canner; repeat for remaining vegetables and hot liquid.

• Cover canner; bring water to a boil. At altitudes up to 1,000 ft (305 m), process – *boil filled jars* – **10 minutes.** Remove jars without tilting. Cool upright, undisturbed 24 hours; DO NOT RETIGHTEN screw bands. After cooling check jar seals. *Sealed lids curve downward.* Remove screw bands; wipe and dry bands and jars. Store screw bands separately or replace loosely on jars, as desired. Label and store jars in a cool, dark place.

FOR BEST QUALITY USE LIGHT RECIPES WITHIN 6 TO 9 MONTHS. TO ENSURE SAFE AND DELICIOUS "SPECIAL DIET PICKLES", DO NOT ALTER QUANTITIES, MEASURE ACCURATELY AND FOLLOW THE DIRECTIONS EXACTLY. HEAT PROCESSING FILLED JARS IS ABSOLUTELY ESSENTIAL.

REDUCED SODIUM SWEET PICKLES

4 lb (1.8 kg) pickling cucumbers, 3 to 4 inch
  (7.5 to 10 cm) long
3 1/2 cups (875 ml) granulated sugar, divided
1 tbsp (15 ml) pickling salt
1 tbsp (15 ml) mustard seed
5 2/3 cups (1375 ml) white vinegar, divided
1 tbsp (15 ml) whole allspice
2 1/4 tsp (11 ml) celery seed

Thoroughly wash cucumbers, scrubbing lightly with a soft vegetable brush and removing all dirt and sand. Discard stem and blossom ends. Cut cucumbers into 1/4 inch (0.5 cm) slices.

• In a large stainless steel saucepan, combine 1/2 cup (125 ml) sugar, pickling salt, mustard seed and 4 cups (1000 ml) vinegar; bring to a boil. Add cucumbers; boil gently 5 to 7 minutes, just until cucumbers change colour from bright to dull green. Drain cucumbers, discarding cooking solution.

• In a separate saucepan, prepare pickling liquid – combine 3 cups (750 ml) sugar, allspice, celery seed and 1 2/3 cups (400 ml) vinegar; bring to a boil. ◀◀◀

Yield – about 5 x 500 ml jars

REDUCED SODIUM POLISH DILL PICKLES

4 lb (1.8 kg) small to medium pickling cucumbers
4 tbsp (60 ml) granulated sugar
2 tbsp (25 ml) pickling salt
3 3/4 cups (900 ml) white vinegar
2 1/2 cups (625 ml) water
6 cloves garlic
6 tsp (30 ml) peppercorns
12 bay leaves
18 heads fresh dill

Thoroughly wash cucumbers, scrubbing lightly with a soft vegetable brush and removing all dirt and sand. Discard stem and blossom ends. Cut cucumbers into spears or slice lengthwise or cut into coins.

• Prepare pickling liquid – combine sugar, salt, vinegar and water in a large stainless steel or enamel saucepan; bring to a boil.

• In a hot jar, place 1 clove garlic, 1 tsp (5 ml) peppercorns, 2 bay leaves and 3 heads fresh dill. Pack cucumbers into jar and proceed as directed in main recipe. ◀◀◀

Yield – 6 x 500 ml jars

LIGHT PICKLED BEETS

4.5 lb (2 kg) beets of similar size
4 1/2 cups (1125 ml) white vinegar
1 1/2 cups (375 ml) water
3 cups (750 ml) granular sugar replacement (artificial sweetener)
1 tbsp (15 ml) pickling spice, *optional*

Scrub beets, leaving root and 2 inches (5 cm) of stem intact to prevent bleeding. Place beets saucepan; cover with water. Boil until tender. Drain, discard liquid and slip off the skins removing tap root and stems. Leave baby beets whole, slice or quarter larger beets.

• Prepare pickling liquid – combine vinegar, water and pickling spice, if using, in a stainless steel saucepan; boil gently 5 minutes. Stir in artificial sweetener and keep liquid hot. ◀◀◀

Yield – 6 x 500 ml jars

REDUCED SODIUM SWEET DILL PICKLES

4 lb (1.8 kg) small to medium pickling cucumbers
3 cups (750 ml) granulated sugar
2 tbsp (30 ml) pickling salt
6 cups (1500 ml) vinegar
2 tbsp (30 ml) mixed pickling spice
6 heads fresh dill

Prepare pickling liquid – combine sugar, salt and vinegar in a large stainless steel or enamel saucepan. Tie pickling spices in a cheesecloth square, creating a spice bag and add to liquid. Bring to a boil, reduce heat, cover and boil gently, 15 minutes; keep hot. Discard spice bag.

• Thoroughly wash cucumbers, scrubbing lightly with a soft vegetable brush and removing all dirt and sand. Discard stem and blossom ends. Cut cucumbers into spears or slice lengthwise or cut into coins.

• In a hot jar, place 1 head dill. Pack cucumbers into jar and proceed as directed in main recipe. ◀◀◀

Yield – 6 x 500 ml jars

LIGHT BREAD & BUTTER PICKLES

4.5 lb (2 kg) medium pickling cucumbers
1 lb (500 g) onion, 2 medium-large
1/3 cup (75 ml) pickling salt
4 1/2 cups (1125 ml) white vinegar
4 1/2 cups (1125 ml) granular sugar replacement (artificial sweetener)
2 tbsp (25 ml) *Each:* **celery seed & mustard seed**
1/2 tsp (2 ml) ground turmeric

Thoroughly wash cucumbers, scrubbing lightly with a soft vegetable brush and removing all dirt and sand. Discard stem and blossom ends. Slice cross-wise into 1/8 inch (2.5 mm) thick coins. Peel and slice onions to the same thickness. Layer cucumbers and onions in a glass or stainless steel container, lightly sprinkling each layer with pickling salt. Cover and let stand in a cool place 3 hours.

• Drain cucumbers and onions; rinse in cool water and drain thoroughly.

• Prepare pickling liquid – combine vinegar, artificial sweetener, celery seed, mustard seed and turmeric and bring to a boil. Add vegetables and return to a boil. Remove from heat. ◀◀◀

Yield – 6 x 500 ml jars

INTERNATIONAL PICKLES

Beyond Dills and Sweets, pickling embraces an infinite treasury of tantalizing textures and tastes to accent your daily diet. Use this recipe sampler to open the door to marvelous taste adventures.

TRADITIONAL PRESERVED LIMES

THESE LIMES ARE FERMENTED IN SALT AND LIME JUICE AND THEN STORED IN THE REFRIGERATOR. THEY ARE THE MAIN INGREDIENT IN LIME PICKLE BUT CAN BE USED ON THEIR OWN AS A CONDIMENT OR INGREDIENT IN SALADS OR RICE DISHES. USE THE LIMES WHOLE OR CUT THEM INTO WEDGES.

20 limes, preferably organic, about 3 lb (1.4 kg)
1/2 cup (125 ml) pickling salt
4 jalapeño peppers, *optional*
6 cloves garlic, peeled, *optional*

• Place 1 clean 1 L mason jar on a rack in a large saucepan or boiling water canner; fill canner with water, cover and boil hard 10 minutes to sterilize jar.
• Scrub 10 limes in warm water, removing dirt and wax. Dry well with paper towels. Slice off stem ends. From stem end, cut each lime into quarters without cutting through the bottom end, leaving the limes intact. Alternatively, cut 10 limes into quarters.
• Juice remaining 10 limes; measure 1 1/2 cups (375 ml) juice.
• If using, wash peppers, remove stems. Cut each pepper lengthwise into 8 strips.
• Drain sterilized jar; measure 1 tbsp (15 ml) salt into jar.
• Working over a bowl, measure a heaping teaspoon salt into a lime; close quarters and place lime in jar. Repeat with 2 more limes, then add 1 heaping tablespoon salt and layer in a third of the garlic and jalapeno strips, if using. Repeat for remaining limes, salt, garlic and jalapeños. Push limes down, packing tightly in jar. Cover with any remaining salt.
• If using lime quarters, combine quartered limes, garlic, jalapeño strips and salt in a large bowl; toss until well mixed. Pack into sterilized jar.
• Fill jar with lime juice. Wipe jar rim removing stickiness. Apply a clean SNAP Lid or plastic storage lid.
• Place jar in a dark, cool cupboard or refrigerate 14 to 21 days; shake jar every day to redistribute the salt. After 2 to 3 weeks, the limes are ready to use.

To use – remove pulp and membrane, using only the peel, and rinse under water to remove excess salt; dry with paper towel.
• Refrigerate Preserved Limes up to 6 months; if desired during refrigerated storage time limes may be topped with 1/4 inch (5 mm) vegetable oil.
Yield – one 1 L jar

TRADITIONAL PRESERVED LEMONS

10 lemons, preferably organic, about 3 lb (1.4 kg)
1/2 cup (125 ml) pickling salt
4 bay leaves, *optional*
4 cinnamon sticks, *optional*
1 tsp whole black peppercorns, *optional*

Prepare, marinate and store as directed for Traditional Preserved Limes.

ASIAN CONDIMENTS

• Place required number of mason jars on a rack in a boiling water canner; cover jars with water and heat to a simmer (180°F/82°C). Set screw bands aside; heat SNAP Lids in hot water, NOT boiling (180°F/82°C). Keep jars and SNAP Lids hot until ready to use.

 Measure and prepare selected recipe as directed.

▶▶▶ **Ladle mixture into a hot jar to within 1/2 inch (1 cm) of top rim (headspace).** Using nonmetallic utensil, remove air bubbles. Wipe jar rim removing any stickiness. Centre SNAP Lid on jar; apply screw band *securely & firmly* until resistance is met – *fingertip tight. Do not overtighten.* Place jar in canner; repeat for remaining mixture.
• Cover canner; bring water to a boil. At altitudes up to 1,000 ft (305 m), process – *boil filled jars* – 125 and 250 ml jars – **10 minutes**; 500 ml jars – **15 minutes**. Remove jars without tilting. Cool upright, undisturbed 24 hours; DO NOT RETIGHTEN screw bands. After cooling check jar seals. *Sealed lids curve downward.* Remove screw bands; wipe and dry bands and jars. Store screw bands separately or replace loosely on jars, as desired. Label and store in a cool, dark place.

LIME PICKLE

TRADITIONAL LIME PICKLE INCORPORATES VEGETABLE OIL INTO THE RECIPE. FOR HOME CANNING, PRESERVE THIS RECIPE AS DIRECTED, THEN STIR VEGETABLE OIL INTO THE MIXTURE AFTER OPENING THE JAR OR JUST BEFORE SERVING.

1 tsp (5 ml) fenugreek
1/2 cup (125 ml) lime juice
2 tsp (10 ml) black mustard seeds
1/4 cup (50 ml) coriander seeds
2 tbsp (25 ml) cumin seeds
2 tsp (10 ml) fennel seeds
1/3 cup (75 ml) coarsely chopped garlic
  (about 1 head garlic)
1/2 cup (125 ml) coarsely chopped gingerroot
1 1/2 cups (375 ml) water
8 Preserved Limes & 1/4 cup (50 ml) preserving
  liquid *(recipe page 92)*
1 cup (250 ml) cider vinegar
1 tbsp (15 ml) honey
1 tsp (5 ml) turmeric
2 tsp (10 ml) chili flakes
4 jalapeño peppers, finely chopped, including seed

In small bowl soak fenugreek seeds in lime juice, 1 hour.

• In dry skillet on high heat, toast black mustard seeds 1 minute or until they start to pop. Set aside. In same dry skillet on high heat, toast coriander, cumin, and fennel seeds 1 minute.

• Grind all toasted seeds in spice grinder or blender. Combine ground seeds, soaked fenugreek mixture, garlic, gingerroot, water and 1/4 cup (50 ml) liquid from Preserved Limes in blender, purée until smooth.

• In a stainless steel saucepan combine purée, cider vinegar, honey, turmeric and chili flakes. Bring to a boil; reduce heat and boil gently, stirring occasionally, 15 minutes.

• Meanwhile, rinse Preserved Limes under running water to remove salt; discard pulp and membrane and slice peel into 1/2 inch (1 cm) pieces. Add limes and peppers to spice mixture; boil gently 5 minutes. ◄◄◄

Yield – about 4 x 250 ml or 8 x 125 ml jars.

HARISSA-STYLE SAUCE

HARISSA IS A MOROCCAN CONDIMENT TRADITIONALLY MADE BY POUNDING FRESH GARLIC AND DRIED CHILIES IN A MORTAR AND PESTLE WITH SEASONINGS AND OLIVE OIL. THIS HOME CANNED VERSION COMBINES A LARGE QUANTITY OF MILD, DRIED CHILIES WITH GARLIC THEN TEMPERS THE FLAVOUR WITH TOMATOES, ONIONS AND A LITTLE SUGAR. IF DESIRED, STIR IN OLIVE OIL JUST BEFORE SERVING.

4 oz (125 g) New Mexico dried chilies, or other
  mild chilies like Ancho or Mulato
4 cups (1000 ml) chopped plum tomatoes (12-14),
  skins and seeds removed
2 cups (500 ml) chopped onion
1/2 cup (125 ml) chopped sweet red bell pepper
3/4 cup (175 ml) lightly packed brown sugar
1 cup (250 ml) cider vinegar
2 1/2 tsp (12 ml) ground cumin
1 1/4 tsp (6 ml) ground coriander
4 tbsp (60 ml) chopped garlic
1 tbsp (15 ml) pickling salt

Remove stems and seeds from dried chilies; cover with warm water. Place a weight (small bowl or cup) on chilies to keep them submerged. Soak 20 minutes or longer. Drain chilies, reserving water. Coarsely chop chilies.

• Prepare and measure tomatoes, onions and red bell pepper; set aside.

• In a large stainless steel saucepan combine tomatoes, onions, red bell pepper, sugar, vinegar, cumin and coriander. Bring to a boil; reduce heat and simmer 25 minutes, stirring frequently.

• In blender or small food processor, combine chopped dried chilies, garlic, salt and 3 tbsp soaking water. Process until a smooth paste is formed.

• Add paste to tomato mixture; cook and stir 5 minutes longer. Remove from heat. ◄◄◄

Yield – about 6 x 250 ml jars or 12 x 125 ml jars.

ASIAN CONDIMENTS, cont.

• Place required number of mason jars on a rack in a boiling water canner; cover jars with water and heat to a simmer (180°F/82°C). Set screw bands aside; heat SNAP Lids in hot water, NOT boiling (180°F/82°C). Keep jars and SNAP Lids hot until ready to use.

 Measure and prepare selected recipe as directed.

▶▶▶ Using nonmetallic utensil, remove air bubbles. Wipe jar rim removing any stickiness. Centre SNAP Lid on jar; apply screw band *securely & firmly until resistance is met – fingertip tight. Do not overtighten.* Place jar in canner; repeat for remaining mixture.
• Cover canner; bring water to a boil. At altitudes up to 1,000 ft (305 m), process – *boil filled jars –* **for time specified in individual recipe.** Remove jars without tilting. Cool upright, undisturbed 24 hours; DO NOT RETIGHTEN screw bands. After cooling check jar seals. *Sealed lids curve downward.* Remove screw bands; wipe and dry bands and jars. Store screw bands separately or replace loosely on jars, as desired. Label and store in a cool, dark place.

ACHAR (ASIAN RELISH)

SERVE THIS CHUNKY CONDIMENT WITH TANDOORI CHICKEN, TANGINES OR CURRIES.

5 English cucumbers, unpeeled
2 medium carrots, peeled
5 cups (1250 ml) cauliflower flowerettes
1/2 cup (125 ml) unsalted roasted peanuts
4 tbsp (60 ml) sesame seeds
2 medium cooking onions, quartered
15 small dried chilies, about 1 inch (2 cm) each
1 1/2 inch (4 cm) piece gingerroot
4 cloves garlic
2 1/2 cups (625 ml) vinegar
1 cup (250 ml) granulated sugar
2 tbsp (25 ml) pickling salt
1 tbsp (15 ml) ground tumeric

 Wash cucumbers, Remove blossom and stem ends; quarter lengthwise and seed. Cut cucumbers into 1 1/2 inch (4 cm) sticks. Cut carrots into similarly-sized sticks. Place cucumber, carrot and cauliflower on a towel to dry while preparing other ingredients.

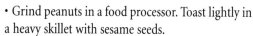

• Grind peanuts in a food processor. Toast lightly in a heavy skillet with sesame seeds.
• Combine onions, chilies, gingerroot and garlic in a blender or food processor. Purée to a paste. In a large, deep stainless steel saucepan, combine purée, vinegar, sugar, salt and tumeric. Bring mixture to a full rolling boil. Stirring frequently to prevent scorching, boil gently, uncovered, 5-10 minutes, or until mixture thickens slightly.
• Add peanut mixture and vegetables to sauce. Stirring frequently, return mixture to a boil; reduce heat and boil gently, uncovered, 5 minutes.
• Ladle achar into a hot jar to within 1/2 inch (1 cm) of top rim (headspace). ◀◀◀
Heat process – *boil filled jars* – **15 minutes.**
Yield – about 7 x 500 ml jars

VIETNAMESE CARROT & DAIKON PICKLE

THESE PRETTY STRANDS OF ORANGE AND WHITE PICKLE ARE THE PERFECT ACCOMPANIMENT TO ANY SOUTH ASIAN MEAL. A MANDOLINE OR BENRINER SPEEDS CUTTING VEGETABLES INTO JULIENNE. DAIKON LOOKS LIKE A LARGE WHITE CARROT AND CAN BE FOUND IN ASIAN GROCERS AND MANY SUPERMARKETS. STAR ANISE ADDS A WONDERFUL FLAVOUR TO THIS UNIQUE PICKLES BUT IT IS OPTIONAL. DO TRY IT IN AT LEAST ONE JAR!

2 lb (1 kg) *Each:* **carrots, daikon**
3 cups (750 ml) *Each:* **white vinegar, water**
1 1/2 cup (375 ml) granulated sugar
2 tsp (10 ml) grated gingerroot
6 whole star anise, *optional*
4 1/2 tsp (24 ml) Bernardin Pickle Crisp™, *optional*

 Peel carrots and daikon; cut into julienne strips 1/4 inch (5 mm) thick.
• In a large, deep stainless steel saucepan combine vinegar, water, sugar and gingerroot; bring to a boil.
• Place one star anise, if using, in a hot jar and fill with carrot and daikon to within 3/4 inch (2 cm) of top rim. Add 3/4 tsp (4 ml) Pickle Crisp, if using.
• Add hot liquid to cover vegetables to within 1/2 inch (1 cm) of top rim (headspace). ◀◀◀
Heat process – *boil filled jars* – **10 minutes.**
Yield – about 6 x 500 ml jars

PICKLED SPICED RED CABBAGE

EASTERN EUROPEANS HAVE THOUSANDS OF DELICIOUS WAYS TO SERVE CABBAGE. THIS COLOURFUL PICKLED CABBAGE IS BUT ONE OF THE MULTITUDES OF WAYS SAVVY COOKS USE THIS VERSATILE KOHL VEGETABLE.

12 lb (5.5 kg) shredded red cabbage, about
  3 large heads
1/2 cup (125 ml) pickling salt
1 cup (250 ml) lightly packed brown sugar
1/2 cup (125 ml) *Each:* mustard seed, ground mace
8 cups (2 L) red wine vinegar
1/4 cup (50 ml) *Each:* whole cloves, whole allspice,
  peppercorns & celery seed
2 sticks cinnamon

Remove outer leaves of cabbage; core and shred. Layer cabbage and salt in a large bowl. Cover; let stand 24 hours. Rinse. Drain thoroughly on paper towel-lined trays, about 6 hours.

• Combine sugar, mustard seed, mace and vinegar in a large stainless steel saucepan. Tie cloves, allspice, peppercorns, celery seed and broken cinnamon stick in a large square of cheesecloth creating a spice bag; add to vinegar. Boil 5 minutes. Discard spice bag.

• Pack cabbage into a hot jar to within 3/4 inch (2 cm) of top rim. Add hot liquid to cover cabbage to within 1/2 inch (1 cm) of top rim (headspace). ◀◀◀

Heat process – *boil filled jars* – **20 minutes**.
Yield – about 5 x 1 L jars

HOT PICKLE MIX

4 cups (1000 ml) sliced pickling cucumbers
2 cups (500 ml) cauliflowerettes
1 green pepper, 1 red pepper, cut into strips
1 cup (250 ml) *Each:* sliced carrots and
  pickling onions
3 cups (750 ml) hot yellow peppers, cut into
  1 1/2 inch (3 cm) pieces
1 large garlic clove
8 1/2 cups (2125 ml) water, divided
2/3 cup (150 ml) pickling salt
8 1/2 cups (2125 ml) white vinegar
3/4 cup (175 ml) granulated sugar
2 tbsp (25 ml) prepared horseradish
3 to 9 jalapeño peppers, halved and seeded

Combine prepared cucumbers, cauliflowerettes, green and red peppers, carrots and pickling onions in a large stainless steel or glass container. Dissolve salt in 7 cups (1750 ml) water. Pour salt water mixture over vegetables; let stand 1 hour.

• Drain vegetables; rinse well and drain thoroughly. Add hot yellow peppers and mix well.

• Combine remaining ingredients, except jalapeño peppers in a large stainless steel saucepan. Bring to a boil; boil gently 15 minutes. Remove garlic.

• Pack vegetables and 1 to 3 jalapeño pepper(s) into a hot jar to within 3/4 inch (2 cm) of top rim. Add hot liquid to cover vegetables to within 1/2 inch (1 cm) of top rim (headspace). ◀◀◀

Heat process – *boil filled jars* – **10 minutes**.
Yield – about 6 x 500 ml jars

95

JARDINIÈRE

ADD THESE TANGY PICKLED VEGETABLES TO A RELISH PLATE OR SERVE AS A CONDIMENT WITH GRILLED MEATS AND SEAFOOD. FOR A QUICK ANTIPASTO – STIR IN TUNA, MUSHROOMS, OLIVES, OLIVE OIL AND TOMATO PASTE.

2 cups (500 ml) small cauliflower florets
1 1/2 cups (375 ml) small white onions
3 stalks celery, sliced 1/4 inch (0.5 cm) thick
2 carrots, cut into 1 1/2 inch (4 cm) strips
1 small zucchini, sliced 1/4 inch (0.5 cm) thick
2 sweet red peppers, cut in strips
1 *Each:* sweet yellow and green peppers, cut in strips
4 cups (1000 ml) white vinegar
2 cups (500 ml) water
2 cups (500 ml) granulated sugar
1 tbsp (15 ml) pickling salt
3 bay leaves
6 whole peppercorns
3 cloves garlic, thinly sliced

• Place 5 clean 500 ml mason jars on a rack in a boiling water canner; cover jars with water and heat to a simmer (180°F/82°C). Set screw bands aside; heat SNAP Lids in hot water, NOT boiling (180°F/82°C). Keep jars and SNAP Lids hot until ready to use.

• Wash and prepare vegetables as stated in ingredient list.

• Combine vinegar, water, sugar and pickling salt in a large stainless steel saucepan: bring to a boil. Tie bay leaves, peppercorns and garlic in a large square of cheesecloth, creating a spice bag; add to liquid. Continue to boil liquid, covered, 5 minutes.

• Add prepared cauliflower, onions, celery, carrots and zucchini; return to a boil. Remove from heat; add peppers. Discard spice bag.

• Pack vegetables into a hot jar to within 3/4 inch (2 cm) of top rim. Add hot liquid to cover vegetables to within 1/2 inch (1 cm) of top rim (headspace). Using non-metallic utensil, remove air bubbles. Wipe jar rim removing any stickiness. Centre SNAP Lid on jar; apply screw band *securely & firmly* until resistance is met – *fingertip tight. Do not overtighten.* Place jar in canner; repeat for remaining vegetables and hot liquid.

• Cover canner; bring water to a boil. At altitudes up to 1,000 ft (305 m), process – *boil filled jars* – **10 minutes**. Remove jars without tilting. Cool upright, undisturbed 24 hours; DO NOT RETIGHTEN screw bands. After cooling check jar seals. *Sealed lids curve downward.* Remove screw bands; wipe and dry bands and jars. Store screw bands separately or replace loosely on jars, as desired. Label and store jars in a cool, dark place.

Yield – about 5 x 500 ml jars

DILLED BEANS

GREEN AND YELLOW WAX BEANS STEEPED IN A ZESTY DILL BRINE MAKE DELICIOUS AND COLOURFUL PICKLES.

2.2 lb (1 kg) green beans
2.2 lb (1 kg) yellow waxed beans
3 small red peppers, sliced into thin strips
3 cups (750 ml) *Each:* white vinegar and water
3 tbsp (45 ml) pickling salt
18 peppercorns
3 tsp (15 ml) dill seed or 6 sprigs fresh dill
6 cloves garlic

• Place 6 clean 500 ml mason jars on a rack in a boiling water canner; cover jars with water and heat to a simmer (180°F/82°C). Set screw bands aside; heat SNAP Lids in hot water, NOT boiling (180°F/82°C). Keep jars and SNAP Lids hot until ready to use.

• Wash and trim beans. Cut into jar-length pieces. In a large stainless steel saucepan, combine vinegar, water and pickling salt. Bring to a boil. Add beans and pepper strips; return mixture to a boil. Remove from heat.

• Place 3 peppercorns, 1/2 tsp (2 ml) dill seed or 1 sprig fresh dill and 1 clove garlic in each jar. Fill jar with beans.

• Pack prepared vegetables into a hot jar to within 3/4 inch (2 cm) of top rim. Add hot liquid to cover vegetables to within 1/2 inch (1 cm) of top rim (headspace). Using nonmetallic utensil, remove air bubbles. Wipe jar rim removing any stickiness. Centre SNAP Lid on jar; apply screw band *securely & firmly* until resistance is met – *fingertip tight. Do not overtighten.* Place jar in canner; repeat for remaining vegetables and hot liquid.

• Cover canner; bring water to a boil. At altitudes up to 1,000 ft (305 m), process – *boil filled jars* – **10 minutes**. Remove jars without tilting. Cool upright, undisturbed 24 hours; DO NOT RETIGHTEN screw bands. After cooling check jar seals. *Sealed lids curve downward.* Remove screw bands; wipe and dry bands and jars. Store screw bands separately or replace loosely on jars, as desired. Label and store jars in a cool, dark place.

Yield – about 6 x 500 ml jars

Hot 'n Spicy Beans are popular garnishes for cocktails. They also add pizzazz to vegetable relish trays and they're easy to make. When making Dilled Beans, simply add about 1 tsp (5 ml) crushed chilies or 1 to 3 fresh hot chili peppers to each jar before packing the beans.

Spicy Asparagus Spears – Substitute asparagus spears for green beans. For easy removal, pack asparagus tips-down into straight-sided, wide mouth 500 ml jars.

LOW ACID FOODS

Make your own ready-to-heat homemade soups, entrées, sauces, vegetables, meat, fish and seafood. Sound inviting? Preserving jars of these delicious foods is just one step beyond cooking and well within the skill set of any home canner equipped with a pressure canner. Because these are all low acid foods, they must be heat processed at higher temperatures than that of boiling water.

Cook once – enjoy soup several times. For shelf-stable storage, filled jars must be heat processed in a pressure canner. Soup in jars can also be refrigerated.

Pressure canned
SOUPS

• Place the required number of clean mason jars on rack in pressure canner or large saucepan; add water and heat jars to a simmer (180°F/82°C). Set screw bands aside; heat SNAP Lids in hot water, NOT boiling (180°F/82°C). Keep jars and SNAP Lids hot until ready to use.

 Measure and prepare ingredients as specified in individual recipes.

▶▶▶ *Ladle hot soup into a hot jar to within 1 inch (2.5 cm) of top rim (headspace).*

• Using nonmetallic utensil, remove air bubbles. Wipe jar rim removing any stickiness. Centre SNAP Lid on jar; apply screw band *securely & firmly until resistance is met – fingertip tight. Do not overtighten.* Place jar in canner; repeat for remaining soup. *If stacking jars, place a second rack between layers of jars.*

• When pressure canner is full, adjust water to level as directed by canner manufacturer. Lock canner lid in place and follow manufacturer's heating instructions. Vent canner – *allow steam to escape steadily* – for 10 minutes; close vent.

• When canner reaches the pressure appropriate for your altitude and type of pressure canner, begin counting processing time. Process – *heat filled jars* – **in pressure canner for time indicated for jar size in each recipe.** NOTE: processing times indicated in each recipe are for weighted gauge pressure canners used at altitudes up to 1,000 ft (305 m). When canning at higher elevations, adjust pressure according to chart on page 12.

• When processing time is complete turn off heat. *Allow canner to stand undisturbed until pressure drops to zero.* Wait 2 minutes, and then remove cover, tilting it away from your face. Remove jars without tilting. Cool upright, undisturbed 24 hours; DO NOT RETIGHTEN screw bands. After cooling check jar seals. *Sealed lids curve downward.* Remove screw bands; wipe and dry bands and jars. Store screw bands separately or replace loosely on jars, as desired. Label and store in a cool, dark place.

CHICKEN SOUP

16 cups (4000 ml) chicken stock
3 cups (750 ml) diced chicken, about one 3 lb/ 1.5 kg chicken
1 1/2 cups (375 ml) diced celery, about 2 stalks
1 1/2 cups (375 ml) sliced carrots
1 cup (250 ml) diced onion, about 1 medium
Salt and pepper to taste
3 chicken bouillon cubes, *optional*

Combine chicken stock, chicken, celery, carrots and onion in a large stainless steel saucepan. Bring mixture to a boil. Reduce heat and simmer 30 minutes. Season with salt and pepper to taste. Add bouillon cubes, if desired. Cook until bouillon cubes are dissolved. ◀◀◀

Yield: 8 x 500 ml or 4 x 1 L jars. Heat process 500 ml jars – **75 minutes**; 1 L jars – **90 minutes** at 10 lb (68 kPa) in weighted gauge pressure canner.

VEGETABLE SOUP

8 cups (2000 ml) chopped, peeled tomatoes
6 cups (1500 ml) cubed, peeled potatoes
6 cups (1500 ml) thickly sliced carrots
4 cups (1000 ml) lima beans
4 cups (1000 ml) whole kernel corn
2 cups (500 ml) thickly sliced celery
2 cups (500 ml) chopped onion
6 cups (1500 ml) water
Salt & pepper

Combine all ingredients, except salt & pepper, in a large stainless steel saucepan. Bring to a boil; reduce heat and simmer 15 minutes. Season to taste with salt and pepper. ◀◀◀

Yield: 14 x 500 ml jars or 7 x 1 L jars. Heat process 500 ml jars – **55 minutes**; 1 L jars **85 minutes** at 10 lb (68 kPa) in weighted gauge pressure canner.

BEAN SOUP

2 cups (500 ml) dried pea or navy beans
1 ham hock or 1/4 lb (125 g) salt pork
1/2 cup (125 ml) chopped onion
1 small carrot, chopped
1 small hot pepper, seed & chopped, *optional*
1 bay leaf
Salt

Cover beans with cold water; soak 12 to 18 hours in a cool place. Drain. Place beans in a large stainless steel saucepan; add water to cover beans by 2 inches (5 cm). Add meat, onion, carrot and pepper, if using; bring to a boil; cover and boil gently 2 to 3 hours or until beans are tender. Remove meat; cut into small pieces. Discard bay leaf. If desired, press remaining ingredients through a sieve. Return meat to soup and reheat to a boil. ◀◀◀

Yield: 5 x 500 ml or 4 x 2 L jars. Heat process 500 ml jars – **75 minutes**; 1 L jars – **90 minutes** at 10 lb (68 kPa) in weighted gauge pressure canner.

SPICED TOMATO SOUP

16 cups (4000 ml) chopped, peeled & cored tomatoes
3 1/2 cups (875 ml) chopped onions
2 1/2 cups (625 ml) chopped celery
2 cups (500 ml) chopped red peppers
1 cup (250 ml) sliced carrots
7 bay leaves
1 tbsp (15 ml) whole cloves
1 clove garlic
1 cup (250 ml) lightly packed brown sugar
Salt & pepper

Combine tomatoes, onions, celery, peppers, carrots, bay leaves, cloves and garlic in a large stainless steel saucepan. Bring to a boil; reduce heat and boil gently until vegetables are tender. Discard bay leaves. Purée soup in small batches. Return puréed soup to saucepan. Add sugar and season to taste with salt and pepper. Heat soup to a boil. ◀◀◀

Yield: 4 x 500 ml jars. Heat process 500 ml jars – **20 minutes** at 10 lb (68 kPa) in weighted gauge pressure canner.

HABITANT SOUP

16 oz (454 g) dried split peas
8 cups (2000 ml) water
1 1/2 cups (375 ml) chopped carrots
1 cup (250 ml) chopped onion
1 cup (250 ml) diced cooked ham
1 bay leaf
Salt & pepper

Combine dried peas and water in a large stainless steel saucepan. Bring to a boil; reduce heat, cover and boil gently until peas are soft, about 1 hour. If desired, purée mixture and return to saucepan. Add carrots, onion, ham and bay leaf; boil gently 30 minutes. If soup is very thick, thin with boiling water. ◀◀◀

Yield: 5 x 500 ml jars or 2 x 1 L jars. Heat process 500 ml jars – **75 minutes**; 1 L jars – **90 minutes** at 10 lb (68 kPa) in weighted gauge pressure canner.

Stock your pantry with jars of homemade ready-to-heat entrées that have seasonings adjusted to your family's preference.

Pressure canned
ENTRÉES IN A JAR

• Place the required number of clean mason jars on rack in pressure canner or large saucepan; add water and heat jars to a simmer (180°F/82°C). Set screw bands aside; heat SNAP Lids in hot water, NOT boiling (180°F/82°C). Keep jars and SNAP Lids hot until ready to use.

 Measure and prepare ingredients as specified in individual recipes.

▶▶▶ *Ladle hot prepared recipe into a hot jar to within 1 inch (2.5 cm) of top rim (headspace).*

• Using nonmetallic utensil, remove air bubbles. Wipe jar rim removing any stickiness. Centre SNAP Lid on jar; apply screw band *securely & firmly until resistance is met – fingertip tight. Do not overtighten.* Place jar in canner; repeat for remaining recipe. *If stacking jars, place a second rack between layers of jars.*

• When pressure canner is full, adjust water to level as directed by canner manufacturer. Lock canner lid in place and follow manufacturer's heating instructions. Vent canner – *allow steam to escape steadily* – for 10 minutes; close vent.

• When canner reaches the pressure appropriate for your altitude and type of pressure canner, begin counting processing time. Process – *heat filled jars* – **in pressure canner for time indicated for jar size in each recipe.** NOTE: processing times indicated in each recipe are for weighted gauge pressure canners used at altitudes up to 1,000 ft (305 m). When canning at higher elevations, adjust pressure according to chart on page 12.

• When processing time is complete turn off heat. *Allow canner to stand undisturbed until pressure drops to zero.* Wait 2 minutes, and then remove cover, tilting it away from your face. Remove jars without tilting. Cool upright, undisturbed 24 hours; DO NOT RETIGHTEN screw bands. After cooling check jar seals. *Sealed lids curve downward.* Remove screw bands; wipe and dry bands and jars. Store screw bands separately or replace loosely on jars, as desired. Label and store in a cool, dark place.

BAKED BEANS

4 cups (1000 ml) dried pea or navy beans
8 oz (225 g) salt pork, cut into pieces
3 large onions, chopped
2/3 cup (150 ml) lightly packed brown sugar
2 tsp (10 ml) *Each:* salt & dry mustard
2/3 cup (150 ml) molasses

Cover beans with cold water; let stand 12 to 18 hours in a cool place. Drain beans; cover with 12 cups (3000 ml) water; bring to a boil. Reduce heat, cover and boil gently until bean skins begin to crack. Drain, reserving liquid. Pour beans into a baking dish; add salt pork and onions. Combine brown sugar, salt, mustard and molasses with 4 cups (1000 ml) reserved cooking liquid. (Add water if needed to meet this measure.) Pour sauce over beans; cover and bake at 350°F (180°C) about 3 1/2 hours. To home can Baked Beans, mixture must be "soupy". If necessary, add water. Ladle beans and liquid into jars. ◀◀◀

Yield: 6 x 500 ml or 3 x 1 L jars. Heat process 500 ml jars – **80 minutes;** 1 L jars – **95 minutes** at 10 lb (68 kPa) in weighted gauge pressure canner.

GOULASH

4 lb (1.8 kg) lean, boned beef chuck or pork leg roast
1 tbsp (15 ml) salt
3 tbsp (45 ml) paprika
2 tsp (10 ml) dry mustard
1/3 cup (75 ml) vegetable oil
1 1/2 cups (375 ml) water
20 peppercorns
3 bay leaves
2 tsp (10 ml) caraway seeds, *optional*
6 stalks celery, cut in half
4 large carrots, cut in half
3 medium onions, cut in half
1/3 cup (75 ml) vinegar

Cut meat into 1-inch (2.5 cm) cubes. Combine salt, paprika and dry mustard. Coat meat with spice mixture. Heat half of oil in heavy frypan. Working in small batches, brown meat cubes and transfer to large stainless steel saucepan. When all meat is browned, add water to frypan pan. Cook and stir to loosen any bits from frypan; add to meat along with any excess spices. Tie whole spices in cheesecloth square creating a spice bag. Add spice bag to meat with celery, carrots, onion and vinegar. Stirring constantly, bring mixture to a boil. Reduce heat, cover and cook slowly, stirring occasionally, until meat is tender. Discard spice bag and vegetables. ◀◀◀

Yield: 4 x 500 ml or 2 x 1 L jars. Heat process 500 ml jars – **75 minutes;** 1 L jars – **90 minutes** at 10 lb (68 kPa) in weighted gauge pressure canner.

BEANS WITH PORK & TOMATO SAUCE

4 cups (1000 ml) dried navy beans, about 2 lb/900 g
4 cups (1000 ml) tomato juice
1 cup (250 ml) chopped onion, about 1 medium
3 tbsp (45 ml) sugar
2 tsp (10 ml) salt
1/4 tsp (1 ml) *Each:* cloves & allspice
1/4 lb (125 g) salt pork, cut into equal pieces

Cover beans with cold water; let stand 12 to 18 hours in a cool place. Drain beans; cover with boiling water by 2 inches (5 cm); boil 3 minutes. Remove from heat; let stand 10 minutes; drain.

• Combine tomato juice, onion, sugar, salt and spices; heat to boiling.

• Pack 1 cup (250 ml) beans into a hot jar. Top with a piece of salt pork; fill jar 3/4 full with beans. Ladle hot tomato sauce to cover beans to within 1 inch (2.5 cm) of top rim (headspace). ◀◀◀

Yield: 6 x 500 ml or 3 x 1 L jars. Heat process 500 ml jars – **65 minutes**; 1 L jars – **75 minutes** at 10 lb (68 kPa) in weighted gauge pressure canner.

BEEF IN WINE SAUCE

2 lb (1 kg) round steak, cut into 1 inch (2.5 cm) cubes
1 tbsp (15 ml) vegetable oil
1 cup (250 ml) *Each:* shredded apples & shredded carrots
3/4 cup (175 ml) sliced onion
3/4 cup (175 ml) water, divided
1/2 cup (125 ml) dry red wine
1 tsp (5 ml) salt
2 cloves garlic, minced
2 beef bouillon cubes
2 bay leaves
5 tsp (25 ml) cornstarch
1/2 tsp (2 ml) browning & seasoning sauce (Kitchen Bouquet), *optional*

Brown meat in vegetable oil. Add apple, carrot, onion, 1/2 cup (125 ml) water, wine, salt, garlic, bouillon cubes and bay leaves. Boil gently 1 hour. Discard bay leaves.

• Combine cornstarch and remaining 1/4 cup (50 ml) water; stir into hot beef mixture. Cook until mixture begins to thicken. Add browning and seasoning sauce, if using. ◀◀◀

Yield: 3 x 500 ml or 1 x 1 L jars. Heat process 500 ml jars – **75 minutes**; 1 L jars – **90 minutes** at 10 lb (68 kPa) in weighted gauge pressure canner.

HEARTY CHILI

AT SERVING TIME, ADD COOKED OR CANNED PINTO OR KIDNEY BEANS; HEAT AND SERVE. TO ADJUST THE "HEAT" IN THIS RECIPE, INCREASE OR DECREASE THE QUANTITY OF RED PEPPER FLAKES.

4 lb (1.8 kg) boneless beef chuck
1/4 cup (50 ml) vegetable oil
3 cups (750 ml) diced onion
2 cloves garlic, minced
5 tbsp (75 ml) chili powder
2 tsp (10 ml) *Each:* cumin seed & salt
1 tsp (5 ml) oregano
1/2 tsp (2 ml) *Each:* pepper, coriander, crushed red pepper flakes
6 cups (1500 ml) undrained & chopped canned tomatoes

Cut meat into 1/2 inch (1 cm) cubes, removing excess fat. Lightly brown in hot oil. Add onions and garlic, cook until soft but not brown. Add remaining spices and cook for 5 minutes. Stir in tomatoes. Boil gently 45 to 60 minutes, stirring occasionally. ◀◀◀

Yield: 6 x 500 ml or 3 x 1 L jars. Heat process 500 ml jars – **75 minutes**; 1 L jars – **90 minutes** at 10 lb (68 kPa) in weighted gauge pressure canner.

BEEF STEW WITH VEGETABLES

4-5 lb (1.8-2.3 kg) stew beef
1 tbsp (15 ml) vegetable oil
12 cups (3000 ml) cubed, peeled potatoes
8 cups (2000 ml) sliced carrots
3 cups (750 ml) *Each:* chopped celery & onions
4 tsp (20 ml) salt
1 tsp (5 ml) thyme
1/2 tsp (2 ml) pepper

Cut meat into 1 1/2 inch (3 cm) cubes; brown in oil. Combine meat, vegetables and seasonings in a large stainless steel saucepan. Cover with boiling water; stirring frequently bring mixture to a boil. ◀◀◀

Yield: 14 x 500 ml or 7 x 1 L jars. Heat process 500 ml jars – **75 minutes**; 1 L jars – **90 minutes** at 10 lb (68 kPa) in weighted gauge pressure canner.

Make-ahead foods are the perfect saviour for time-pressed cooks. Serve versatile sauces with pasta, potatoes or rice. Or, add more ingredients to make easy one-dish meals.

Pressure canned
SAVOURY SAUCES

• Place the required number of clean mason jars on rack in pressure canner or large saucepan; add water and heat jars to a simmer (180°F/82°C). Set screw bands aside; heat SNAP Lids in hot water, NOT boiling (180°F/82°C). Keep jars and SNAP Lids hot until ready to use.

 Measure and prepare ingredients as specified in individual recipes.

▶▶▶ *Ladle hot prepared sauce into a hot jar to within 1 inch (2.5 cm) of top rim (headspace).*

• Using nonmetallic utensil, remove air bubbles. Wipe jar rim removing any stickiness. Centre SNAP Lid on jar; apply screw band *securely & firmly* *until resistance is met – fingertip tight. Do not overtighten.* Place jar in canner; repeat for remaining sauce. *If stacking jars, place a second rack between layers of jars.*

• When pressure canner is full, adjust water to level as directed by canner manufacturer. Lock canner lid in place and follow manufacturer's heating instructions. Vent canner – *allow steam to escape steadily* – for 10 minutes; close vent.

• When canner reaches the pressure appropriate for your altitude and type of pressure canner, begin counting processing time. Process – *heat filled jars* – **in pressure canner for time indicated for jar size in each recipe.** NOTE: processing times indicated in each recipe are for weighted gauge pressure canners used at altitudes up to 1,000 ft (305 m). When canning at higher elevations, adjust pressure according to chart on page 12.

• When processing time is complete turn off heat. *Allow canner to stand undisturbed until pressure drops to zero.* Wait 2 minutes, and then remove cover, tilting it away from your face. Remove jars without tilting. Cool upright, undisturbed 24 hours; DO NOT RETIGHTEN screw bands. After cooling check jar seals. *Sealed lids curve downward.* Remove screw bands; wipe and dry bands and jars. Store screw bands separately or replace loosely on jars, as desired. Label and store in a cool, dark place.

SPAGHETTI SAUCE WITH MEAT

30 lb (13.5 kg) tomatoes
2 1/2 lb (1125 g) ground beef or sausage
5 cloves garlic, minced
1 cup (250 ml) *Each:* chopped onion, green pepper or celery
1 lb (454 g) fresh mushrooms sliced, *optional*
2 tbsp (30 ml) dried oregano
4 tbsp (60 ml) chopped parsley
4 tsp (20 ml) salt
2 tsp (10 ml) black pepper
1/4 cup (50 ml) brown sugar

Core and quarter tomatoes. Boil 20 minutes, uncovered in a large stainless steel saucepan. Put through sieve or food mill to remove seeds and skins. Return tomato sauce to large saucepan.

• Sauté meat until it looses pink colour. Add garlic, onion, green pepper or celery, and mushrooms, if using. Add meat mixture and brown sugar to tomatoes; bring to a boil. Boil 5 minutes. Adjust seasonings to taste. ◀◀◀

Yield: 9 x 500 ml or 5 x 1 L jars. Heat process 500 ml jars – **60 minutes**; 1 L jars – **70 minutes** at 10 lb (68 kPa) in weighted gauge pressure canner.

MEAT SAUCE

5 lb (2.3 kg) lean ground beef or pork
2 cups (500 ml) chopped onions
1 cup (250 ml) chopped green pepper
9 cups (2250 ml) canned or cooked tomatoes, including juice
2 2/3 cups (650 ml) tomato paste
1/4 cup (50 ml) chopped parsley
2 tbsp (25 ml) brown sugar
4 tsp (20 ml) salt
1 tbsp (15 ml) dried herbs, such as oregano, basil, thyme
1/2 tsp (2 ml) *Each:* pepper, ginger & allspice
2 tbsp (25 ml) vinegar

In large frypan, brown meat in small batches. Drain off excess fat and transfer meat to large stainless steel saucepan. Add onions and pepper to meat; cook and stir until vegetables are tender crisp. Stir in remaining ingredients; cook and stir until mixture boils. Continue cooking until sauce reduces slightly. Skim off excess fat, if necessary. ◀◀◀

Yield: 6 x 500 ml or 3 x 1 L jars. Heat process 500 ml jars – **60 minutes**; 1 L jars – **75 minutes** at 10 lb (68 kPa) in weighted gauge pressure canner.

Homemade stock is easy and economical to make – unfortunately, once made it has a limited shelf-life unless canned or frozen. Jars of stock are handy time-savers year round.

Pressure canned
STOCK

- Place the required number of clean mason jars on rack in pressure canner or large saucepan; add water and heat jars to a simmer (180°F/82°C). Set screw bands aside; heat SNAP Lids in hot water, NOT boiling (180°F/82°C). Keep jars and SNAP Lids hot until ready to use.

Measure and prepare ingredients as specified in individual recipes.

▶ ▶ ▶ *Ladle hot stock into a hot jar to within 1 inch (2.5 cm) of top rim (headspace).* Using nonmetallic utensil, remove air bubbles.

- Wipe jar rim removing any stickiness. Centre SNAP Lid on jar; apply screw band *securely & firmly until resistance is met – fingertip tight. Do not overtighten.* Place jar in canner; repeat for remaining stock. *If stacking jars, place a second rack between layers of jars.*

- When pressure canner is full, adjust water to level as directed by canner manufacturer. Lock canner lid in place and follow manufacturer's heating instructions. Vent canner *– allow steam to escape steadily –* for 10 minutes; close vent.

- When canner reaches the pressure appropriate for your altitude and type of pressure canner, begin counting processing time. Process *– heat filled jars –* **in pressure canner for time indicated for jar size in each recipe.** NOTE: processing times indicated in each recipe are for weighted gauge pressure canners used at altitudes up to 1,000 ft (305 m). When canning at higher elevations, adjust pressure according to chart on page 12.

- When processing time is complete turn off heat. *Allow canner to stand undisturbed until pressure drops to zero.* Wait 2 minutes, and then remove cover, tilting it away from your face. Remove jars without tilting. Cool upright, undisturbed 24 hours; DO NOT RETIGHTEN screw bands. After cooling check jar seals. *Sealed lids curve downward.* Remove screw bands; wipe and dry bands and jars. Store screw bands separately or replace loosely on jars, as desired. Label and store in a cool, dark place.

BEEF STOCK

4 lb (1.8 kg) meaty beef bones
16 cups (4000 ml) water
1 *Each:* bay leaf, onion, chopped; carrot and celery stalk, sliced
Beef bouillon cubes or granules, *optional*
Salt

Combine bones and water in large stainless steel saucepan. Bring to a boil over high heat; reduce heat and skim foam. Add vegetables; cover and simmer 2 to 3 hours. For stronger flavour, simmer longer or add bouillon. Remove bones, strain liquid and skim excess fat from top of stock. Season to taste with salt. Reheat stock and ladle into jars. ◀ ◀ ◀
Yield: 4 x 500 ml or 2 x 1 L jars. Heat process 500 ml jars **– 20 minutes;** 1 L jars **– 25 minutes** at 10 lb (68 kPa) in weighted gauge pressure canner.

CHICKEN STOCK

3 to 4 lb (1.4 to 1.8 kg) chicken
16 cups (4000 ml) water
2 *Each:* bay leaves; celery stalks and onions, quartered
10 peppercorns
Salt

Combine chicken and water in large stainless steel saucepan. Bring to a boil over high heat; reduce heat and skim foam. Add vegetables; cover and simmer 2 hours or until chicken is well cooked. Remove chicken reserving meat for another use. Strain liquid through cheesecloth lined sieve. Cool and skim excess fat from top of stock. Reheat stock; season to taste with salt, and ladle into jars. ◀ ◀ ◀
Yield: 4 x 500 ml or 2 x 1 L jars. Heat process 500 ml jars **– 20 minutes;** 1 L jars **– 25 minutes** at 10 lb (68 kPa) in weighted gauge pressure canner.

VEGETABLE STOCK

1 lb (454 g) carrots, cut into small pieces
6 stalks celery, cut into small pieces
3 medium onions, quartered
2 *Each:* red peppers, coarsely chopped; large tomatoes, seeded & chopped; medium turnips, finely chopped
3 cloves garlic, crushed
3 bay leaves
1 tsp (5 ml) thyme and 8 peppercorns
28 cups (7000 ml) water

Combine all ingredients in a large stainless steel saucepan. Bring to a boil; reduce heat. Cover, boil gently 2 hours. Uncover, cook 2 hours longer. Strain stock through a cheesecloth lined strainer. Discard vegetables and seasonings. Reheat stock and ladle into jars. ◀ ◀ ◀
Yield: 8 x 500 ml or 4 x 1 L jars. Heat process 500 ml jars **– 30 minutes;** 1 L jars **– 35 minutes** at 10 lb (68 kPa) in weighted gauge pressure canner.

Like all prepared foods, the flavour and texture of home canned meats and poultry is largely dependent upon the quality of the original product. Always start with top quality, fresh meat or poultry.

Pressure canned
MEATS & POULTRY

• Place the required number of clean mason jars on rack in pressure canner or large saucepan; add water and heat jars to a simmer (180°F/82°C). Set screw bands aside; heat SNAP Lids in hot water, NOT boiling (180°F/82°C). Keep jars and SNAP Lids hot until ready to use.

 Prepare meat or poultry as directed in individual recipes.

▶▶▶ *Pack prepared meat into a hot jar to within 1 1/4 inch (3 cm) of top rim.* Add hot cooking liquid or broth to within 1 inch (2.5 cm) of top rim (headspace).

• If desired, season each jar with salt: 1/2 tsp (2 ml) per 500 ml jar; 1 tsp (5 ml) per 1 L jar.

• Using nonmetallic utensil, remove air bubbles. Wipe jar rim removing any stickiness. Centre SNAP Lid on jar; apply screw band **securely & firmly** *until resistance is met – fingertip tight. Do not overtighten.* Place jar in canner; repeat for remaining meat. *If stacking jars, place a second rack between layers of jars.*

• When pressure canner is full, adjust water to level as directed by canner manufacturer. Lock canner lid in place and follow manufacturer's heating instructions. Vent canner – *allow steam to escape steadily* – for 10 minutes; close vent.

• When canner reaches the pressure appropriate for your altitude and type of pressure canner, begin counting processing time. Process – *heat filled jars* – **in pressure canner for time indicated for jar size and specific recipe.** NOTE: processing times indicated in each recipe are for weighted gauge pressure canners used at altitudes up to 1,000 ft (305 m). When canning at higher elevations, adjust pressure according to chart on page 12.

• When processing time is complete turn off heat. *Allow canner to stand undisturbed until pressure drops to zero.* Wait 2 minutes, and then remove cover, tilting it away from your face. Remove jars without tilting. Cool upright, undisturbed 24 hours; DO NOT RETIGHTEN screw bands. After cooling check jar seals. *Sealed lids curve downward.* Remove screw bands; wipe and dry bands and jars. Store screw bands separately or replace loosely on jars, as desired. Label and store in a cool, dark place.

CHOPPED MEAT – BEEF, PORK, VEAL, LAMB, MUTTON

Grind fresh meat. Sear meat in hot skillet. For each 4 cups (1000 ml) seared meat, add 1 to 1 1/2 cups (250-375 ml) boiling water, broth or tomato juice. Pack hot meat into hot jars. Season, add hot liquid. ◀◀◀
Heat process 500 ml jars – **75 minutes**; 1 L jars – **90 minutes** at 10 lb (68 kPa) in weighted gauge pressure canner.

PORK SAUSAGE

Grind fresh pork. Season pork to taste with spices and herbs such as salt, black pepper, cayenne pepper, thyme, oregano and basil. (As a seasoning, avoid sage because it can become bitter during storage.) Shape mixture into patties or 3- to 4-inch (7-10 cm) links. Cook until lightly browned. Drain. Pack hot sausage into hot jars. Season, add hot broth. ◀◀◀
Heat process 500 ml jars – **75 minutes**; 1 L jars – **90 minutes** at 10 lb (68 kPa) in weighted gauge pressure canner.

PORK TENDERLOIN

RAW PACK – Slice pork tenderloin across grain into 1/2 to 1-inch (1 to 2 cm) pieces. Pack tenderloin into hot jars. Season, add hot broth. ◀◀◀
Heat process 500 ml jars – **75 minutes**; 1 L jars – **90 minutes** at 10 lb (68 kPa) in weighted gauge pressure canner.

HOT PACK – Cook whole tenderloin until a third to half done. Slice tenderloin across grain into 1/2 to 1-inch (1 to 2 cm) pieces. Pack hot tenderloin pieces into hot jars. Season, add hot broth. ◀◀◀
Heat process 500 ml jars – **75 minutes**; 1 L jars – **90 minutes** at 10 lb (68 kPa) in weighted gauge pressure canner.

ROAST – BEEF, PORK, VEAL, VENISON, LAMB, MUTTON

Cut meat into 1/2 to 1-inch (1 to 2 cm) thick jar-length strips. Roast meat until well browned but not done. Meat also may be browned in a small quantity of fat. Pack hot meat into hot jars. Season, add hot broth. ◀◀◀
Heat process 500 ml jars – **75 minutes**; 1 L jars – **90 minutes** at 10 lb (68 kPa) in weighted gauge pressure canner.

STEAKS AND CHOPS – BEEF, PORK, VEAL, VENISON, LAMB, MUTTON

RAW PACK – Cut meat into 1-inch (2.5 cm) slices. Remove large bones. Pack meat into hot jars. Season, add hot broth. ◀◀◀
Heat process 500 ml jars – **75 minutes**; 1 L jars – **90 minutes** at 10 lb (68 kPa) in weighted gauge pressure canner.

HOT PACK – Cut meat into 1-inch (2.5 cm) slices. Remove large bones. Quickly sear meat until browned in a small quantity of fat. Pack hot meat into hot jars. Season, add hot broth. ◀◀◀
Heat process 500 ml jars – **75 minutes**; 1 L jars – **90 minutes** at 10 lb (68 kPa) in weighted gauge pressure canner.

SPARERIBS

Crack ribs evenly. Cook until about half done. Remove bones. Cut meat into squares. Pack hot meat into hot jars. Season, add hot broth. ◀◀◀
Heat process 500 ml jars – **75 minutes**; 1 L jars – **90 minutes** at 10 lb (68 kPa) in weighted gauge pressure canner.

STEW MEAT

Use beef, pork or other suitable meats for stewing. Cut into 1 1/2 to 2-inch (3 to 5 cm) cubes. Remove fat and gristle. Place meat in saucepan, cover with water; heat and stir until meat is heated through. Pack hot meat into hot jars. Season, add hot broth. ◀◀◀
Heat process 500 ml jars – **75 minutes**; 1 L jars – **90 minutes** at 10 lb (68 kPa) in weighted gauge pressure canner.

POULTRY – CHICKEN, DUCK, GOOSE, TURKEY, GAME BIRDS

ONE TO TWO-YEAR OLD FOWL IS BEST FOR HOME CANNING. WASH FOWL THOROUGHLY, REMOVE ENTRAILS AND WASH AGAIN. CUT INTO PIECES. RINSE AND DRY BUT DO NOT SALT. CHILL 6 TO 12 HOURS BEFORE CANNING.

RAW PACK – Separate bird into pieces at joints. Leave bones in or debone as desired. Pack meat into hot jars. Season, add hot broth. ◀◀◀
Heat process DEBONED MEAT 500 ml jars – **75 minutes**; 1 L jars – **90 minutes** at 10 lb (68 kPa) in weighted gauge pressure canner; BONE-IN MEAT 500 ml jars – **65 minutes**; 1 L jars – **75 minutes** at 10 lb (68 kPa) in weighted gauge pressure canner.

HOT PACK – Boil, steam or bake poultry or game bird until about two-thirds done. Separate into pieces at joints. Leave bones in or debone as desired. Pack hot meat into hot jars. Season, add hot broth. ◀◀◀
Heat process DEBONED MEAT 500 ml jars – **75 minutes**; 1 L jars – **90 minutes** at 10 lb (68 kPa) in weighted gauge pressure canner; BONE-IN MEAT 500 ml jars – **65 minutes**; 1 L jars – **75 minutes** at 10 lb (68 kPa) in weighted gauge pressure canner.

BROTH FOR HOME CANNED MEAT

Remove meat from cooking pan. Add 1 cup (250 ml) boiling water or broth for each 2 tbsp (25 ml) fat in pan. Boil 2 to 3 minutes. Do not add thickening agent such as flour or cornstarch before canning. Thicken liquids only when prepared for serving.

Regardless of your choice or source of vegetables – they are all low acid foods. A pressure canner is the essential piece of equipment required to safely heat process all home canned vegetables.

Pressure canned
VEGETABLES

• Place the required number of clean mason jars on rack in pressure canner or large saucepan; add water and heat jars to a simmer (180°F/82°C). Set screw bands aside; heat SNAP Lids in hot water, NOT boiling (180°F/82°C). Keep jars and SNAP Lids hot until ready to use.

Prepare vegetables as directed in individual recipes using your choice of **RAW PACK** and **HOT PACK** methods, where available.

▶▶▶ *Pack prepared vegetables into a hot jar to within 1 1/4 inch (3 cm) of top rim.*

• If desired season each jar with salt: 1/4 tsp (1 ml) per 250 ml jar; 1/2 tsp (2 ml) per 500 ml jar; 1 tsp (5 ml) per 1 L jar.

RAW PACK vegetables, add boiling water to cover vegetables to within 1 inch (2.5 cm) of top rim (headspace).

HOT PACK vegetables, add hot cooking liquid or fresh boiling water as specified in individual vegetable directions to within 1 inch (2.5 cm) of top rim (headspace).

• Using nonmetallic utensil, remove air bubbles. Wipe jar rim removing any stickiness. Centre SNAP Lid on jar; apply screw band *securely & firmly until resistance is met – fingertip tight. Do not overtighten.* Place jar in canner; repeat for remaining vegetables. *If stacking jars, place a second rack between layers of jars.*

• When pressure canner is full, adjust water to level as directed by canner manufacturer. Lock canner lid in place and follow manufacturer's heating instructions. Vent canner – *allow steam to escape steadily* – for 10 minutes; close vent.

• When canner reaches the pressure appropriate for your altitude and type of pressure canner, begin counting processing time. Process – *heat filled jars* – **in pressure canner for time indicated for specific vegetable and jar size.** NOTE: processing times indicated in each recipe are for weighted gauge pressure canners used at altitudes up to 1,000 ft (305 m). When canning at higher elevations, adjust pressure according to chart on page 12.

• When processing time is complete turn off heat. *Allow canner to stand undisturbed until pressure drops to zero.* Wait 2 minutes, and then remove cover, tilting it away from your face. Remove jars without tilting. Cool upright, undisturbed 24 hours; DO NOT RETIGHTEN screw bands. After cooling check jar seals. *Sealed lids curve downward.* Remove screw bands; wipe and dry bands and jars. Store screw bands separately or replace loosely on jars, as desired. Label and store in a cool, dark place.

ASPARAGUS

For each 1 L jar, select 3 1/2 lb (1.6 kg) tender-tipped spears, 4 to 6 inches (10 to 15 cm) long. Wash, trim off tough scales. Break off tough stem ends; wash again. Cut into pieces or pack whole.

RAW PACK – Pack asparagus – whole or cut into 1-inch (2.5 cm) pieces – as tightly as possible without crushing into hot jars. Ladle boiling water over asparagus. ◀◀◀

Heat process 500 ml jars – **30 minutes**; 1 L jars – **40 minutes** at 10 lb (68 kPa) in weighted gauge pressure canner.

HOT PACK – Cut asparagus into 1-inch (2.5 cm) pieces. Boil 3 minutes. Pack hot asparagus into hot jars and cover with hot cooking liquid. ◀◀◀

Heat process 500 ml jars – **30 minutes**; 1 L jars – **40 minutes** at 10 lb (68 kPa) in weighted gauge pressure canner.

BEANS – GREEN, SNAP & WAXED

Select young, tender crisp beans only. Discard diseased or rusted beans. Wash beans; drain. Remove string, trim ends; break or cut freshly gathered beans into 2-inch (5 cm) pieces.

RAW PACK – Tightly pack beans into hot jars. Season, add liquid & close jars as directed in Basic Recipe. ◀◀◀

HOT PACK – Place beans in saucepan; cover with water. Bring to a boil; boil 5 minutes. Pack hot beans into hot jars. Season, add liquid. ◀◀◀

Heat process RAW OR HOT PACKED 500 ml jars – **20 minutes**; 1 L jars – **25 minutes** at 10 lb (68 kPa) in weighted gauge pressure canner.

BEETS

Use firm, ripe freshly harvested beets with roots intact to prevent bleeding. Trim tops, leaving root and 2 inches (5 cm) stem. Scrub well. Place in saucepan; cover with boiling water; boil until skins slip off easily. Rinse in cold water; remove skins, trim off stems and roots. Pack baby beets whole, slice or cube medium or large beets. Season, add liquid. ◀◀◀

Heat process 500 ml jars – **30 minutes**; 1 L jars – **35 minutes** at 10 lb (68 kPa) in weighted gauge pressure canner.

CARROTS

Use small carrots 1 to 1 1/4 inches (2.5 to 3 cm) in diameter. Larger carrots may be fibrous. Wash, peel and rewash carrots. Slice, dice or leave small carrots whole. Place in saucepan, cover with water.

RAW PACK – Tightly pack carrots into hot jars. Season, add liquid & close jars as directed in Basic Recipe. ◀◀◀

HOT PACK – Place carrots in saucepan; cover with water. Bring to a boil; boil 5 minutes. Pack hot carrots into hot jars. Season, add liquid. ◀◀◀

Heat process RAW OR HOT PACKED 500 ml jars – **25 minutes**; 1 L jars – **30 minutes** at 10 lb (68 kPa) in weighted gauge pressure canner.

CORN – CREAM STYLE

Use ideal eating quality ears with slightly immature kernels. Husk corn, remove silk and wash ears. Blanch 4 minutes in boiling water. Cut corn from cob at center of kernel leaving tip ends. Scrape cob to extract pulp and milk. Measure kernels, pulp and milk together. For each 2 cups (500 ml), add 1 cup (250 ml) water. Bring to a boil; reduce heat, boil gently 3 minutes. Ladle corn and liquid into 500 ml jars; do not use 1 L jars. Season and close as directed in Basic Recipe. ◀◀◀

Heat process 500 ml jars – **85 minutes** at 10 lb (68 kPa) in weighted gauge pressure canner.

LEGUMES – DRIED BEANS OR PEAS

For each 1 L jar, select 2 1/4 lb (1 kg) dried beans such as kidney, navy, pinto. Wash legumes thoroughly, discarding any shriveled or discoloured beans. Place beans or peas in a large stainless steel saucepan; cover with cold water. Let stand 12 to 18 hours in a cool place. Drain. Cover soaked beans with 2 inches (5 cm) fresh water. Bring to a boil; boil 30 minutes stirring frequently. Pack hot beans into hot jars. Season, ladle hot cooking liquid over beans. ◀◀◀

Heat process 500 ml jars – 75 minutes; 1 L jars – **90 minutes** at 10 lb (68 kPa) in weighted gauge pressure canner.

Use only jar sizes recommended for each vegetable.

CORN – WHOLE KERNEL

Use ideal eating quality ears with slightly immature kernels. The sugar content in ears of some varieties of immature corn can cause browning. Husk corn, remove silk & wash ears.

RAW PACK – Cut kernels from cob; do not scrape. Pack kernels loosely into jars. Season & add liquid. ◀◀◀

Heat process 500 ml jars – **55 minutes**; 1 L jars – **85 minutes** at 10 lb (68 kPa) in weighted gauge pressure canner.

HOT PACK – Cut corn from cob; do not scrape cob. Measure corn into saucepan. For each 4 cups (1 L) corn add 1 cup (250 ml) water. Bring to boil; reduce heat, boil gently 5 minutes. Pack loosely into hot jars. Season, add liquid. ◀◀◀

Heat process 500 ml jars – **55 minutes**; 1 L jars – **85 minutes** at 10 lb (68 kPa) in weighted gauge pressure canner.

MIXED VEGETABLES

7 cups (1750 ml) *Each:* **sliced carrots, corn kernels and lima beans**

6 cups (1500 ml) cubed zucchini

1 cup (250 ml) chopped red pepper

Combine vegetables in a large stainless steel saucepan; add water to cover. Boil vegetables 5 minutes. Pack hot vegetables into hot jars. Season, add liquid. ◀◀◀

Heat process 500 ml jars – **75 minutes**; 1 L jars – **90 minutes** at 10 lb (68 kPa) in weighted gauge pressure canner.

MUSHROOMS, CULTIVATED

Do not home can wild mushrooms. Clean dirt from mushrooms with a soft brush. Rinse under cold water. Trim stem ends. Leave small mushrooms whole; cut large mushrooms in half. Place mushrooms in a stainless steel saucepan; add water to cover. Bring to a boil; boil 5 minutes. Pack hot mushrooms into 250 ml or 500 ml jars only. Do not use larger volume jars. Add hot cooking liquid. ◀◀◀

Heat process 250 and 500 ml jars – **45 minutes** at 10 lb (68 kPa) in weighted gauge pressure canner.

PEAS, GREEN OR ENGLISH, SHELLED

Select well filled pods containing young, tender, and sweet peas. Shell peas; wash again.
RAW PACK – Pack peas loosely into hot jars; do not shake or press down. Season, add liquid & close jars as directed in Basic Recipe. ◄◄◄
Heat process 500 ml or 1 L jars – **40 minutes** at 10 lb (68 kPa) in weighted gauge pressure canner.
HOT PACK – Place peas in a large stainless steel saucepan. Cover with water. Bring to boil; boil small peas (less than 1/4 inch/0.5 cm) 3 minutes; medium peas, 5 minutes. Drain; rinse in hot water; drain again. Pack hot peas into hot jars. Season, add fresh boiling water. ◄◄◄
Heat process 500 ml or 1 L jars – **40 minutes** at 10 lb (68 kPa) in weighted gauge pressure canner.

PEPPERS – SWEET GREEN

Select mature, firm peppers. Wash peppers; remove stem and seeds and cut into quarters. Place in a stainless steel saucepan; cover with water. Bring to a boil; boil 3 minutes. Drain. Pack peppers into 250 ml or 500 ml jars only. Do not use larger jars. Add 1 1/2 tsp (7 ml) vinegar to each 250 ml jar; 1 tbsp (15 ml) vinegar to each 500 ml jar. Season, add fresh boiling water. ◄◄◄
Heat process 250 ml or 500 ml jars – **35 minutes** at 10 lb (68 kPa) in weighted gauge pressure canner.

POTATOES, SWEET

Use small to medium sweet potatoes that are mature but not too fibrous. Can within 1 to 2 months of harvest. Do not mash or purée sweet potatoes. Wash; drain. Boil or steam potatoes until peel can be easily removed and potatoes are partially soft. Peel and cut into uniform pieces. Pack hot potatoes into hot jars. Season, add fresh boiling water. ◄◄◄
Heat process 500 ml jars – **65 minutes**; 1 L jars – **90 minutes** at 10 lb (68 kPa) in weighted gauge pressure canner.

> *Processing times are for weighted gauge pressure canners at 10 lb (68 kPa) at altitudes up to 1,000 ft (305 m).*
> *For dial gauge canners or higher elevations, see page 12.*

POTATOES, WHITE

Use small to medium mature potatoes. Tubers stored below 45°F (7°C) may discolour when canned. Wash, peel and wash again. Potatoes 1 to 2 inches (2.5 to 5 cm) in diameter may be packed whole. Cut larger potatoes into small uniform cubes. Place in colour protection solution (see page 38); drain. Place in stainless steel saucepan; cover with water. Bring to boil; boil small cubes 2 minutes and small potatoes 10 minutes. Drain. Pack hot potatoes into hot jars. Season, add fresh boiling water. ◄◄◄
Heat process 500 ml jars – **35 minutes**; 1 L jars – **40 minutes** at 10 lb (68 kPa) in weighted gauge canner.

PUMPKIN, SQUASH

Use pumpkins with hard rind & stringless, mature pulp. Small sugar or pie pumpkins give best results. **Do not mash or purée pumpkin or squash.** Wash; remove seeds. Remove peel or rind and cut flesh into 1 inch (2.5 cm) cubes. Place cubes in stainless steel saucepan; cover with boiling water. Bring to a boil; boil 2 minutes. Pack hot cubes loosely into hot jars. Season, add fresh boiling water. ◄◄◄
Heat process 500 ml jars – **55 minutes**; 1 L jars – **90 minutes** at 10 lb (68 kPa) in weighted gauge pressure canner.

TURNIPS, PARSNIPS

Use firm, medium unblemished root vegetables. Wash vegetables; drain. Prepare vegetables as for cooking, peeling and cutting to desired sized pieces. Place prepared vegetables in a large stainless steel saucepan; cover with cold water. Bring to a boil; boil 3 minutes. Pack hot vegetables into hot jars. Season, add liquid. ◄◄◄
Heat process 500 ml jars – **30 minutes**; 1 L jars – **35 minutes** at 10 lb (68 kPa) in weighted gauge pressure canner.
• Parsnips may be canned but freezing results in a better quality product.
• Rutabagas can be canned following above method but usually discolour and tend to develop a strong flavour.

PRESSURE CANNED TOMATOES

WHOLE OR HALVED TOMATOES

For each 1 L jar, select 2 1/2 to 3 1/2 lb (1.1-1.6 kg) tomatoes. Blanch, peel & core tomatoes. Pack whole, halved or quartered into hot jars. See tomato recipe directions, *page 53*.

Acidify tomatoes *(required)*. Season with salt *(optional)*.

PACKED IN WATER

RAW PACK – Pack tomatoes into hot jars leaving **1 inch (2.5 cm) headspace.** Ladle boiling water over tomatoes.

Heat process 500 ml and 1 L jars – **10 minutes** at 10 lb (68 kPa) in weighted gauge pressure canner.

HOT PACK – Place prepared tomatoes in a large stainless steel saucepan; cover with water. Bring to a boil, stirring occasionally. Boil gently 5 minutes. Pack hot tomatoes & cooking liquid into hot jars leaving **1 inch (2.5 cm) headspace.**

Heat process 500 ml and 1 L jars – **10 minutes** at 10 lb (68 kPa) in weighted gauge pressure canner.

PACKED RAW (IN OWN JUICE)

Pack prepared tomatoes into hot jars, pressing gently on tomatoes until natural juice fills the spaces between individual tomatoes. Leave **1 inch (2.5 cm) headspace.**

Heat process 500 ml and 1 L jars – **10 minutes** at 25 lb (68 kPa) in weighted gauge pressure canner.

TO ACIDIFY TOMATOES ADD TO EACH JAR:

Jar size	Citric Acid	Bottled Lemon Juice	Salt *(optional)*
500 ml	1/4 tsp (1 ml)	1 tbsp (15 ml)	1/2 tsp (2 ml)
1 L	1/2 tsp (2 ml)	2 tbsp (25 ml)	1 tsp (5 ml)

Note: 1.5 L jars are not recommended for pressure canning.

TOMATO SAUCE

Prepare sauce as directed on page 54 for boiling water canner. Acidify each jar as directed and ladle hot sauce into hot jars leaving **1 inch (2.5 cm) headspace.**

Heat process 500 ml and 1 L jars – **15 minutes** at 25 lb (68 kPa) in weighted gauge pressure canner.

TOMATO JUICE

Prepare juice as directed on page 55 for boiling water canner. Acidify each jar as directed and ladle hot sauce into hot jars leaving **1 inch (2.5 cm) headspace.**

Heat process 500 ml and 1 L jars – **15 minutes** at 25 lb (68 kPa) in weighted gauge pressure canner.

Prepare freshly caught fish as for cooking. Leave backbone in small fish; debone large fish. Home can fish and seafood in 250 or 500 ml jars only.

Pressure canned
SEAFOOD

BECAUSE SEAFOOD IS VERY LOW IN ACIDITY, HEAT PENETRATION OF LARGE JARS MAY BE INADEQUATE TO DESTROY BACTERIAL SPORES. i.e. DO NOT ATTEMPT TO HOME CAN FISH IN 1 L JARS.

• Place the required number of clean mason jars on rack in pressure canner or large saucepan; add water and heat jars to a simmer (180°F/82°C). If canning chilled fish, do not heat jars.

• Set screw bands aside; heat SNAP Lids in hot water, NOT boiling (180°F/82°C). Keep hot until used.

 Prepare seafood as directed in individual recipes.

▶▶▶ *Pack prepared seafood into prepared mason jar to within 1 inch (2.5 cm) of top rim.* When specified in individual recipe, add liquid or broth indicated in specific recipe to within 1 inch (2.5 cm) of top rim (headspace).

• If desired, season each jar with salt: 1/4 tsp (1 ml) per 250 ml jar; 1/2 tsp (2 ml) per 500 ml jar.

• Using nonmetallic utensil, remove air bubbles. Wipe jar rim removing any stickiness. Centre SNAP Lid on jar; apply screw band **securely & firmly** until resistance is met – fingertip tight. *Do not overtighten.* Place jar in canner; repeat for remaining fish. *If stacking jars, place a second rack between layers of jars.*

• When pressure canner is full, adjust water to level as directed by canner manufacturer. Lock canner lid in place and follow manufacturer's heating instructions. Vent canner – *allow steam to escape steadily* – for 10 minutes; close vent.

• When canner reaches the pressure appropriate for your altitude and type of pressure canner, begin counting processing time. Process – *heat filled jars* – **in pressure canner for time indicated for jar size and specific recipe.** NOTE: processing times indicated in each recipe are for weighted gauge pressure canners used at altitudes up to 1,000 ft (305 m). When canning at higher elevations, adjust pressure according to chart on page 12.

• When processing time is complete turn off heat. *Allow canner to stand undisturbed until pressure drops to zero.* Wait 2 minutes, and then remove cover, tilting it away from your face. Remove jars without tilting. Cool upright, undisturbed 24 hours; DO NOT RETIGHTEN screw bands. After cooling check jar seals. *Sealed lids curve downward.* Remove screw bands; wipe and dry bands and jars. Store screw bands separately or replace loosely on jars, as desired. Label and store in a cool, dark place.

CLAMS

Keep clams alive, moist and chilled until ready to can. Scrub clams. Steam and open shells; remove meat and reserve juice. Discard any clams that do not open. Drop clam meat into salt water brine – 1/2 cup (125 ml) pickling salt dissolved in 16 cups (4000 ml) water. Boil clam meat 2 minutes. Drain. Heat reserved juice. Pack hot clam meat into hot jars. Add hot juice. ◀◀◀
Heat process 250 ml jars – **60 minutes**; 500 ml jars – **70 minutes** at 10 lb (68 kPa) in weighted gauge pressure canner.

CRAB MEAT – KING, DUNGENESS

Keep crabs alive, moist and chilled until ready to can. Wash crabs using several changes of cold water. In a large stainless steel saucepan, bring 16 cups (4000 ml) water to a boil with 1/4 cup (50 ml) bottled lemon juice and 2 tbsp (25 ml) pickling salt. Add crabs; boil 20 minutes. Drain cooked crabs and cool in cold water. Drain.

• Prepare a brine of 16 cups (4000 ml) cold water, 2 tbsp (25 ml) pickling salt plus 4 cups (1000 ml) vinegar or 2 cups (500 ml) bottled lemon juice. Remove back shell; remove meat from body and claws and place crab meat in brine. Soak crab meat 2 minutes.

• Drain, squeezing excess liquid from meat. Pack 6 oz (170 g) crab meat and 2 tbsp (25 ml) bottled lemon juice into each 250 ml jar; 12 oz (340 g) crab and 4 tbsp (60 ml) bottled lemon juice in each 500 ml jar. Remove air bubbles. ◀◀◀
Heat process 250 ml and 500 ml jars – **80 minutes** at 10 lb (68 kPa) in weighted gauge pressure canner.

When canning chilled fish, do not heat jars. Add room temperature water to pressure canner.

FISH – ALL VARIETIES
See separate recipe for Tuna and Salmon

Clean fish within 2 hours after it is caught. Keep cleaned fish chilled until ready to can. Make a brine of 16 cups (4000 ml) water and 1 cup (250 ml) salt. Cut fish into jar-sized pieces. Place in brine and soak 1 hour. Drain 10 minutes. Note: if fish has been refrigerated, do not heat jars prior to filling. Pack fish into prepared jars, skin side next to glass. Do not add liquid. Remove air bubbles. When canning chilled fish, add room temperature water to pressure canner to level specified by manufacturer. ◀◀◀

Heat process 250 ml and 500 ml jars – **100 minutes** at 10 lb (68 kPa) in weighted gauge pressure canner.

OYSTERS

Keep oysters alive and chilled until ready to can. Wash shells. Bake oysters at 400°F (200°C) for 5 to 7 minutes. Quickly cool in ice water. Drain. Remove oyster meat from shells. Wash meat in salt water (1/2 cup/125 ml salt dissolved in 16 cups/4000 ml water). Drain. Pack oysters into hot jars; add hot water. ◀◀◀

Heat process 250 ml and 500 ml jars – **75 minutes** at 10 lb (68 kPa) in weighted gauge pressure canner.

TUNA

RAW PACK – Fillet raw tuna. Remove skin; lightly scrape surface to remove blood vessels and any discoloured flesh. Cut fish into quarters; remove all bones; discard dark flesh. Cut quarters crosswise into jar-sized pieces. Pack fish into prepared mason jars with 1/2 tsp (2 ml) salt for 250 ml jars (double for 500 ml jars). Do not add liquid. ◀◀◀

Heat process 250 ml and 500 ml jars – **100 minutes** at 10 lb (68 kPa) in weighted gauge pressure canner.

HOT PACK – Place cleaned tuna on a rack in a large baking pan. Bake at 350°F (180°C) for 1 hour or until internal temperature reaches 165°-175°F (74°-79°C). Refrigerate overnight. Remove skin and lightly scrape surface to remove blood vessels and any discoloured flesh. Cut fish into quarters, removing all bones. Discard all dark flesh. Cut quarters crosswise into jar-sized pieces. Pack fish into prepared mason jars. Add 1/2 tsp (2 ml) salt and 1 tbsp (15 ml) vegetable oil or water to each 250 ml jar. (Double quantities for 500 ml jars.) Do not add liquid. ◀◀◀

Heat process 250 ml and 500 ml jars – **100 minutes** at 10 lb (68 kPa) in weighted gauge pressure canner.

NOTE: *Crystals of magnesium ammonium phosphate may form in canned tuna. There is no way to prevent crystals from forming but they usually dissolve when tuna is heated. Crystals are safe to eat.*

For safe salmon home canning, please see tips and follow directions carefully. Processing salmon in a pressure canner is essential to eliminate the risk of Botulism. Do not home can salmon in jars larger than 500 ml.

Pressure canned
SALMON

Fresh Salmon

Salt, *optional*

• Use properly eviscerated fish. Chill cleaned fish on ice or refrigerate until ready to can.

• To prepare salmon, remove and discard salmon head, tail and fins. Wash fish carefully removing all blood. (If desired, remove skin and/or bones). Cut fish into pieces suitable for jars.

• Wash required number of clean 250 or 500 ml mason jars.

• Set screw bands aside; heat SNAP Lids in hot water, NOT boiling (180°F/82°C). Keep SNAP Lids hot until ready to use.

• Pack salmon tightly into a clean mason jar to within 1 inch (2.5 cm) of top rim (headspace). If desired, add 1/2 tsp (2 ml) salt per 250 ml jar or 1 tsp (5 ml) salt per 500 ml jar. Using nonmetallic utensil, remove air bubbles.

• Wipe jar rim clean with a wet paper towel moistened with vinegar. (Clean rims are essential to good seals.) Centre SNAP Lid on jar; apply screw band *securely & firmly until resistance is met – fingertip tight. Do not overtighten.* Place jar in canner; repeat for remaining salmon.

• As each jar is filled, set it on rack in pressure canner. Arrange jars allowing space for steam to flow around jars. *If stacking jars, place a second rack between layers of jars.*

• When pressure canner is full, add room temperature water to level directed by canner manufacturer. Lock canner lid in place and follow manufacturer's heating instructions. Vent canner – *allow steam to escape steadily* – for 10 minutes; close vent.

• When canner reaches the pressure appropriate for your altitude and type of pressure canner, begin counting processing time. Process – *heat filled jars* – 250 ml or 500 ml jars **100 minutes** at 10 lb (68 kPa) pressure in weighted gauge pressure canner.

• When processing time is complete turn off heat. *Allow canner to stand undisturbed until pressure drops to zero.* Wait 2 minutes, then remove cover, tilting it away from yourself. Remove jars without tilting. Cool upright, undisturbed 24 hours; DO NOT RETIGHTEN screw bands. After cooling check jar seals. *Sealed lids curve downward.* Remove screw bands; wipe and dry bands and jars. Store screw bands separately or replace loosely on jars, as desired. Label and store in a cool, dark place.

SALMON CANNING TIPS

• **Handle raw seafood safely.** Thoroughly wash your hands, utensils and work surfaces (such as cutting boards) after handling raw seafood. Do not let raw seafood come into contact with cooked seafood.

• When canning salmon, a fatty fish, use nonporous equipment that can be cleaned easily and thoroughly. i.e. acrylic cutting board. Cover work surfaces with a layer of paper such as freezer wrap. Use disposable paper towels rather than cloth for clean-ups.

• Fill only the number of jars that fit in your canner for processing. Refrigerate any leftover, unpacked fish until ready to pack the next batch of jars.

• Salt is a flavouring and may be omitted.

• If packing salmon with skin on, place skin side next to glass.

• Frozen salmon may be home canned. However, it MUST be thawed in the refrigerator before you begin. Do not pack frozen fish into jars.

• Salmon is a fatty fish. Adding oil when canning salmon is not required and is NOT recommended. During processing, lots of natural juices and fats in fresh salmon are released to provide plenty of liquid in canned product.

• Glasslike crystals of magnesium ammonium phosphate sometimes form in home canned salmon. There is no way to prevent their formation, but they usually dissolve when heated and are not harmful to eat.

• Salmon is rich in Omega 3 fatty acids and calcium. The calcium is found mainly in the bones which soften during the pressure canning process. To reap the full nutritional benefits of salmon, include the salmon juices and bones in recipes prepared from home canned salmon. The bones easily flake into mixtures and become indistinguishable from the fish.

Smoked Salmon – For long-term storage, smoked salmon must be frozen or canned. Fully smoked fish that is dry enough to eat tends to be too dry and strong-flavoured after home canning. **Do not reduce processing time** to lessen these quality changes. The smoking technique must be modified when smoked salmon is to be home canned. *For specific Smoked Salmon canning directions, contact Bernardin Ltd. 1-888-430-4231.*

Processing times are for weighted gauge pressure canners at 10 lb (68 kPa) at altitudes up to 1,000 ft (305 m). For dial gauge canners or higher elevations, see page 12.

FREEZING

Savvy cooks and busy families soon learn that a freezer can hold the key to quick, easy and delicious meals. But just like home canning, freezing food for utmost quality and flavour requires attention to a few important details. Freezing meats, vegetables and fruits in meal-sized prepared portions also helps you take advantage of seasonal money-saving bargains.

Food preservation by freezing is based on the principle that extreme cold retards growth of microorganisms and slows down enzyme activity and oxidation. Starting with quality raw ingredients is essential to ensure a high quality frozen product. Prepare food in sanitary conditions and store foods at or below 0°F (-17°C). Proper packaging is essential to protect against freezer burn. Use packaging that is moisture/vapour proof, odourless, tasteless, grease proof and capable of being closed tightly to eliminate as much air as possible. Once food is correctly packaged, freeze it in single layers, leaving 1 inch (2.5 cm) of space between packages in the coldest spot in your freezer. Most foods will freeze in 12 to 24 hours. Once packages are completely frozen, restack them in more compact arrangements.

FREEZING BASICS

EQUIPMENT & STORAGE CONTAINERS

Most well stocked kitchens have the equipment required for freezing foods.

Rigid containers such as Bernardin mason jars and plastic freezer containers come in a variety of sizes and are best used with soft or liquid food like fruit packed in syrup, butter, eggs, stews and meats with gravy. Use only straight-walled mason jars for freezing i.e. 250 ml Preserve n' Serve, 125 ml, 250 ml, or 500 ml Decorative Mason Jars.

For irregular shapes such as meats, fish and vegetables, use flexible bags and wraps such as plastic freezer bags, plastic lined freezer paper or aluminum foil.

To extend the storage life of frozen foods, vacuum packaging is recommended. Packaging foods with the FoodSaver® vacuum packaging system removes air and seals the package – a process that extends the quality storage life of frozen foods three to five times longer than other methods. Because little or no air contacts the food, natural deterioration is slowed down and quality is enhanced. To achieve this extended freezer storage quality it is important to use FoodSaver® Bags or FoodSaver® Rolls.

The FoodSaver can also be used to vacuum seal SNAP Lids on straight-walled mason jars for perishable foods stored in the refrigerator or freezer as well as non-perishable items stored at room temperature.

STORAGE TIMES

Gradual loss of quality occurs in all frozen foods. To maintain the best quality for the longest possible storage period, maintain your freezer at 0°F (-17°C) or lower.

Frozen Food Storage – Recommended Time at 0°F (-17°C).

BAKERY	MONTHS
Breads, Quick (Baked)	2
Breads, Yeast (Baked)	4-8
Breads, Yeast (Unbaked)	1/2 (15 days)
Cakes	6
Cakes, Fruit	12
Cookies (Baked)	6
Cookies (Unbaked)	4
Pastry (Unbaked)	2
Pies (Baked)	1
Pies (Unbaked)	3

DAIRY	MONTHS
Butter	5-6
Cheese, Cottage	1
Cheese, Hard or Semi-Hard	6-12
Cheese, Soft	4
Eggs	12
Ice Cream, Sherbet	1-3
Milk	1

FRUITS	MONTHS
Fruits (Citrus)	3-4
Fruits (Except Citrus)	12

MEAT, POULTRY, SEAFOOD AND GAME	MONTHS
Beef, Lamb, Mutton, Veal, Venison	8-12
Fish	2-3
Ground Meat	3-4
Liver	3
Rabbit	6-8
Crab, Fish Roe, Lobster, Oysters	3-4
Pork (Cured)	1-2
Pork (Fresh)	6-8
Sausage	4-6
Shrimp	6
Turkey, Chicken	12

PREPARED FOODS	MONTHS
Candies	12
Gravy	2
Pizza	1
Prepared Main Dishes i.e. Lasagna	3-6
Salads	2
Sandwiches	1
Soups, Stews	6

SOFT SPREADS	MONTHS
Freezer Jams & Jellies	12

VEGETABLES	MONTHS
Onions	3-6
Vegetables (Cooked)	1
Vegetables (Uncooked, blanched)	12

Not all foods freeze well. Foods not recommended for freezer storage include:
- cake icings
- cream fillings and soft frostings
- custard and cream-pie fillings
- egg whites
- fried foods (exceptions are french fries and onion rings)
- pasta and some rice
- mayonnaise
- meringue
- peppers, onions, cloves, synthetic vanilla
- potatoes (Irish) in stews and soups
- sauces (tend to separate unless beaten or stirred when reheated)
- vegetables (raw)

THAWING FROZEN FOOD

Do not thaw more food at one time than is actually needed; when frozen food is thawed, it spoils more rapidly than fresh. Thaw each product to the desired point by placing the sealed package:
a. in the refrigerator (this is the best method)
b. at room temperature for two hours; completely thaw in the refrigerator
c. in the microwave oven on the defrost cycle, following manufacturer's instructions
d. in cold water (never hot)

REFREEZING

Do not refreeze thawed product. If absolutely necessary partially thawed foods – some ice crystals present – may be refrozen. Remember, refreezing partially thawed product reduces quality.

COOKING AND SERVING

Cook frozen foods immediately after thawing and serve them as soon as the correct internal temperature is reached.
1. Serve still frozen – cookies, candies, ice cream and similar foods.
2. Serve immediately after thawing – cakes, sandwiches and similar foods.
3. Heat to serving temperature – soups, meat dishes, stews and similar dishes.
4. Cook frozen – uncooked pies, rolls and combinations dishes.

FREEZING FRUIT

Three methods of freezing fruit are recommended.

- **Dry pack** – pack selected prepared fruit into containers/bags. Seal, label and freeze.
- **Sugar pack** – combine fruit with sugar in quantities suggested, let stand if indicated. Pack into freezer containers, leaving 1/2 inch (1 cm) headspace. Seal, label and freeze.
- **Syrup pack** – Pack fruit into freezer container. Cover with suggested syrup leaving 1/2 inch (1 cm) headspace. Seal, label and freeze.

SYRUP TYPE	% SUGAR	SUGAR	WATER	YIELD
Extra-Light	20	1 1/4 cups (300 ml)	5 1/2 cups (1375 ml)	6 cups (1500 ml)
Light	30	2 1/4 cups (550 ml)	5 1/4 cups (1300 ml)	6 1/2 cups (1725 ml)
Medium	40	3 1/4 cups (800 ml)	5 cups (1250 ml)	7 cups (1750 ml)
Heavy	50	4 1/4 cups (1050 ml)	4 1/4 cups (1050 ml)	7 cups (1750 ml)

Most fruit does not require blanching prior to freezing. Blanch fruits such as peaches to loosen the skin. Prepare fruit using selected PACK METHOD (indicated for each fruit), place in chosen package removing as much air as possible, seal and freeze. When freezing fruit in mason jars or firm containers, allow a minimum of 1/2-inch (1 cm) headspace.

FREEZE NOW, JAM LATER!

If you don't have time to make all the jam you want during the harvest season, freeze freshly-picked fruit and berries for quick and easy jam-making session at a later date. Freeze fruit in recipe-sized batches with no added sugar. For best results, wash and peel or hull fruit, arrange in single layer on tray. Place this tray in the freezer just until fruit freezes, then transfer it to airtight freezer packaging. When you are ready to make the jam, **partially** thaw fruit in the refrigerator. Thaw only until fruit is crushable. A ✻ indicates those fruits that are suitable for this freezing technique when the fruits are destined for jam-making.
Some fruits make better jellies when frozen than when fresh because freezing and thawing releases juices and colours. For jellies, extract the juice as directed in jelly recipe; measure and freeze the juice, without sugar, in recipe-sized portions.

Apples – Select crisp, firm apples. Wash, peel and core. Cut into 1/4 inch (0.5 cm) slices. Treat with FRUIT-FRESH® to prevent darkening. SYRUP PACK – Package apples with heavy syrup. DRY PACK pie apples: blanch slices 2 minutes; cool in ice water; drain.

✻ **Berries – blackberries, mulberries, raspberries** – Select fully ripe firm berries. Wash in cold water. Drain and dry. Discard soft, under-ripe or defective berries. Remove stems if required. SUGAR PACK – Mix 1 part sugar with 4 parts berries. SYRUP PACK – Pack drained berries in heavy syrup, shaking the container to pack berries.

✻ **Berries – blueberries, huckleberries, elderberries and gooseberries** – Select fully ripe firm berries. Wash in cold water. Drain and dry. Remove stems. Discard under ripe or defective berries. DRY PACK. SUGAR PACK – 2/3 cup (150 ml) sugar to 4 cups (1000 ml) berries. SYRUP PACK in heavy syrup.

✻ **Cherries** – Select tender skinned, bright red cherries. Wash and drain. Stem and pit. SUGAR PACK – sour cherries in 1 part sugar to 4 parts sour cherries. SYRUP PACK sour or sweet cherries in heavy syrup.

Cranberries – Select firm cranberries of uniform colour. Wash in cold water and drain. Dry and stem. DRY PACK.

✻ **Currants** – Select ripe currants. Wash in cold water, drain and stem. DRY PACK. SUGAR PACK – crush currants lightly. Combine 3 parts currants with 1 part sugar. Let stand until sugar dissolves, about 10 minutes.

Grapes – Select ripe, firm sweet grapes. Wash, drain and stem. SYRUP PACK in medium syrup.

Melons cantaloupe, cranshaw, honeydew, Persian and watermelon – Select fully ripe fruit. Remove seeds and peel. Cut into 3/4 inch (2 cm) cubes, slices or balls. DRY PACK. Best when served partially thawed.

✻ **Peaches, nectarines, apricots** – Select fully ripe fruit. Wash and drain. Peel, pit and slice fruit. Treat with FRUIT FRESH® to prevent darkening. SUGAR PACK – mix 2/3 cup (150 ml) sugar, 2 tsp (10 ml) FRUIT-FRESH®. Sprinkle over 4 cups (1000 ml) fruit. Let stand until sugar dissolves syrup, about 10 minutes. SYRUP PACK in heavy syrup.

✻ **Pears** – Select full flavoured pears that are crisp and firm. Wash, peel and core pears. Leave in halves or cut into quarters. Treat with FRUIT-FRESH® to prevent darkening. SYRUP PACK in medium syrup; blanch prepared pears in syrup 2 minutes before packing.

✱ **Rhubarb** – Select rhubarb with crisp, tender, red stalks. Early spring cuttings are best for freezing. Remove leaves and woody ends; discard blemished and tough stalks. Wash under running water; cut into 1 inch (2.5 cm) pieces. DRY PACK. SUGAR PACK – mix 1 part sugar to 4 parts rhubarb. SYRUP PACK in heavy syrup.

✱ **Strawberries** – Select fully ripe, firm strawberries. Wash, then remove caps, hulls. DRY PACK. SUGAR PACK. – slice berries length wise into halves or thirds. Mix 1 part sugar to 6 parts strawberries. Allow to stand until sugar dissolves, about 10 minutes. SYRUP PACK in heavy syrup leaving berries whole or sliced.

MEAT

Freezing preserves the natural, fresh qualities of meat better that any other method of preservation. As with all other types of food preservation cleanliness and sanitary conditions are a must. For large cuts of meat wrap individually in plastic freezer bags, foil, plastic wrap or vacuum packaging. Steaks or chops wrap individually in plastic freezer bags, foil, plastic wrap or vacuum packaging. To ease separation of cuts place a double layer of moisture/vapour proof material between each piece of meat. Ground meat is best packaged in family size servings packed in plastic freezer bags, foil, plastic wrap or vacuum packaging.

POULTRY

Package poultry in the same manner as meat. **Do not freeze whole stuffed poultry!**

SEAFOOD

Only freeze fresh seafood. It must be cleaned and prepared for freezing shortly after being caught. Ensure your seafood is kept under refrigeration at all times prior to freezing. Whole fish can be wrapped in freezer film, foil or paper and then packed into a freezer bag. Alternately vacuum package. Steaks of fillets should be dipped in a 5 percent salt solutions (2/3 cups [150 ml] salt to 4 cups [1 L] water) for 30 seconds. Pack as suggested with whole fish.

VEGETABLES

Blanching is an essential step to prepare vegetables for freezing. It must be done carefully. The only exceptions to the "blanch first" rule are those to be used exclusively for their flavour, such as green onions, hot peppers and herbs.

Blanching:
• cleanses vegetables of surface dirt and microorganisms,
• brightens the colour,
• helps retain vitamins,
• reduces the action of enzymes that can destroy the flavour.

FREEZING VEGETABLES

• Wash, drain, sort, trim and cut the vegetables as directed for each.
• Bring water to a rolling boil in a large stainless steel saucepan. Place vegetables in a basket, coarse mesh bag or perforated metal strainer; lower into vigorously boiling water. Use approximately 16 cups (4000 ml) water per 1 lb (454 g); twice this quantity for leafy vegetables. Begin counting blanching time as soon as the vegetables are placed in the boiling water. Keep the heat on high and stir the water or keep the container covered. Under blanching stimulates enzyme activity and is worse than no blanching.
• When blanching time is complete, cool quickly. Immerse vegetables in ice water. Stir several times during cooling time that should not be longer than the blanching time.
• Drain cooled vegetables well and pack loosely without seasoning in meal-sized, airtight, moisture/vapour-proof packaging. When packing in rigid containers, leave 1/2 inch (1 cm) headspace.

Asparagus – Select young, tender asparagus with tightly closed tips. Wash thoroughly and sort into sizes. Trim stalks by removing scales with a sharp knife. Cut into even lengths to fit freezer container. BLANCH small spears 1 1/2 minutes, medium spears 2 minutes and large spears 3 minutes.

Beans, snap – Select young, tender bean pods. Trim ends; cut into 2 to 4 inch (5-10 cm) lengths or lengths to fit freezer container. BLANCH 3 minutes.

FREEZING VEGETABLES

Beets – Select uniformly deep red beets. Leave 2 inch (5 cm) stem and tap root; wash; cook until tender. Cool and remove skins, stem and tap root. Leave whole, quarter, slice or dice.

Broccoli, Cauliflower – Select tender firm compact heads. Wash and remove leaves and woody portions. Separate heads into convenient size sections and immerse in brine (1 cup/250 ml pickling salt to 16 cups/4000 ml water) for 30 minutes to remove insects. Rinse and drain. BLANCH medium size sections 3 minutes; large size sections 4 minutes blanch.

Brussel sprouts – Select dark green sprouts with compact heats. Remove coarse outer leaves; wash and sort into small, medium and large sizes. BLANCH small 3 minutes, medium 4 minutes and large 5 minutes.

Carrots – Select young, tender, coreless medium length carrots. Wash, peel, wash again and dice or quarter. Small carrots may be frozen whole. BLANCH cut carrots 3 minutes; whole 5 minutes.

Corn on the cob or whole – Remove husks and silk. BLANCH 1 1/2 inch (3 cm) diameter ears 6 minutes; 2-inch (5 cm) ears 8 minutes; larger ears 10 minutes. Wrap ears individually in moisture/vapour proof film. Pack wrapped ears in freezer bags or vacuum package. For corn kernels, BLANCH ears 5-6 minutes; cool, drain and cut corn from cob.

Eggplant – Select uniformly dark colour eggplant before seeds mature. Wash, peel and slice slightly less than 1/2 inch (1 cm) thick. BLANCH 4 minutes in 16 cups (4000 ml) boiling water containing 3 tbsp (45 ml) FRUIT FRESH® or 1/2 cup (125 ml) lemon juice.

Greens – Select young, tender greens. Wash thoroughly and cut off woody stems. BLANCH 2 minutes and avoid matting leaves.

Herbs – Wash, drain and dry herbs. Wrap a few sprigs or leaves in plastic wrap and place in plastic freezer bags. No blanching required. (Frozen, thawed herbs will be limp and are best chopped, used in cook dishes.)

Onions – For mature bulbs, remove peel as for eating. Wash and chop green onions. BLANCH mature bulbs 3-7 minutes until core is heated. Do not blanch green onions.

Parsnips, Turnips – Choose firm, smooth skim parsnips/turnips. Remove tops, wash thoroughly and peel. Slice, dice or cut lengthwise. BLANCH 3 minutes.

Peas, green or garden, snow or sugar – Select young, tender green or garden peas that have not become starchy. Wash, shell and wash again. Select firm, unblemished snow or sugar pods, wash. BLANCH green and snow 2 minutes.

Peppers, hot or sweet – Select crisp, tender ripe pods. Wash and drain, leave whole. Select crisp, tender sweet pods. Wash, cut out seams and remove seeds. Leave whole or cut in halve, strips or dice. No blanching is required for hot or sweet peppers.

Pumpkin – Select mature cooking pumpkin that has uniform colour and a stem that breaks easily from the vine. Wash; peel and remove seeds. Cut pumpkin into sections; steam until soft. Purée pulp. If desired, add 1 part sugar to 6 parts purée. Pack leaving 1/2 inch (1 cm) headspace.

Squash, spaghetti – Cut squash in half; remove seeds. Place in baking dish, cut side down; add 1/2 inch (1 cm) water and bake at 350°F (180°C) until fork tender. Using a fork, rake pulp away from peel. Place squash in a bowl and set in ice water to cool.

Squash, summer – Choose young squash with tender skin. Wash, slice. BLANCH 3 minutes.

Squash, winter – Select fully mature squash with a hard rind. Wash; cut into halves; scoop out seeds and membrane. Place in baking dish, cut side down. Add 1/4 inch (0.5 cm) water and bake at 375°F (190°C) until tender. Scoop out pulp. Purée in a food processor or food mill.

Tomatoes, sauce or juice – Prepare sauce or juice, pack into freezer container leaving 1/2 inch (1 cm) headspace.

DEHYDRATED FOODS

For families on the run nothing is quicker than grabbing a handful of dried fruit to fill the hunger gap. Why pay for expensive commercially dried products? The best part is that dehydration is simple. And remember, dehydrated vegetables and jerky are a great way to add high density nutrition to everyday meals.

Preserving food by drying harkens back to antiquity. Ancient dehydration methods utilized heavy concentrations of salt and sugar that no longer appeal to today's tastes. Many foods, especially fruit and vegetables can be easily and successfully dehydrated to produce delicious products that weigh little and require minimal storage space. Dehydrated foods have particular appeal to outdoor enthusiasts and persons concerned about the quality and source of their food supply.

Dehydration removes moisture from food reducing the opportunity for microbial growth and enzymatic action. It retards deterioration and spoilage but doesn't necessarily prevent it indefinitely. Drying does not eliminate bacteria. Like all food preservation, dehydration requires use of up-to-date methods and attention to detail.

GENERAL GUIDELINES

• Start with the best, top quality *freshly harvested* produce or prime cuts of fresh meat. Do not dehydrate lesser quality produce or meat. Freshness is imperative for successful dehydration. Enzymatic action increases and microorganisms multiply exponentially as food ages. Freshly harvested produce has lower levels of problematic microorganisms.

• Commercial dehydrators are preferred for efficient food dehydration. Normal kitchen ovens, particularly convection ovens, can be used but require constant attention & rack rotation over several hours drying time. Drying in a baking/roasting oven lacks energy efficiency; some ovens aren't built to maintain the low temperatures (140°-195°F/ 60°-90°C) required for dehydration. Consult your oven manufacturer for special dehydration instructions.

• **Check dehydrator temperature regulator**. Before using a commercial dehydrator, first determine its actual operating temperature. Place a shallow dish of vegetable oil in the dehydrator and heat it to a chosen level selected on the dehydrator's regulator. After 1 hour, use candy thermometer to test temperature of oil. Compare it to the temperature expected from the appliance's temperature regulator. Repeat with one or two alternate temperatures. Record and make adjustments as needed when using the appliance.

• Pretreatment – Some produce benefits from pretreatment that retards enzymatic action, preserves colour, enhances dried texture or taste and minimizes vitamin loss.

  • Steam blanch fruit – steam prepared fruit over boiling water until heated through. Break a piece in half to assure that it feels hot at the centre.

  • Syrup blanch – Heat 1 part sugar, 1 part white corn syrup with 2 parts water in a large stainless steel saucepan until combined. Add prepared fruit and bring to a boil; simmer 10 minutes. Remove from heat and let stand 35 minutes. Drain thoroughly.

  • Sodium bisulfite (available at wine stores). Dissolve 1/4 tbsp (4 ml) in 4 cups (1000 ml) water. Immerse prepared fruit in solution; soak slices 5 minutes, quartered fruit or larger pieces 15 minutes. Drain, rinse in running water and drain again.

  • Steam blanch vegetables – Because vegetables have heavier bacterial content, adding 2 tbsp (30 ml) sodium bisulfite for each 4 cups (1000 ml) water in steamer is recommended.

• Produce may also be treated with sulfur. This procedure must be done outside and requires construction of a special smoking device. Obtain detailed directions before attempting this procedure.

• Dehydrate foods slowly at low temperatures to prevent "case hardening." When dehydrated too rapidly, a hard shell forms on the exterior of the food and prevents interior moisture from escaping. Failure to remove adequate moisture will cause mold growth during storage.

• Dehydrate food at recommended temperature for recommended time. Test for doneness. If additional dehydration is required, reduce temperature to 130°F (55°C) and continue drying food until it tests positive for doneness.

• Do not attempt to dehydrate milk or egg products at home. Use commercially dehydrated milk and egg products. Fish must be brined in salt solutions and dehydrated in refrigerated conditions. For greatest safety, purchase commercially dehydrated fish.

DEHYDRATION MEASURE

Weight is a good way to determine that fruit or vegetables have been adequately dehydrated. The average water content of fresh fruits and vegetables is included with dehydration directions for each of the produce items. The following chart illustrates how to calculate the amount of moisture that must be removed for each produce item.

WEIGHT OF PRODUCE TO BE DEHYDRATED = FRESH WEIGHT

Multiply:
Fresh weight of produce **X** water content **= initial water content**

Multiply:
Vegetables: Initial water content **X** 95% **= water weight to be removed**
Fruit: Initial water content **X** 80% **= water weight to be removed**

Subtract:
Fresh weight **–** water weight to be removed **= Target weight of dehydrated produce**

STORAGE

Store dehydrated foods in food-safe containers that will protect them from air, moisture, light and insects. Home canning jars are excellent, see-through storage containers for dehydrated foods. Wash and rinse jars in hot water and dry thoroughly before packing with dried product. Vacuum sealing jars or bags of dehydrated food, extend shelf life by 3 to 5 times.

Store containers of dehydrated products in a cool (68°F/20°C), dry location. Storage life doubles or triples when storage temperature is dropped to 50°F (10°C). Vacuum packaging using FoodSaver® Bags and FoodSaver® Rolls also helps extend shelf life. Depending on storage temperature, most dehydrated fruit and vegetables can be stored safely from 6 months to 1 year.

FRUIT

Fruits such as grapes, plums and blueberries have a natural waxy coating or "bloom" that must be removed by dipping the fruit in boiling water prior to dehydration. Stone fruits like peaches, plums and apricots, benefit from a technique called "popping the backs" – push the peel side inward to expose more of the surface during dehydration.

Bite into a piece of fruit to test doneness. Most fruit is dried until pliable and leathery with no moisture pockets. Dry apples and bananas until slightly crisp; citrus peel until very crisp. Fruits are dry when **80% of the moisture** initially present is removed. Condition dehydrated fruit before storage. As soon as dehydrated fruit is cool, place it in large jar and apply lid. Let stand one week to allow moisture levels of individual pieces to equalize. After conditioning, repack dried fruit in small containers for storage.

If there was any concern about pest infestation of the initial produce or during dehydration, freeze dehydrated fruit 48 hours prior to final packaging. Freezing kills infestation that may have taken place during the dehydration process. Dehydrated fruit may also be pasteurized by heating in an 175°F (80°C) oven for 15 minutes or 160°F (70°C) oven for 30 minutes.

Apples, *84% water* – Select tart, crisp, firm apples. Wash, peel and core. Slice into 1/4 to 1/2 inch (0.5-1 cm) slices. Pretreat by dipping in sodium bisulfite. Dry at 150°F (65°C) 2 to 3 hours or until pliable.

Apricots, *85% water* – Select firm, ripe apricots with deep yellow orange colour. Wash, cut in half and remove pit. Pretreat by dipping, if desired. Dry at 158°F (70°C) 2 to 3 hours or until pliable, with no moisture pockets.

Bananas, *65% water* – Select large, slightly brown spotted yellow bananas. Peel and slice into 1/4 to 1/2 inch (0.5-1 cm) slices. Dry at 150°F (65°C) 1 to 2 hours until pliable and almost crisp.

Blueberries, – Select large, ripe, dark blue berries. Wash in cold water, remove stems. Blanch in boiling water for 30 seconds to "check" skins. Dry at 130°F (55°C) until leathery.

Cherries, *82% water, sweet or sour* – Wash, remove stem, cut in half and discard pit. Dry at 158°F (70°C) 2 hours. Test for doneness, reduce temperature to 130°F (55°C) and continue drying until leathery and slightly sticky.

Citrus peel, *grapefruit, lemon, lime, orange or tangerine* – Wash to remove dirt, pesticides and any waxes. Using a sharp knife carefully remove the coloured zest/peel avoiding the white pith. Dry at 130°F (55°C) 1 to 2 hours until crisp.

Coconut, *51% water* – Select fresh heavy coconuts. Pierce eyes to drain milk. Crack outer shell with hammer. Remove coconut meat, discard dark outer skin. Grate or thinly slice. Dry at 130°F (55°C) until crisp.

Cranberries – Drying cranberries requires an extra dose of patience, persistence and a few extra steps. Select firm, fully ripe cranberries; wash and drain thoroughly. Halve berries using slicer or a sharp knife. Alternatively, submerge cranberries in hot water just until the skins pop; drain thoroughly. (Bring water to a boil and remove pot from heat before adding berries). Then dip berries in a 50% sugar syrup – combine equal parts water and sugar; cook until sugar is completely dissolved. Drain berries; place in single layer on a cookie

sheet and freeze until hardened. Transfer prepared berries to dehydrator trays. Dry at 140°F (60°C) until shriveled and light in weight. Home dried cranberries are best stored in a very cool place.

Grapes, *81% water* – *Thompson seedless or red seedless* – Select ripe, firm grapes. Wash, remove stems. Dip in boiling water 30 to 60 seconds to "check" skins. Dry at 158°F (70°C) 1 to 2 hours until pliable, with no moisture pockets.

Nectarines, *82% water* – Select fully ripe, plump fruit with deep orange colour. Wash, cut in half and remove pit. Pretreat by dipping in sodium bisulfite, if desired. Slice into 1/4 to 1/2 inch (0.5-1 cm) slices. Place in tray peel side down. Dry at 158°F (70°C) until pliable, with no moisture pockets.

Peaches, *89% water clingstone or freestone varieties* – Select firm, fully ripe peaches with no green areas. Wash peaches, blanch for 1 minute, immediately immerse in ice water to remove skins. Remove pits and slice into 1/2 inch (1 cm) slices or rings. Pretreat by dipping in sodium bisulfite. Dry at 150°F (65°C) 2 to 3 hours until pliable, with no moisture pockets.

Pears, *83% water, winter or summer varieties* – Select fully ripe pears that are crisp and firm. Wash, peel and core pears. Slice into 1/2 inch (1 cm) slices, quarters or halves. Pretreat by dipping, if desired. Dry at 158°F (70°C) 2 to 3 hours until pliable, with no moisture pockets.

Pineapple, *86% water* – Select fully ripe pineapples with a yellowish brown peel. Wash, peel and core pineapple. Cut into 1/2 inch (1 cm) slices. Dry at 158°F (70°C) 1 to 2 hours until leathery and no longer sticky.

Plums, *81% water, any variety of sweet plums* – Select fully ripe plums. Wash, cut in half and remove pits. Slice into 1/4 to 1/2 inch (0.5-1 cm) slices. Dry at 158°F (70°C) 1 to 2 hours until pliable.

Prune plums, *81% water* – Select ripe prune plums that are soft with a sweet flesh. Wash, cut in half and remove pits. "Pop the back" of the fruit to increase surface area. Dry peel side down at 158°F (70°C) 1 to 2 hours until pliable, with no moisture pockets.

Strawberries, *90% water* – Select fully ripe, firm and juicy strawberries. Wash, then remove caps, hulls. Slice into 1/2 inch (1 cm) slice. Dry at 150°F (65°C) 1 to 2 hours until pliable to crisp.

FRUIT LEATHERS

Thoroughly wash & drain fruit immediately before it is to be puréed and dehydrated. Press purée of heavily seeded berries – raspberries, blackberries, Saskatoon berries, etc – through sieve to remove seeds. Pour 1/4 inch (6 mm) thick layer of purée onto heavy plastic wrap and place on drying trays. (Do not use waxed paper or aluminum foil.) Dehydrate at 140°F (60°C) for 6 to 8 hours until leather is dry but still pliable. Cut fruit leather into 4-inch (10 cm) squares and roll *immediately* after dehydration while still warm.

VEGETABLES

Although potentially more problematic for dehydration, vegetables can be dried successfully with attention to detail. Vegetables contain less natural sugar and acid, so **95% of water must be removed** when dehydrating vegetables. i.e. they are dried until crisp or brittle.
Because vegetables have stronger cell walls, most require steam blanching in boiling water to break down their strong cell wall structure so that moisture can be released during dehydration.
Dehydrate vegetables at suggested temperature for 1 to 3 hours. Test, if not dry after 3 hours dehydration, reduce temperature to 130°F (55°C) and continue dehydration until vegetables are crisp to brittle.
Rehydrate vegetables by pouring boiling water over dehydrated vegetables; let stand 30 minutes. Do not allow vegetables to rehydrate at room temperature longer than 2 hours.

Asparagus, *92% water* – Select young, tender asparagus with tightly closed tips. Wash and cut off tough ends. Steam blanch 3 minutes. Dry until brittle. Dry until brittle. Initial dehydration temperature: 130°F (55°C). Rehydrate and use in soups or serve with a sauce.

Beans, *green or wax, 90% water,* – Select any type with crisp, thick walls and small seeds. Wash and trim ends; cut diagonally into 1 inch (2.5 cm) lengths or French cut. Steam blanch 4 to 6 minutes. To tenderize dehydrated beans,

freeze prepared beans 30 minutes prior to drying. Dry until brittle. Initial dehydration temperature: 140°F (60°C).

Beets, *87% water* – Select uniformly deep red beets. Leave 2 inch (5 cm) stem and tap root; wash; steam until tender, approximately 30 minutes. Cool and remove skins, stem and tap root. Cut into 1/2 inch (1 cm) slices or dice. Dry until leathery. Initial dehydration temperature: 125°F (52°C).

Carrots, *88% water* – Select mature, deep orange varieties. Wash, peel, wash again and slice crosswise or dice. Steam blanch 3 to 4 minutes. Dry until almost brittle. Initial dehydration temperature: 140°F (60°C).

Corn, *sweet,*
73% water – Select yellow
varieties with tender sweet kernels. Husk corn, remove silks and wash. Steam until milk is set. Allow to cool. Cut kernels carefully from cob. Dry until brittle. Initial dehydration temperature: 150°F (65°C).

Mushrooms, *90% water* – Select only edible, cultivated mushrooms with small closed caps. Wash quickly to remove dirt. Slice into 1/4 inch (0.5 cm) slices. Dry until brittle. Initial dehydration temperature: 130°F (55°C).

Onions, *red, white or yellow varieties, 89% water* – Large, pungent white varieties are best. Trim end, remove papery cover and slice 1/4 inch (0.5 cm) thick. Dry until crisp. Initial dehydration temperature: 158°F (70°C).

Peas, *78% water* – Select medium peas. Shell and wash. Steam blanch 3 minutes. Dry until brittle. Initial dehydration temperature: 130°F (55°C).

Peppers, *fresh red, green sweet or hot, 93% water* – Sweet (red, green, yellow) peppers – wash, remove stem and seed; dice. Hot peppers – wash and slice 1/4 to 1 inch (0.5 to 2.5 cm) thick. Dry hot peppers until crisp; sweet peppers until leathery. Crush or grind. Initial dehydration temperature: 140°F (60°C).

Potatoes, *sweet and yams, 71% water* – Select thick orange potatoes free from decay and blemishes. Wash, peel and slice into 1/4 inch (0.5 cm) slices. Steam blanch 3 minutes. Dry until brittle. Initial dehydration temperature: 158°F (70°C).

Potatoes, *white or Irish, 80% water* – Select any white variety. Wash well to remove surface dirt. Slice 1/4 inch (0.5 cm) thick. Steam blanch 5 to 6 minutes. Rinse in cold water to remove starch. Dry until crisp. Initial dehydration temperature: 158°F (70°C).

Tomatoes, *94% water* – Select plum or paste type tomatoes. Wash, blanch in boiling water 30 seconds to remove skins. Core and slice 1/4 inch (0.5 cm) thick. Dry until crisp. Initial dehydration temperature: 150°F (65°C).

Turnips and Rutabagas, *turnips, 92% water* – *rutabagas, 87% water* – Select firm round turnips and rutabagas. Wash, cut off tops and peel. Slice 1/4 inch to 1/2 inch (0.5 to 1 cm) thick. Steam blanch 3 to 5 minutes. Dry until brittle. Initial dehydration temperature: 140°F (60°C).

Zucchini, *94% water* – Select young, slender zucchini. Wash and cut into 1/4 inch (0.5 cm) or thinner slices or chips. Dry until brittle. Initial dehydration temperature: 130°F (55°C).

JERKY

Select top quality flank, inside or outside round or sirloin tip cuts. Corned beef may also be dehydrated for jerky.

To kill parasites that might be present in game, freeze game meat at 0°F (-18°C) for 60 days before using game for dehydration.

Cut meat across grain of muscle fibers, place in shallow container and marinate **in refrigerator** 8 to 12 hours or overnight. Marinades add flavour to jerky and reduce the pH of the meat. Liberally salt meat on both side and place in marinades containing your choice of ingredients such as Worcestershire, soy, A1 and other commercial meat sauces plus seasonings such as chili, onion or garlic to taste. When using marinades containing liquid smoke, be sure meat is tightly covered before placing in refrigerator.

Dry meat at 155°F (68°C) 3 to 4 hours. Test for doneness. If jerky is not dry, reduce temperature to 131°F (55°C) and continue dehydration process, testing frequently for doneness.

Properly dehydrated jerky will crack when bent. If jerky breaks it has been dried too long.

HERBS

To prevent loss of their volatile oils, dehydrate herbs at cooler temperatures 95°F (35°C). Dry fresh herbs until 70 to 85% of their original moisture is removed. The best quality dried herbs are produced when herbs leaves are removed from stems.

To test for doneness – place dehydrated herbs in plastic bag; close bag. If condensation builds up in bag, herbs must be returned to dehydration device for more time.

With care and patience, herbs can be successfully dehydrated in small batches in a microwave. Arrange herbs in thin layer on tray in oven. Microwave at Medium power 2 to 3 minutes, check dryness; and continue microwaving in 30 seconds bursts at Medium power until sufficiently dehydrated.

CRAFTS

GIFTS IN

GLASS

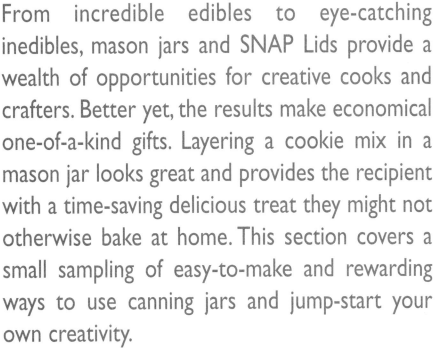

From incredible edibles to eye-catching inedibles, mason jars and SNAP Lids provide a wealth of opportunities for creative cooks and crafters. Better yet, the results make economical one-of-a-kind gifts. Layering a cookie mix in a mason jar looks great and provides the recipient with a time-saving delicious treat they might not otherwise bake at home. This section covers a small sampling of easy-to-make and rewarding ways to use canning jars and jump-start your own creativity.

INCREDIBLE EDIBLES

Ingredients for baked goods attractively layered in mason jars make eye-catching, greatly appreciated gifts.

LAYERED RECIPES IN A JAR

Each jar holds the time-saving convenience of a commercial mix made especially for the recipient. He or she can bake that one-of-a-kind treat at a time of his/her choice. When the ingredients are used, the recipient can reuse the gift container for kitchen storage or food preservation. These gifts are especially handy for those who normally don't keep a stock of baking ingredients.

Better yet, you can make your own layered recipes in a jar for less than half the price they demand at craft shows. Add your own special touches with ribbons or decorative tags to suit the occasion. Or save time, use BERNARDIN Collection Elite Lids and decorative jars for that extra touch of class.

The recipes shown here are but a small sampling of ways this idea can be adapted. Each recipe makes one jar.

Tips:

• Thoroughly wash, rinse and dry mason jar and lid before filling.

• Layer ingredients in order specified. Using a non-metallic utensil such as a bendable rubber scrapper, gently but firmly press each layer in place before adding the next. Press each layer into place, to assure all ingredients fit the jar.

• Convert your own recipes for baked goods to layered recipes in a jar. Add eye-appeal to the jar by selecting recipes with a variety of different textured and coloured ingredients. Combine leavening ingredients with flour before placing in jar. Choose recipes that will fill the jar brimful.

• Be sure to attach an Instruction Tag to each jar detailing the quantities of additional ingredients, mixing directions, pan size plus cooking time and temperature.

• Make more than one jar, but measure and combine ingredients for each jar separately when preparing baked goods. This will assure the correct single recipe proportions are in each jar. Soup and spice mixtures can be prepared in larger batches and then divided among several jars.

TRADITIONAL SCONES

2 cups (500 ml) all purpose flour
4 tbsp (60 ml) buttermilk powder
1/4 cup (50 ml) granulated sugar
2 1/2 tsp (12 ml) baking powder
1/2 tsp (2 ml) *Each:* baking soda & salt
1/2 cup (125 ml) currants
500 ml BERNARDIN mason jar &
  2-piece SNAP Lid

Combine flour, buttermilk powder, sugar, baking powder, baking soda and salt. Spoon 2/3 of mixture into jar. Tap and press the mixture to form an angled surface for the first layer.

Add currants, pushing them to the front of the jar and pressing down. Carefully spoon in remaining flour mixture. Cover tightly with a SNAP Lid and attach Instruction Tag.

Instruction Tag:
Preheat oven to 425°F (220°C). Empty contents of jar into bowl. With pastry cutter or two knives, cut in 1/2 cup (125 ml) cold butter until mixture resembles coarse crumbs. Stir in 3/4 cup (175 ml) water. With lightly floured hands, press dough into ball. Knead gently 8 to 10 times on lightly floured surface. Pat out dough into 3/4 inch (2 cm) thick round. Using floured cutter, cut into 10 scones. Place on baking sheet; sprinkle lightly with sugar. Bake 10 to 12 minutes until golden.

SCOTCH HERMITS

2 cups (500 ml) quick rolled oats, divided
1/2 cup (125 ml) raisins
1/2 cup (125 ml) chopped dried apricots
1/2 cup (125 ml) sweetened dried cranberries
1 cup (250 ml) lightly packed brown sugar
1 cup (250 ml) all purpose flour
1 tsp (5 ml) baking soda
1/2 tsp (2 ml) *Each:* salt, ground cinnamon
1 L BERNARDIN mason jar & 2-piece SNAP Lid

Pour 2/3 cup (150 ml) rolled oats into jar. Using a spoon or scoop, gently tap oats down to an even layer. Top with raisins, arranging them in a 1/2 inch (1 cm) deep circle against jar wall. Repeat with a 2/3 cup (150 ml) rolled oats layer. Place chopped apricots in a circle against jar wall. Add remaining rolled oats and tap down. Add dried cranberries in a circle against jar wall. Add brown sugar and press down firmly on all layers. Combine flour, baking soda, salt and cinnamon until well mixed; add to jar. Cover tightly with a SNAP Lid and attach Instruction Tag.

Instruction Tag:
Preheat oven to 350°F (180°C). Cream 3/4 cup (175 ml) softened butter or margarine. Add 2 eggs and beat until light and fluffy. Empty contents of jar into large bowl; mix well. Incorporate butter mixture, mixing thoroughly. Dough will be stiff; mix thoroughly with spoon or clean hands. With a teaspoon, drop 1 1/2 inch (4 cm) balls onto baking sheet, allowing 2 inches (5 cm) between cookies. Dip bottom of jar in water and use to flatten cookies to 1/2 inch (1 cm) thickness. Bake 10 to 12 minutes until light golden. Do not over-bake. Remove from oven and cool 5 minutes on cookie sheet. Remove cookies to cooling rack; cool thoroughly. Store in airtight container. **Makes 30-40 cookies.**

WHITE CHOCOLATE SCONES

1 2/3 cups (425 ml) all purpose flour
1/4 cup (50 ml) granulated sugar
1 tbsp (15 ml) baking powder
1/8 tsp (0.5 ml) salt
1/2 cup (125 ml) white chocolate pieces or chips
1/3 cup (75 ml) dried cherries
500 ml BERNARDIN mason jar &
  2-piece SNAP Lid

In a bowl combine flour, sugar, baking powder and salt; mix well. Stir in chocolate and cherries. Place funnel in jar and pack in scone mix. Frequently tap jar down as mix is added. Cover tightly with a SNAP Lid and attach Instruction Tag.

Instruction Tag:
• *Preheat oven to 425°F (220°C). Line baking sheet with parchment paper or lightly grease.*
• *Empty contents of jar into bowl. With a pastry knife cut in 1/4 cup (50 ml) chilled butter until mixture is crumbly. Stir in 1/2 cup (125 ml) milk. Turn dough out onto a lightly floured surface. Knead gently 5 times. Roll out dough 3/4 inch (2 cm) thick. Cut into 2 inch (5 cm) rounds using cookie cutter. Bake for 10 minutes or until golden brown.*
Makes 12 scones.

CHOCOLATE CHIP COOKIES

3/4 cup (175 ml) granulated sugar
3/4 cup (175 ml) lightly packed brown sugar, divided
1 cup (250 ml) chocolate chips or coloured chocolate candies
2 1/4 cups (550 ml) all purpose flour
1 tsp (5 ml) baking soda
1/2 tsp (2 ml) baking powder
1/2 tsp (2 ml) salt
1 L BERNARDIN mason jar & 2-piece SNAP Lid

Pour granulated sugar into jar forming a level layer. Add half of brown sugar, tap down firmly. Top with chocolate chips. Add remaining brown sugar. Combine flour, baking soda, baking powder and salt until well mixed; add to jar. Cover tightly with a SNAP Lid and attach Instruction Tag.

Instruction Tag:
Preheat oven to 375°F (190°C). Cream 1/2 cup (125 ml) softened butter or margarine. Add 2 eggs and 1 tbsp water; beat until light and fluffy. Empty contents of jar into large bowl. Incorporate butter mixture, mixing thoroughly. Dough will be stiff; mix thoroughly with spoon or clean hands. Drop heaping teaspoonful onto baking sheet, allowing 2 inches (5 cm) between cookies. Bake 8 to 10 minutes until light golden. Do not over-bake. Remove from oven and cool 5 minutes on cookie sheet. Remove cookies to cooling rack; cool thoroughly. **Makes 35-40 cookies.**

BROWNIES IN A JAR

3/4 cup (175 ml) all purpose flour
1/2 tsp (2 ml) baking powder
1/4 tsp (1 ml) salt
2/3 cup (150 ml) lightly packed brown sugar
2/3 cup (150 ml) granulated sugar
1/2 cup (125 ml) cocoa powder
3/4 cup (175 ml) semi-sweet chocolate chips
2/3 cup (150 ml) chopped walnuts
1 L BERNARDIN mason jar & 2-piece SNAP Lid

Combine flour, baking powder and salt. Starting with flour mixture, layer ingredients, in order listed, tapping and pressing each down firmly. Cover tightly with a SNAP Lid and attach Instruction Tag.

Instruction Tag:
Preheat oven to 350°F (180°C). Cream 3/4 cup (175 ml) softened butter or margarine. Add 3 eggs and beat until light and fluffy. Empty contents of jar into large bowl; mix well. Incorporate butter mixture, mixing thoroughly. Pour into an 8 or 9 inch greased square pan, spread mixture evenly. Bake 30 to 35 minutes. Do not over-bake. Remove from oven and score into 36 squares with a sharp knife. Cool completely, cut into squares and store in air-tight container. **Makes 36 brownies.**

IRISH SODA BREAD

1 1/4 cups (300 ml) rolled oats
4 tbsp (60 ml) buttermilk powder
2 1/2 cups (625 ml) all purpose flour
3 tbsp (45 ml) granulated sugar
1 1/2 tsp (7 ml) *Each:* baking powder & baking soda
1/3 cup (75 ml) golden shortening
1/2 cup (125 ml) raisins
1 L BERNARDIN mason jar
  & 2-piece SNAP Lid

Set 1/4 cup (50 ml) rolled oats aside. Pulse remaining oats until ground. Stir reserved rolled oats and buttermilk powder into ground oats.

Combine flour, sugar, baking powder and soda together. Cut in shortening until fine crumbs are formed.
Layer half of oat mixture, followed by half of flour mixture into a 1 L jar. Add raisins and repeat oat and flour mixtures.

Instruction Tag:
Empty jar contents into bowl. Stir in 1 cup (250 ml) water to make soft dough. Knead 1 to 2 minutes. Shape into 6-inch (15 cm) round loaf. Place on baking sheet; cut a deep X about 1/4 way through loaf. Bake in 375°F (190°C) 35 to 45 minutes until golden. Remove and brush with butter, if desired.

Not all edible gifts in glass require the recipient to cook or bake. Imaginative cooks package ready-to-eat sweet and savoury treats in decorative mason jars and SNAP Lids. This packaging protects the food and lets the giver present it with no additional wrapping. Spiced Nuts is just one of many tasty treats you can make in quantity, then pack in mason jars. Savvy cooks stow small candies, gourmet chocolates, tiny cookies and crunchy cereal mixes in mason jars to have on hand when a last-minute gift is required.

SPICED NUTS

2 tbsp (25 ml) butter, melted
1/4 cup (50 ml) liquid honey
1 tsp (5 ml) ground cinnamon
1/2 tsp (2 ml) ground nutmeg
pinch *Each:* ground allspice & cloves
3/4 lb (340 g) assorted unsalted nuts – almonds, Brazil nuts, cashews, hazelnuts, pecan halves, peanuts
3 x 236 ml Collection Elite Mason Jar Storage Pots and 2-piece SNAP Lids

Combine butter, honey and spices. Add nuts and stir to thoroughly coat; spread onto greased cookie sheet. (Blanched nuts with outer brown skins removed work best.)

Stirring every 5 minutes, roast coated nuts in 325°F (160°C) oven, until evenly coated, about 15 minutes. Remove, cool completely; pack nuts into jars and apply lids. **Yield – 3 x 236 ml jars.**

RUM BALLS

RUM-LACED BON BONS THAT IMPROVE WITH AGE, IF THEY LAST THAT LONG! LEFTOVER ICING SUGAR ADDS WONDERFUL FLAVOUR TO ICINGS AND OTHER RECIPES.

100 g ground pecans, hazelnuts, almonds or walnuts (1 cup + 2 tbsp / 280 ml)
1 1/2 cups (375 ml) vanilla wafer or graham cracker crumbs
4 tbsp (60 ml) liquid honey
3 tbsp (45 ml) rum
Icing sugar
3 x 236 ml Collection Elite Storage Pots and 2-piece SNAP Lids

Combine nuts, crumbs, honey and rum; mix until well blended and sticky. Generously cover bottom of large baking pan with icing sugar. Spoon rounded half teaspoon portions of nut mixture onto icing sugar; roll into balls. Repeat sugar coating several times until balls are thickly coated. Place balls and a dusting of the icing sugar in jars; cover tightly with SNAP Lids.

Yield – 3 x 236 ml jars. (Double recipe if desired).

SOUP MIX IN A JAR

Combine legumes, pasta, dehydrated vegetables and bouillon powder to create a delicious variety of ready-to-cook hearty soups or stews in a jar. Or, stock up on a variety of legumes, measure and mix them then divide among several jars to save shopping and measuring time in the future.

Ready to use soup mixes make wonderful gifts, but don't give them all away. Stow some away to use on those days when you're stuck for an idea of what to cook or when time is short. Carefully layered to display each ingredient or simply mixed and poured into a jar, these combination recipes are eye-catching as well as practical ways to make efficient use of economical, large-bag or bulk purchases of legumes and pasta.

LENTIL SOUP OR SALAD MIX

THIS COMBO CAN BECOME A SOUP OR A SALAD.

2/3 cup (150 ml) red lentils, divided
1 cup (250 ml) green lentils, divided
1 tbsp (15 ml) chicken boullion powder
1/3 cup (75 ml) white or brown rice
2 tbsp (30 ml) *Each:* bacon bits, dehydrated onions
   500 ml BERNARDIN mason jar & 2-piece SNAP Lid

Pour boullion into jar and top with half of the red lentils, to form first layer; top with half of the green lentils. Combine bacon bits and onion for next layer. Top with rice, then the remaining red and green lentils. Apply lids and attach cooking instructions.
   Yield – 1 x 500 ml jar.

Cooking Instructions:
Salad: *Combine contents of jar with 3 jars of water (6 cups/1500 ml) in large saucepan. Bring to a boil; reduce heat and boil gently, until lentils are al dente. Drain well; transfer to a bowl. While warm, toss mixture with grated peel and juice of 1/2 lemon, olive oil, salt and freshly ground pepper to taste. If desired, add chopped green onion and red pepper.*
Soup: *Combine contents of jar with 4 jars of water (8 cups/2000 ml) cook until lentils are soft; mash or purée, if desired. Season to taste with salt and pepper and serve garnished with thin lemon slices and chopped green onion.*

ALPHABET SOUP

ALPHABET SOUP IN A JAR IS A QUICK WAY TO WARM UP ON A COLD WINTER DAY.

3/4 cup (175 ml) dried alphabet pasta
2 tbsp (30 ml) bouillon base (chicken, beef or vegetable)
1 tbsp (15 ml) dehydrated vegetable mix
1/2 tbsp (7 ml) *Each:* dried parsley & dehydrated minced onion
250 ml BERNARDIN mason jar & 2-piece SNAP Lid

In a bowl combine all ingredients; mix well. Pour into mason jar; apply lid and cooking instructions.
Yield – 1 x 250 ml jar.

Cooking Instructions:
Combine contents of jar with 6 cups (1500 ml) water in large saucepan. Bring to a boil; boil gently until pasta is al dente, about 5 to 10 minutes.
Makes 4 to 6 servings.

HEARTY VEGETABLE SOUP MIX

1 cup (250 ml) *Each:* pinto, kidney, small lima & white navy beans
1 cup (250 ml) *Each:* yellow & green split peas
1 cup (250 ml) *Each:* whole green lentils and pearl barley
4 x 500 ml BERNARDIN mason jars & 2-piece SNAP Lids
Chili powder, divided
Ground cloves, divided

Combine beans, peas, lentils and barley; mix well. Divide equally, pouring into 4 mason jars. Add 2 tsp (10 ml) chili powder and 1/4 tsp (1 ml) ground cloves to each jar. Apply lids and attach cooking instructions.
Yield – 4 x 500 ml jars.

Cooking Instructions:
Pour contents of jar into large saucepan; add water to generously cover beans and let stand overnight. Drain water; add 8 cups (2000 ml) water to soaked beans. Bring to boil; reduce heat & simmer 1 1/2 hours. Add 1 chopped onion, 2 diced carrots, 1/2 lb (250 g) smoked sausage or cubed ham and 1 L jar of home canned tomatoes (or a 28 oz/796 ml can); cook 30 minutes longer. Stir in 2 tbsp (30 ml) sherry, if desired, and 1 tbsp (15 ml) lemon juice.
Makes 8 to 10 servings.

SOUTHWESTERN BEAN STEW MIX

A JAR OF YOUR OWN HOME CANNED TOMATOES IS THE PERFECT PARTNER FOR THIS SOUP-MIX-IN-A-JAR.

1/4 cup (50 ml) beef bouillon powder
2 tbsp (25 ml) chili powder
2 tsp (10 ml) garlic powder
1 cup (250 ml) *Each:* red kidney, white kidney, black turtle and pinto beans
3/4 cup (175 ml) sun-dried tomatoes
1/2 cup (125 ml) dehydrated onions
3-4 dried chili peppers
1 L BERNARDIN mason jar & 2-piece SNAP Lid

Combine bouillon, chili and garlic powders; pour into mason jar. Add two layers of beans. Place chili peppers upright against glass; add a layer of sun-dried tomatoes and top with dehydrated onions.

Layer in remaining two beans. Apply lids and attach cooking instructions. **Yield – 1 x 1 L ml jar.**

Cooking Instructions:
Pour contents of jar into large saucepan; add water to cover beans by 2 inches (10 cm). Bring mixture to a boil; boil 2 minutes, cover and remove from heat. Let stand 1 to 2 hours. Return mixture to a boil; reduce heat and simmer until beans are nearly tender, about 1 hour. Stir occasionally and add more water, if necessary. Add 3/4 lb (340 g) cooked chorizo or spicy Italian sausage and 1 L jar of home canned tomatoes. Cook 30 minutes longer; adjust seasonings to taste. **Makes 8 to 10 servings.**

SEASONING MIXES

BUSY COOKS AND NON-COOKS ALIKE APPRECIATE READY-MADE SEASONING BLENDS THAT CAN COMBINED WITH YOGOURT, SOUR CREAM OR CREAM CHEESE FOR DIPS; WHISKED WITH VINEGAR AND OIL FOR QUICK SALAD DRESSINGS; OR, USED TO SEASON GRILLED FOODS. EACH RECIPE FILLS ONE 125 ML BERNARDIN MASON JAR.

VEGETABLE SPICE MIX

USE THIS MIX TO CREATE A MOUTHWATERING BAGEL SPREAD.

3 tbsp (45 ml) buttermilk powder
2 tbsp (30 ml) dehydrated minced onion
2 tbsp (30 ml) dehydrated vegetable mix
1 tbsp (15 ml) *Each:* dehydrated minced garlic, freeze dried chives
1 tsp (5 ml) *Each:* basil leaves, oregano leaves, thyme leaves and dried parsley
1/2 tsp (2 ml) salt

GARDEN HERB MIX

PERFECT FOR SALAD DRESSINGS OR SEASONING RUBS FOR BARBECUED FOODS.

2 tbsp (30 ml) *Each:* dried parsley, freeze-dried chives, buttermilk powder
1/2 tbsp (7 ml) *Each:* garlic powder, onion powder, ground pepper and dried tarragon
1 tsp (5 ml) *Each:* dried oregano leaves, salt

CAJUN SPICE MIX

ADD SIZZLE TO EVERY DAY COOKING. THIS MIX CREATES A FESTIVE CHEESE BALL. IT CAN ALSO BE USED TO SEASON FAJITA.

2 tbsp (30 ml) dehydrated onions
1 tbsp (15 ml) *Each:* dehydrated minced garlic, paprika, cayenne pepper, dried parsley
2 tsp (10 ml) dried oregano leaves
1 tsp (5 ml) *Each:* salt, ground pepper and dried thyme
1/2 tsp (2 ml) ground cumin

EXAMPLE: GIFT TAG FOR SEASONING MIXES:
Salad Dressing: *Combine 2 tbsp (25 ml) mix with 1 cup (250 ml) buttermilk and 1 cup (250 ml) salad dressing. Mix well and chill.*
Veggie Dip: *Combine 2 tbsp (25 ml) mix with 1 cup (250 ml) sour cream or yogourt and 1 cup (250 ml) salad dressing. Mix well and chill.*

INCREDIBLE IN-EDIBLES

Versatile mason jars are perfect containers for a wealth of creative and artistic endeavours.

MASON JAR CANDLES

Decorative and plain, large to small mason jars are perfect containers for candle making. Although you can make candles with melted paraffin wax, layering wax granules into a jar is far easier. Today's craft stores stock wax granules in a multitude of colours. You simply secure a wick in your choice of mason jars, then add several layers of coloured granules in a pattern of your own design.

Gel candles provide another creative alternate to melted paraffin. Consult the manufacturer's instructions for specific preparation instructions. Add scents and colour tints to your heart's content.

Two-piece SNAP Lids complete your candle in style. These closures keep the candle clean and fresh until it is used. When the candle is lighted, unscrew the band and remove the lid to use as a coaster under the jar. Reapply the screw band to give the lighted candle a decorative touch.

FRAGRANT POTPOURRI
(not pictured)

PRESERVING SUMMER IN A JAR CAN MEAN MORE THAN FRUITS AND VEGETABLES! POTPOURRIS CREATED FROM FLOWERS IN YOUR GARDEN PLUS KITCHEN INGREDIENTS MAKE TREASURED MEMORIES FOR FAMILY AND FRIENDS. HOMEMADE POTPOURRIS LET YOU CUSTOMIZE COLOURS AND AROMAS TO MATCH ANY COLOUR SCHEME.

1/2 cup (125 ml) dried eucalyptus pieces
1/2 cup (125 ml) dried rose petals
2 tbsp (25 ml) pickling salt
4-inch (10 cm) cinnamon sticks, broken into pieces
1 dried orange slice, quartered
1 dried quince slice, quartered
1/4 tsp (1 ml) vanilla extract

In large bowl, combine eucalyptus and rose petals. Add salt, cinnamon sticks, orange and quince; mix well. Sprinkle vanilla over mixture; toss gently. Let mixture dry 30 minutes before filling jars and tightly applying lids.

CANDLES & POTPOURRI

Preserve and present! SNAP Lids and mason jars are perfect for candle makers, especially when fragrances are added. SNAP Lids seal in the fragrance and together with the decorative glass design add a distinction to the completed package. For extra appeal, seal potpourri or homemade candles in mason jars with decorative Collection Elite 2-piece SNAP Lids. When using the potpourri or candles, the SNAP Lid becomes a coaster while the screw band stays in place to add a decorative touch.

SNOW GLOBE

FASCINATING TO WATCH, SNOW GLOBES ARE FUN AND EASY TO PERSONALIZE WHEN YOU CRAFT THEM YOURSELF. ALTHOUGH SNOW GLOBES REQUIRE MINIMAL EFFORT AND LITTLE TIME TO CONSTRUCT, ALLOWING AMPLE TIME TO THOROUGHLY DRY OR CURE THE SILICONE AT VARIOUS STAGES OF CONSTRUCTION WILL PRODUCE THE BEST, LONG-LASTING GLOBE. WATER-PROOF SILI-CON SEALANTS ARE AVAILABLE IN AQUARIUM SUPPLY STORES.

2-piece SNAP Lid
Silicon caulk for water-tight seals
Decorative figurine
BERNARDIN mason jar
Distilled water
Glycerin
Plastic glitter, cutout shapes or snow beads

• Run a bead of silicone around top edge of SNAP Lid. Invert lid and press firmly into screw band, sealing lid into band and creating a one-piece closure. Let dry.
• Test figurine fit and positioning – place figurine in jar. Note that screw band covers base of jar, so some figurines look best when elevated on plastic cap or block. If using, affix figurine to block and block to lid with silicon. Centre figurine/block on inside of lid and affix with silicon. If desired, apply additional silicon with additional tiny decorations. Do not allow silicon or decorations to flow onto red lid sealing compound.
• Determine required water level: fill jar brimful with water. Loosely apply figurine/lid to jar and then remove it and mark water level on jar. Discard water and dry jar rim.
• Refill jar to marked level with distilled water. Stir in 1 tsp (5 ml) glycerin. Add 1/2 to 1 tsp (2 to 5 ml) glitter or snow beads. Let stand until glitter settles to bottom of jar.
• Reapply figurine/lid on jar, screwing on as tightly as possible. Apply a thin bead of silicon between base of screw band and jar. Allow jar to stand upright until silicon drys thoroughly.

CHAMOMILE-MINT BATH SALTS

COMBINE COMMON KITCHEN INGREDIENTS TO CREATE AN ALL-NATURAL GIFT. TREAT YOUR FRIENDS TO A SKIN-SOOTHING TREAT-MENT OF CHAMOMILE AND RELAXING EFFECTS OF PEPPERMINT AROMAS. SMALL PORTIONS OF THESE BATH SALTS CAN BE ADDED DIRECTLY TO WARM WATER. TIE LARGER PORTIONS INTO HOMEMADE CHEESECLOTH SACHETS TO AVOID FLOATING TEA LEAVES.

For each 236 or 250 ml jar:
1/2 cup (125 ml) Epsom Salts
1/4 cup (50 ml) sea salt
4 tsp (20 ml) peppermint tea or 2 tea bags
4 tsp (20 ml) chamomile tea or 2 tea bags
1/2 tsp (1 ml) vanilla extract
1/2 tsp (1 ml) peppermint extract

• In large bowl, combine Epsom and sea salts. Add chamomile and peppermint tea; mix well. Sprinkle vanilla and peppermint extracts over salt mixture; stir and mix to thoroughly blend extracts.
• Pour into dry jars and tightly apply 2-piece lids.

JUST FOR KIDS

Create special homemade gifts for kids of all ages. Mason jars and lids provide compact, see-through storage for collectibles and all those small pieces for games, construction sets and other toys and crafts.

ALTHOUGH THIS PLAY CLAY IS NOT MEANT TO BE EATEN, ALL THE COMPONENTS ARE FOODS SO YOUNGSTERS WHO SNEAK A TASTE WON'T BE HARMED.

TINTING THE DOUGH WITH DRINK CRYSTALS PRODUCES VIBRANT COLOURS AND A PLEASANTLY SCENTED PRODUCT.

SMALL MASON JARS CLOSED WITH PLASTIC STORAGE LIDS ARE JUST THE RIGHT SIZE FOR MOLDABLE CLAY – EASY FOR SMALL HANDS TO REMOVE. AND THE CLOSED CONTAINER CAN BE EASILY WASHED OFF AFTER EACH USE.

MAKE SEVERAL BATCHES TO CREATE A RAINBOW OF COLOURED MOLDING DOUGH FOR THOSE SPECIAL YOUNGSTERS IN YOUR LIFE. TO MAKE A COMPLETE PLAY KIT, PAIR POTS OF FUN WITH A SHORT PIECE OF DOWEL (FOR ROLLING), A STURDY PLASTIC KNIFE AND SMALL COOKIE CUTTERS.

2/3 cup (150 ml) all purpose flour
2 1/2 tbsp (37 ml) pickling salt
4 tsp (20 ml) cream of tartar
2/3 cup (150 ml) water
1 tbsp (15 ml) vegetable oil
1 1/2 tsp (7 ml) unsweetened drink crystals
2 x 125 ml BERNARDIN mason jars
2 BERNARDIN Standard Plastic Storage Lids

• In a saucepan combine flour, salt and cream of tartar. Stir in water and vegetable oil; mix well. Sprinkle in drink crystals, stirring until colour is evenly distributed.

• Stirring constantly, cook over medium heat until mixture forms a ball in centre of saucepan, 3 to 5 minutes. Remove from heat and cool. Knead dough for 1 minute. Lightly coat inside surface of mason jars with vegetable oil to assist in dough removal. Press dough into jars; apply lids securely.

Yield – 2 x 125 ml jars

HIDE & SEEK

LOOKING FOR WAYS TO KEEP YOUNGSTERS OCCUPIED IN THE CAR OR ON RAINY DAYS?

Fill a 1 L BERNARDIN mason jar with bird seed or rice add a selection of small plastic or wooden toys; tightly apply a two-piece SNAP Lid or plastic storage lids. Tie a tag on the jar, listing the objects inside the jar.

Each player turns or shakes the jar to identify each object. Allow about one inch (2.5 cm) headspace in the jar.

It's easy to adjust this homemade toy to different interests, ages and skill levels. Select trinkets or toys themed to a child's interests – i.e. plastic farm or zoo animals, miniature balls representing various sports or small artificial fruits and vegetables. Stores usually stock a wide selection of miniatures in craft and notions departments. For younger children use only a few larger objects or colourful shapes. For competitive play, time each player's search. To increase the difficulty, draw a circle on the jar and instruct players to shake the jar to move the identified piece into the circle before scoring a point.

TROUBLE SHOOTING

CONDITION	CAUSE	PREVENTION/SOLUTION
Seals & processing		
Seal failure Note: correct cause and reprocess within 24 hours, use or refrigerate food immediately.	Many factors can contribute to seal failure: not preparing lids correctly, improper adjustment of SNAP Lids (over-or under-tightening screw band), food particles on jar rim, not processing food or underprocessing food.	**Carefully follow instructions for using home canning jars and SNAP Lids and follow correct processing methods and times for the recipe.**
Jar seals then unseals – do not use. If spoilage is evident, do not use food.	1. Minimum vacuum seal caused by underprocessing or skipping the essential step of heat processing filled jars. 2. Particles of food left on the sealing surface. 3. Crack or chip in jar rim. 4. Air bubbles not removed before adjusting SNAP Lid.	**1. Process each food by recommended length of time. 2. Wipe jar rim and threads of the jar before adjusting SNAP Lid. 3. Check jars; discard ones unsuitable for canning. 4. Use recommended headspace in recipe. 5. Slide nonmetallic utensil between food and jar to release trapped air.**
Buckled lids – appear to warp or bulge upward under the screw bands. If spoilage is evident, do not use food.	1. Buckling that is apparent immediately after heat processing is caused by applying the screw bands too tightly. 2. Buckling during storage is caused by food spoilage, when heat processing is insufficient and does not destroy all spoilage microorganisms.	**1. Apply screw band securely & firmly until resistance is met – fingertip tight. Do not overtighten. 2. Ensure proper heat processing time and method. Foods, on which lids buckle during storage, must be discarded in a manner that neither humans nor animals will consume it.**
Liquid loss – during processing – do not open jar to replace liquid.	1. Food not heated before packing into jars. 2. Food packed too tightly. 3. Air bubbles not removed before adjusting SNAP Lid. 4. Pressure canner not operated correctly. 5. Jars not covered with water in boiling water canner. 6. Starchy foods absorbed liquid. 7. Light band torque – screw bands were applied too loosely.	**1. Use hot pack method. 2. Pack food loosely. 3. Slide nonmetallic utensil between food and jar to release trapped air. 4. Pressure should not be allowed to fluctuate during processing time. Allow pressure to drop to zero naturally; waiting 2 minutes before opening lid. 5. Jars must be covered with water by 1 to 2 inches (2.5 to 5 cm) throughout the processing period. 6. None.**
Liquid loss – immediately following processing (siphoning).	Jars removed from canner before temperatures stabilizes.	**When boiling water canner processing time is complete, turn off heat & remove lid. Wait 5 minutes or until water is still before removing jars. For pressure canner, follow manufacturer's directions for cooling prior to removing canner lid.**
Black spots on underside of metal lid.	Natural compounds in some foods cause a brown or black deposit on the underside of the lid. This deposit is harmless and does not mean the food is unsafe to eat.	**None.**

CONDITION	CAUSE	PREVENTION/SOLUTION
Colour changes		
Food darkens in top of jar.	1. Liquid did not cover food product. 2. Food not processed long enough to inactivated enzymes. 3. Manner of packing and processing did not expel enough air. 4. Air was sealed in the jar either because headspace was too large or air bubbles were not removed.	**1. Completely cover food product with brine, syrup, juice or water before adjusting SNAP Lid.** **2. Process each food for recommended length of time.** **3. Use hot pack when indicated in the recipe.** **4. Use headspace recommended in recipe. Slide nonmetallic utensil between food and jar to release trapped air.**
Fruit darkens after removed from jar.	Fruit has not been processed long enough to inactivate enzymes.	**Process each fruit by recommended method and for recommended length of time. Time is counted when water reaches a rolling boil in the boiling water canner.**
Corn turns brown after processing.	1. Variety of corn was not suitable for canning or corn was not harvested at the correct time. 2. Liquid did not cover corn. 3. Jars were processed at too high a temperature.	**1. Select only varieties of corn recommended for preserving and choose ears of corn with plump, shiny kernels filled with milk.** **2. Cover corn with liquid before adjusting SNAP Lid.** **3. Keep pressure in canner at recommended pounds; dial gauge may be faulty and must be checked.**
Pink, red, blue or purple colour in canned apples, pears, peaches and quinces.	A natural chemical change which occurs when these fruits are cooked.	**None.**
Some food becomes black, brown or gray.	Natural chemical substances (tannins, sulfur compounds and acids) in food react with minerals in water or with metal utensils used in preparing the food.	**Use soft water. Avoid using brass, copper, iron, aluminum, zinc or chipped enamelware and utensils from which tin plate is worn.**
Green garlic – usually in pickled foods.	1. Immature garlic that has not been properly aged. 2. Pickling liquid causes reaction which causes pigment changes. 3. Garlic may also turn green when exposed to sunlight or temperature changes. 4. Some varieties of garlic and/or growing conditions produce garlic that has an excess of natural blue/green pigmentation. This colouring becomes more evident after pickling.	**None – green or blue garlic is still generally safe to eat.**
Pink cauliflower.	Pickling liquid causes reaction which changes pigments.	**None – pink cauliflowers is generally still safe to eat.**

CONDITION	CAUSE	PREVENTION/SOLUTION
Crystals & Sediments		
Crystals in grape products.	Formed by tartaric acid which is naturally found in grapes.	Grape juice should stand overnight after straining; ladle juice from container so as not to disturb sediment that has settled to the bottom; strain again.
White crystals in canned spinach.	Calcium and oxalic acid in spinach combine to form harmless calcium oxalate.	None.
Fruit/Vegetables		
White sediment in bottom of jar of vegetables. If spoilage is evident, do not use food.	1. Starch from the food. 2. Minerals in water used. 3. Bacterial spoilage; liquid is usually murky and food is soft. (Do not use.)	1. None. 2. Use soft water. 3. Process each food by recommended method and for recommended length of time.
Fruit floats in jar.	Fruit is lighter that the syrup.	Use firm, ripe fruit. Heat fruit before packing. Use a light to medium syrup. Pack fruit as tightly as possible without crushing.
Liquid – cloudy If spoilage is evident, do not use food.	1. Food spoilage from underprocessing. 2. Minerals in water. 3. Starch in vegetables. 4. Fillers in table salt.	1. Process each food by recommended method and for recommended length of time. 2. Use soft water. 3. None. 4. Use canning and pickling salt or a salt without additives.
Pickles		
Pickles – hollow.	Faulty growth of cucumbers.	None. Hollow cucumbers are best if used for relish. They can be identified during cleaning, as hollow cucumbers will float in water.
Pickles – white sediment in bottom of jar.	1. Harmless yeast has grown on the surface and then settled. 2. Additives in salt.	1. None. The presence of a small amount of white sediment is normal. 2. Use canning and pickling salt or a salt without additives.
Pickles – shriveled.	1. Too much salt, sugar or vinegar was added to the cucumbers. 2. Whole pickles were not picked before canning. 3. Cucumbers had a wax coating that prevented the brine from penetrating the peel.	1. Gradually add salt, sugar or vinegar until the full amount has been incorporated. 2. Prick whole pickles before canning to allow the brine to saturate and plump the flesh of the cucumber. 3. Use unwaxed pickling cucumbers.

CONDITION	CAUSE	PREVENTION/SOLUTION
Pickles		
Pickles – soft slippery. If spoilage is evident, do not use food.	1. Blossom end was not removed from the cucumber. 2. Brine or vinegar was too weak. 3. Scum was not removed daily from top of brine. 4. Pickles not completely covered with brine. 5. Pickles were underprocessed.	1. Cut 1/16th inch (0.2 cm) off blossom end of cucumber before pickling. 2. Use pure, refined salt or canning and pickling salt, 5% acidity vinegar and a tested recipe. 3. Completely remove scum daily during the brining process. 4. Pickles must be completely covered with liquid during fermentation and in the home canning jar. 5. Process all pickled foods in a boiling water canner.
Pickles – darkened or discoloured.	1. Minerals present in hard water used in making the pickles. 2. Brass, iron, copper, aluminum or zinc utensils were used in making the pickles. 3. Ground spices used. 4. Whole spices left in jars of pickles.	1. Use soft water. 2. Use enamelware, glass, stainless steel or stoneware utensils. 3. Use whole spices. 4. Whole cloves, cinnamon sticks and other whole spices used for flavouring the pickling liquid should be removed before canning.
Pickles – scum on brine.	Surface scum while curing cucumbers is a result of yeast, mold and bacteria that feed on acid thus reducing its concentration if allowed to accumulate.	Remove scum frequently during the brining process.
Pickles – cloudy brine. Do not use if spoilage is evident.	Use of table salt. Minerals in water (hard water).	Use pickling salt. Use soft water.
Pickles – strong, bitter taste.	1. Spices too old, cooked too long in vinegar or too high in quantity. 2. Vinegar too strong. 3. Use of salt substitutes.	1. Follow tested recipe & use fresh spices. 2. Use vinegar with a 5% acidity. 3. Potassium chloride found in salt substitutes is normally bitter.
Jams, Jelly, Soft spreads		
Soft spread – tough or stiff.	1. Too much natural pectin in fruit. 2. Soft spread was cooked too long. 3. Too much sugar used.	1. Use fruit that is fully ripe. 2. When commercial pectin is not added, use Gel Test (see page 15). 3. If commercial pectin is not used 3/4 cup to 1 cup (175 ml to 250 ml) sugar for each cup of juice of fruit should be adequate. Use standard dry measuring cups and level sugar even with the top edge of the cup.
Soft spread – ferments. If spoilage is evident, do not use food.	Soft spread was not brought to the correct temperature before filling jars and/or was underprocessed, preventing all spoilage microorganisms such as yeasts from being destroyed.	Bring soft spread to a rolling boil when using commercial pectin or 220°F (104°C) when preparing a recipe without added pectin. Fill jars and adjust SNAP Lids one at a time. Process in a boiling water canner. Refer to recipe for correct processing time.

CONDITION	CAUSE	PREVENTION/SOLUTION
Jams, Jelly, Soft spreads		
Soft spread – contains glass like particles.	1. Too much sugar used. 2. The mixture may have been undercooked. 3. The mixture may have been cooked too slowly or too long. 4. Undissolved sugar that was sticking to the pan washed into the soft spread as it was poured. 5. If jelly is grape, the crystals may be tartaric acid, the natural substance in grapes from which cream of tartar is made.	1. Follow instructions for Soft Spreads (see pages 14-36). 2. Too short a cooking time results in sugar not dissolving completely and not mixing thoroughly with juice or fruit. 3. Long, slow cooking results in too much evaporation of the water content of the fruit. 4. Carefully wipe side of pan free of sugar crystals with a damp cloth before filling jars. Ladle soft spread into jars instead of pouring. 5. Allow juice to stand in the refrigerator 12 to 24 hours. Ladle juice from bowl, being careful not to disturb sediment that may have settled in the bottom, and strain through a damp jelly bag or several layers of cheesecloth.
Soft spread – weeps.	1. Syneresis or "weeping" occurs in quick-setting soft spreads and is due to the quantity of acid and quality of pectin in the fruit. 2. Storage conditions were not ideal.	1. None. 2. Store soft spreads in a dry, dark place between 50°F and 70°F (10°C to 21°C).
Soft spread, made with added pectin – too soft.	1. Proportions of sugar, juice or fruit, acid and pectin were not in balance. 2. Too large a batch was made at one time. 3. Fruit used was too ripe. 4. Soft spread was not boiled at a "rolling boil" for the time indicated in the recipe. 5. The wrong type of pectin was used. 6. The wrong amount of pectin was used.	1. Follow instructions for Soft Spreads (see pages 14-36). 2. Use no more that 4 to 6 cups (1 L to 1.5 L) of juice or fruit in each batch. Never "double batch" the recipe. 3. Fruit selected should include some fruit that is slightly under-ripe (but not green) along with some fruit that is fully ripe. 4. Soft spread must be brought to a hard boil, one that cannot be stirred down, and boiled hard for the length of time indicated in the recipe. 5. Original powdered, Liquid and No Sugar Needed and Freezer Jam pectins are NOT INTERCHANGEABLE. Use only the type of pectin indicated in the recipe. 6. Package weight for the different brands of commercial pectin is not uniform. Use only the amount of pectin called for in the recipe.
Soft spread, made without added pectin – too soft.	1. Proportions of sugar, juice or fruit, acid and pectin were not in balance. 2. Too large a batch was made at one time. 3. Fruit used was too ripe. 4. Soft spread was not boiled to the correct temperature.	1. Follow instructions for soft spreads (see pages 14-36). 2. Use no more than 4 to 6 cups (1 L to 1.5 L) of juice or fruit in each batch. Never "double batch" the recipe. 3. Fruit selected should include some fruit that is slightly under-ripe (but not green) along with some fruit that is fully ripe. 4. Use Gel Test (see page 15).

CONDITION	CAUSE	PREVENTION/SOLUTION
Jams, Jelly, Soft spreads		
Soft spread – cloudy.	1. Fruit used was too green. 2. Fruit may have been cooked too long before straining. 3. Some fruit pulp may have been extracted when juice was squeezed from fruit. 4. Soft spread was ladled into jars too slowly. 5. Soft spread mixture was allowed to stand before it was ladled into the jars.	1. Fruit should be firm and ripe. 2. Fruit should be cooked only until it is tender. 3. To obtain the clearest jelly possible, let juice drain through a damp jelly bag or several layers of cheesecloth. Do not squeeze jelly bag. 4. Work quickly to fill jars before soft spread starts to set. 5. When cooking period is complete, ladle soft spread into jars and process immediately.
Jelly or soft spread – filled with bubbles. If spoilage is evident, *do not use.*	1. If bubbles are moving when the jar is stationary, the soft spread is spoiling. 2. If bubbles are not moving when the jar is stationary, air was trapped in the soft spread as it gelled.	1. Process all soft spreads in a boiling water canner for the time indicated in the recipe. 2. Ladle soft spread quickly into the jar, holding ladle near the rim of the jar or funnel. 3. Use nonmetallic utensil to free bubbles before applying lid.
Soft spread or fruit mixture – **molds** – *do not use.*	1. Mixture was not fully heated to a temperature high enough to treat mold spores prior to filling jars. 2. Food was not processed long enough to destroy molds, allowing them to grow on the surface of the food. 3. Headspace was too great to allow creation of an adequate vacuum seal.	1. Cook mixtures, such as jams and applesauce, to a full rolling boil that cannot be stirring down prior to filling jars. 2. Heat process all filled jars in a boiling water canner for the time indicated in the tested recipe. 3. Leave 1/4 inch (0.5 cm) headspace in soft spreads; 1/2 inch (1 cm) for fruit.
Soft spreads – mixture gels but fruit solids and clear jelly separate into layers.	1. Use of immature fruit or porous textured fruit. 2. High sugar content in recipe.	1. Use fully ripe, freshly picked fruit and berries, either fresh or frozen. Some imported/out of seasons fruits are firmly textured and tend to float more easily. 2. Measure carefully and be sure to cook mixture at a full rolling boil for time directed. 3. After processing and after lids have snapped down but spread is still hot & liquid, carefully – without disturbing screw band – rotate jar and turn upside briefly to redispurse solids in mixture. 4. Before serving, stir solids into gelled portion.
Tomatoes		
Tomatoes – separation in juice.	Enzymes in tomatoes cause separation of water from tomato solids.	To limit separation, quickly heat a small quantity of quartered or crushed tomatoes to a boil. While maintaining a boil, add tomatoes in small quantities until full batch is boiling.
Tomatoes – colour changes.	Tomatoes are acidic and react with metals when cooked in aluminum, copper, brass or cast iron utensils.	Use stainless steel or glass utensils or enamel pans that have no breaks in enamel.

REMAKE INSTRUCTIONS

COOKED SOFT SPREADS

Unique circumstances – growing conditions, the fruit variety or the fruit itself – occasionally necessitate more than 24 hours for a gel to form. Therefore, wait two weeks to see if the product will gel. Do not disturb or shake the product during this time.

If after two weeks the product still has not formed a good set, it may be recooked.
• Only remake products that have been heat processed and have maintained a good seal.
• First, make one trial batch using 1 cup (250 ml) unset product to assure success.
• Do not recook more than 8 cups (2000 ml) at one time.
• All remade jams and jellies must be processed in a boiling-water canner.

REMAKE COOKED JAM/JELLY USING ORIGINAL FRUIT PECTIN

1. Measure unset jam/jelly to be re-cooked.
2. For each 1 cup (250 ml) product, measure:
   2 tbsp (30 ml) granulated sugar,
   1 tbsp (15 ml) water and
   1 1/2 tsp (7 ml) BERNARDIN *Original Fruit Pectin.*
3. In a large, deep stainless steel saucepan, whisk fruit pectin into water. Stirring constantly to prevent scorching, bring to a boil. Stir in the measured unset soft spread and sugar.
4. Stirring constantly over high heat, bring to a full rolling boil; boil hard 30 seconds. Remove from heat; skim foam, if necessary.
5. Ladle into hot jars, leaving 1/4 inch (0.5 cm) of top rim (headspace). Remove air bubbles. Wipe jar rim removing any stickiness. Center SNAP Lid on jar; apply screw band *securely & firmly* until resistance is met — fingertip tight. Process **10 minutes** in boiling water canner.

REMAKE COOKED JAM/JELLY USING NO SUGAR NEEDED FRUIT PECTIN

1. Measure unset jam/jelly to be re-cooked. Re-cook no more than 4 cups (1000 ml) at a time.
2. For each 1 cup (250 ml) product, measure:
   1 tbsp (15 ml) water and
   1 tsp (5 ml) Bernardin NO SUGAR NEEDED Fruit Pectin.
3. In a large, deep stainless steel saucepan, whisk pectin into water. Stirring constantly to prevent scorching, bring to a boil. Stir in the measured unset soft spread.
4. Stirring constantly over high heat, bring to a full rolling boil; boil hard 30 seconds. Remove from heat; skim foam, if necessary.
5. Ladle into hot jars, leaving 1/4 inch (0.5 cm) of top rim (headspace). Remove air bubbles. Wipe jar rim removing any stickiness. Center SNAP Lid on jar; apply screw band *securely & firmly* until resistance is met – fingertip tight. Process **10 minutes** in boiling water canner.

REMAKE COOKED JAM/JELLY USING LIQUID PECTIN

1. Measure unset product and place in a large, deep stainless steel saucepan.
2. For each 1 cup (250 ml) unset product, measure and set aside:
   3 tbsp (45 ml) granulated sugar,
   1 1/2 tsp (7 ml) lemon juice
   1 1/2 tsp (7 ml) BERNARDIN *Liquid* Pectin.
3. Stirring constantly over high heat, bring soft spread to a boil. Quickly stir in sugar, lemon juice and liquid pectin.
4. Stirring constantly, return mixture to a full rolling boil; boil hard 1 minute. Remove from heat; skim foam, if necessary.
5. Ladle into hot jars, leaving 1/4 inch (0.5 cm) of top rim (headspace). Remove air bubbles. Wipe jar rim removing any stickiness. Center SNAP Lid on jar; apply screw band *securely & firmly* until resistance is met – fingertip tight. Process **10 minutes** in boiling water canner.

LONG BOIL SPREADS MADE WITHOUT ADDED PECTIN

Double check recipe to be sure correct ingredient measures were used. Boil the unset soft spread to the temperature indicated in the original recipe or to the gelling point if a temperature is not given. Ladle into hot jars, leaving 1/4 inch (0.5 cm) headspace. Remove air bubbles. Wipe jar rim removing any stickiness. Centre new SNAP Lid on jar; apply screw band securely until fingertip tight. Process **10 minutes** in boiling water canner.

IDENTIFYING & DISPOSING OF SPOILED FOODS

Examine each jar carefully before using it to ensure a vacuum seal is present. Do not use any product that shows signs of spoilage or the lid is unsealed. Spoilage produces gases that cause the lids to swell and/or break the seal. Do not use jars with lids that lift off without force, i.e. do not require an opener to break the seal. Visually examine jars for other spoilage signs, including:

• Broken seals	• Mold	• Gassiness
• Cloudiness	• Spurting liquid	• Seepage
• Yeast growth	• Fermentation	• Slime
• Disagreeable odours		

Home canned food that displays signs of spoilage must be discarded in a manner that no human or animal will come in contact with the product. Handle carefully all suspect jars of spoiled low acid or tomato products.

Detoxify spoiled vegetables, meats, poultry, seafoods and tomato products to prevent any possible contamination from botulin that could be present.

Place the product, jar, lid and band in a deep saucepan. Cover with 2 inches (5 cm) water. Cover pan and bring water to a boil; boil 30 minutes. Avoid splashing water or product outside the pot. Cool contents of pot. Discard all contents of saucepot.

To clean surfaces that come in contact with suspect product, use a solution of 1 part chlorine bleach to 5 parts water. Allow cleaning solution to stand 5 minutes before rinsing. Dispose of dishcloths and sponges used in the detoxifying process.

PRODUCE PURCHASE GUIDE

APPROXIMATE, AVERAGE WEIGHTS AND VOLUME YIELDS OF COMMON FRUITS AND VEGETABLES. ACTUAL YIELDS WILL VARY BASED ON SIZE OF SELECTED ITEMS AND PREPARATION TECHNIQUE.

VEGETABLES	WEIGHT Imperial	Metric	Purchase Unit	Condition	Prepared Yield VOLUME Imperial	Metric
ASPARAGUS	1 lb	454 g	16-20 medium	1 inch (2.5 cm) pieces	4 cups	1000 ml
BEANS, *green or yellow*	1 lb	454 g			3 cups	750 ml
BEANS *(legumes)*	1 lb	454 g	kidney beans	dried	2 1/2 cups	625 ml
			pea/navy beans	dried	2 1/3 cups	575 ml
BEETS	1 lb	454 g	without tops	peeled, diced	2 cups	500 ml
BROCCOLI	1 lb	454 g		florets	2 cups	500 ml
CABBAGE	3 1/2 lb	1.7 kg	1 large head			
	1 lb	454 g		shredded	3 1/2 - 4 1/2 cups	875 - 1125 ml
CARROTS	1 lb	454 g	5-6 med without tops	sliced	3 cups	750 ml
				shredded	2 1/2 cups	625 ml
CAULIFLOWER	1.7 lb	780 g	1 medium			
	1 lb	454 g		florets	1 1/2 cups	375 ml
CELERY			1 bunch	16 stalks		
	1 lb	454 g	8 stalks	sliced	3 2/3 cups	900 ml
CORN on the COB			1 dozen ears	kernels	5-6 cups	1250 - 1500 ml
CUCUMBER –						
English or field	1/2 lb	225 g	1 medium	sliced or diced	2 cups	500 ml
CUCUMBER *(pickling)*		454 g	5 med			
ONIONS	1 lb	454 g	3 large	chopped	2 - 2 1/2 cups	500 - 625 ml
MUSHROOMS	1 lb	454 g		sliced	2-3 cups	500 - 750 ml
PARSNIPS	1 lb	454 g	4 medium			
PEAS, *green fresh*	1 lb	454 g	fresh in pods	shelled	1 cup	250 ml
PEPPERS, *red, green, sweet or yellow*				whole	3 cups	750 ml
POTATOES	1 lb	454 g	3-4 medium	diced	2 1/4 cups	550 ml
TOMATOES – *round, globe*	1 lb	454 g	2 large, or 3 medium or 4 small	chopped	2 cups	500 ml
				sliced	2 1/2 cups	625 ml
				crushed or puréed	1 1/2 cups	375 ml
1 bushel	53 lb	24 kg				
TOMATOES – *Italian plum*	1 lb	454 g	4 large or 5 medium or 6-7 small	chopped	2 cups	500 ml
				sliced	2 1/2 cups	625 ml
				crushed or puréed	1 1/2 cups	375 ml
1 bushel	53 lb	24 kg				
TURNIPS, RUTABAGA	1 lb	454 kg		cubed	2 1/2 cups	625 ml
ZUCCHINI			1 medium	sliced	1 cup	250 ml

| FRUIT | WEIGHT | | Purchase Unit | Condition | Prepared Yield VOLUME | |
	Imperial	Metric			Imperial	Metric
APPLES	1 lb	454 g	3 medium	peeled & sliced	2 3/4 cups	675 ml
			1 medium	diced	1 cup	250 ml
APRICOTS	1 lb	454 g	8-12 medium	sliced	2 1/2 cups	625 ml
			1 medium	sliced	1/4 cup	50 ml
BANANAS	1 lb	454 g	3 to 4	sliced	2 cups	500 ml
				mashed	1 1/3 cups	325 ml
BLACKBERRIES	12.2 oz	345 g	1 pint container	whole, fresh	2 cups	500 ml
				crushed	1 1/4 cups	300 ml
BLACK CURRANTS	1/2 lb	225 g	1 pint container	whole, fresh	2 cups	250 ml
dried	1 lb	454 g		dried, chopped	3 1/4 cups	800 ml
BLUEBERRIES	12.3 oz	350 g	1 pint container	whole	2 1/3 cups	575 ml
				crushed	1 1/3 cups	325 ml
CHERRIES, *fresh*	1 lb	454 g	1 lb/454 g	unpitted	1 3/4 cups	425 ml
	1 lb	454 g	1 lb/454 g	pitted	2 1/3 cups	575 ml
Red Tart Cherries						
Frozen, pitted	10 lb	4.5 kg	10 lb/4.5 kg bucket		16 cups	4000 ml
CRANBERRIES	3/4 lb	375 g		whole, fresh	3 cups	750 ml
ELDERBERRIES	10 oz	290 g	1 pint container	whole, fresh	2 cups	500 ml
FIGS, *fresh*	1 lb	454 g	12 medium, fresh	whole, fresh		
dried	1 lb	454 g	dried	dried, chopped	2 3/4 cups	675 ml
GOOSEBERRIES	10.5 oz	300 g	1 pint container	whole, fresh	2 cups	500 ml
GRAPEFRUIT	1 lb	454 g	1 medium	sections	1 cup	250 ml
GRAPES	1 lb	454 g	seeded grapes	whole, fresh	2 cups	500 ml
	1 lb	454 g	seedless grapes	whole, fresh	2 1/2 cups	625 ml
LEMONS	1 lb	454 g	4 medium	whole, fresh		
			1 medium	juice	2 1/2 tbsp	40 ml
MELON			1 medium honeydew or cantaloup	cubes or balls	3 cups	750 ml
MULBERRIES	9.8 oz	140 g	1 pint container	whole, fresh	2 cups	500 ml
NECTARINES	1 lb	454 g	3 medium	sliced	2 cups	500 ml
ORANGES	1 lb	454 g	2 to 3	sections	2 cups	500 ml
				juice	2/3 cups	150 ml
PEARS	1 lb	454 g	3 pears	peeled, cored & sliced	2 1/4 cups	650 ml
PEACHES	2.2 lb	1 kg	6-8 medium	sliced	4 1/4 cups	450 ml
				chopped	3 1/3 cups	875 ml
				crushed	3 cups	750 ml
PLUMS	1 lb	454 g	10 plums	sliced	3 1/3 cups	750 ml
PRUNES	1 lb	454 g	dried, pitted	whole	2 1/4 cups	550 ml
RAISINS	1 lb	454 g	seedless	whole	2 3/4 cups	675 ml
RHUBARB	1 lb	454 g	4-8 stalks	chopped	2 cups	500 ml
RASPBERRIES	12.6 oz	358 g	1 pint container	whole, fresh	2 3/4 cups	675 ml
				crushed	1 1/3 cups	325 ml
SASKATOON BERRIES	9.5 oz	270 g	1 pint	whole	2 cups	500 ml
STRAWBERRIES	1.5 lb	675 g	1 quart container	whole, fresh	4 cups	1000 ml
				sliced	3 cups	750 ml
				crushed	2 1/2 cups	625 ml

GLOSSARY

Altitude – the vertical elevation (feet or meters) of a location above sea level.

Antioxidant – An agent, such as lemon juice, ascorbic acid or a blend of ascorbic and citric acids, that inhibits oxidation and controls discolouration of light colour fruits and vegetables.

Ascorbic Acid – A natural component of some fruits and vegetables that is available commercially in a concentrated form as white, crystalline powder or Vitamin C. It is used to control discolouration of light coloured fruits and vegetables.

Bacteria – Microorganism, some of which are harmful, found in the soil, water and air around us. Some bacteria thrive in conditions common in low acid canned food and produce toxins that must be destroyed by heating to 240°F (116°C) for a specified time. For this reason, it is essential to heat process low acid foods in a pressure canner.

Blanch – To loosen the skin/peel or to inactivate enzymes by submerging a food in boiling water or steam. Blanching is immediately followed by rapidly cooling the food in ice water.

Boil – Water or food heated to 212°F (100°C) at sea level. A "boil" is achieved only when the mixture is continuously rolling or actively bubbling.

> **Boil gently or simmer** – To cook food gently just below the boiling point (180°-200°F/82°-93°C). Bubbles rise gently from the pot bottom, only slightly disturbing the surface of the food.

> **Full rolling boil** – a rapid, "rolling" boil (220°F/104°C) usually foaming or spurting, that cannot be stirred down. This stage is essential to achieve a gel when making cooked jams or jellies.

Boiling Water Canner – A large deep pot with a lid and a rack to lift jars off direct heat. The pot must be large enough to completely immerse and fully surround canning jars and deep enough to cover jars with 1 to 2 inches (3-5 cm) water. Boiling water canners are used to heat process high acid foods.

Botulism – A deadly form of food poisoning caused by ingestion of the toxin produced by spores of the bacterium Clostridium botulinum. This bacterium can be present on any food but does not survive in high acid environments. In low acid environments, growth of Clostridium botulinum spores is prevented when filled jars of low acid foods are "heat processed" at a temperature of 240°F (116°C) for the prescribed time in pressure canner.

Bubble Remover – A nonmetallic utensil used to free air bubbles trapped inside a jar before the lid is applied. Bernardin makes a unique utensil for this purpose.

Citric Acid – A natural acid derived from citrus fruits, used to increase the acidity of tomatoes for safe heat processing in a boiling water canner. It is also used in combination with ascorbic acid as an antioxidant to control discolouration of fruits.

Colour Protection Solution – An 'antioxidant' solution used to retard darkening (oxidizing) of cut, light coloured fruits such as apples, peaches, pears.

Options – In 4 cups (1 L) water, dissolve:

2 tbsp (925 ml) Fruit-Fresh® Colour Protector, OR
1/4 tsp (1 ml) ascorbic acid (vitamin C), OR
4 tbsp (60 ml) lemon juice

Condiment – Sweet or savoury sauce used to enhance or garnish entrées.

Conserve – Small pieces of fruit, nuts and/or raisins uniformly distributed in a very thick sauce.

Cool Place – Term used to describe best storage for home canned foods. The ideal place is dark with a consistent temperature of 50° to 70°F (10° to 21°C).

Dehydration (or drying) – The process of removing water from food.

Dry Pack – When freezing food, to pack without added liquid or sugar.

Enzyme – A protein that acts as a catalyst in organisms. In food, enzymes start the process of decomposition, changing the flavour, colour and texture of fruit and vegetables. Enzyme actions slows down in frozen food; increases quickly at temperatures between 85°F and 120°F (29°C and 49°C); stops at temperatures above 140°F (60°C). Following recommended food preservation methods neutralizes enzyme action.

Fermentation – An action caused by yeasts that have not been destroyed during processing of canned food. With the exception of some pickles that use intentional fermentation in preparation, do not consume fermented home canned foods.

Fingertip Tight – The degree to which screw bands are properly applied to home canning jars. Use fingers to apply screw band securely & firmly until resistance is met – fingertip tight. Do not overtighten. Do not use utensil or full force of hand to overtighten bands. Do not retighten bands after processing.

Flash Freezing – Accelerated method of freezing foods. In the home, rapid freezing is accomplished by placing individual food pieces on a baking sheet and placing the sheet in a freezer until the pieces are firm. The frozen pieces are then packed in airtight containers.

Freezer Burn – The result of dehydration of improperly packed frozen foods. Freezer burn results in loss of flavour, texture and colour.

Headspace – In a home canning jar, the unfilled space between the top of the food or liquid and the underside of the lid. The correct amount of headspace is essential for food expansion as jars are heated and for formation of a strong vacuum seal as jars cool.

Hermetic Seal – A seal that secures a product against the entry of microorganisms and maintains commercial sterility.

High Acid Food – Foods that have a natural acidity or pH of 4.6 or lower; also food mixtures composed of low acid foods combined or treated with sufficient quantities of high acid foods such as vinegar, lemon juice or citric acid to achieve an over-all 4.6 pH acidity. High acid foods may be safely heat processed in a boiling water canner at sea level 212°F (100°C).

Hot Pack – Filling jars with preheated, hot food prior to heat processing. Because preheating foods exhausts excess air and permits a tighter pack in the jar, hot packing is the preferred method when using firm food. It reduces food floatation and requires fewer jars.

Jam – Crushed or finely chopped fruit combines with sugar, with or without added pectin, to form a gel.

Jelly – Fruit or acidified vegetable juice cooked with sugar and added pectin, if required, to form a gel.

Jelly Bag – A mesh bag used to strain juice for making jellies. A cheesecloth-lined strainer may be substituted.

Long Boil Jams/Jellies – Sugar and fruit mixtures boiled to concentrate fruit's natural pectin and evaporate moisture until a thick or gelled texture is achieved. Works best with fruits containing naturally high pectin levels. Yields smaller quantities per amount of fruit used; has caramelized fruit flavour. May require smaller measure of sugar (ingredient), but final cooked down product isn't necessarily lower in sugar than other products.

Low Acid Food – Foods that contain little natural acid and have a pH higher than 4.6. Bacteria thrive in low acid foods. The only recommended and practical means to destroy bacteria naturally found in low acid foods is heating at sea level to 240°F (116°C) for a specified time in a pressure canner.

Marmalade – Citrus peel cooked with fruit juice, sugar and/or other fruits or vegetables.

Mason Jar – A glass jar geometrically designed and constructed to seal with two-piece metal closures and to withstand temperatures and reuse associated with home canning. True home canning Mason jars also conform to specific geometrical shapes and volume capacities compatible with established heat processing times.

Microorganism – A living plant or animal of microscopic size, such as molds, yeasts or bacteria, that can cause spoilage in canned or frozen foods.

Mold – Microscopic fungi that grow as silken threads and appear as fuzz on food. Molds thrive on acids and can produce mycotoxins. Mold is easily destroyed at processing temperatures between 140° and 190°F (60° and 88°C).

Pectin – A naturally occurring carbohydrate in fruits and vegetables. Pectin works together with fruit, sugar and acid to form a gel.

pH – Potential Of Hydrogen – A chemistry measuring system used to determine the acidity or alkalinity of a solution. In home canning, foods are classified as High Acid or Low Acid, with specific heat processing techniques required for each.

Pickling – Preserving food, especially cucumbers and vegetables, in a high acid (usually vinegar) solution. Despite this addition of acid, jars of pickled foods still require heat processing in a boiling water canner.

Preserve – Pieces of or small whole fruits suspended in a thick sauce or jelly.

Pressure Canner – A large, heavy, specially designed pot with a lid that can be locked in place to create a pressure-tight seal. The lid is fitted with a safety valve, a vent and a pressure gauge. When heated, the build up of steam inside the pressure canner creates temperatures higher than those of boiling water. This produces heat processing temperatures of 240°F (116°C) necessary to destroy harmful bacteria that thrive in low acid foods.

Pretreatment – Blanching or treating produce with an antioxidant to set colour, slow enzyme action or destroy bacteria.

Process or Heat Process – Heating filled jars of food to a specified temperature for a specified time to inactivate enzymes and to destroy harmful molds, yeasts and bacteria. Heat processing is essential for the food safety of all home canned foods. Processing destroys microorganisms that are naturally present in food and/or enter the jar upon filling. It also allows gasses or air to be "vented" from the jar to create an airtight vacuum as the product cools.

Raw Pack – Filling jars with raw, unheated food prior to heat processing.

Rehydration (or reconstitution) – Restoring water or liquid to dried foods.

SNAP Lid – A specially coated tinplated steel disc with a unique red sealing compound built into the flanged edge. It is applied to mason jars in combination with a metal screw band. The jars must then be heat processed to create vacuum seals for home canned foods.

Syrup or Canning Syrup – The liquid added to canned or frozen food. Common "canning syrups" are sweetened by adding sugar, honey or sugar replacements to water and/or juice.

Vacuum Packaging – A mechanical technique that removes air from a container and seals it to prevent air from reentering the container without heat processing. Because air is removed, vacuum packaged foods tend to retain their quality longer. Vacuum packaging, however, does not replace heat processing required for shelf stability of perishable foods. Vacuum packaged perishable foods must be refrigerated or frozen.

Vacuum Seal – The absence of normal atmospheric (air) pressure in properly heat processed jars of home canned foods.

Venting –

a. In home canning, forcing excess gasses or air to escape filled jar by the application of heat during boiling water or pressure processing.

b. During the period of heat build-up in a pressure canner, permitting air to escape prior to closing the vent and begin counting the required heat processing time.

Yeast – Microscopic fungi grown from spores that cause fermentation in foods. Yeasts are inactive in foods that are frozen and are easily destroyed by heat processing at a temperature of 212°F (100°C).

INDEX